POLICE AND COMMUNITY IN TWENTIETH-CENTURY SCOTLAND

POLICE AND COMMUNITY IN TWENTIETH-CENTURY SCOTLAND

Louise A. Jackson

with Neil Davidson, Linda Fleming,
David M. Smale and Richard Sparks

EDINBURGH
University Press

Edinburgh University Press is one of the leading university presses in the UK. We publish academic books and journals in our selected subject areas across the humanities and social sciences, combining cutting-edge scholarship with high editorial and production values to produce academic works of lasting importance. For more information visit our website: edinburghuniversitypress.com

© Louise A. Jackson, 2020, 2022

First published in hardback by Edinburgh University Press 2020

Edinburgh University Press Ltd
The Tun – Holyrood Road
12 (2f) Jackson's Entry
Edinburgh EH8 8PJ

Typeset in 10/12.5 Adobe Sabon by
IDSUK (DataConnection) Ltd, and
and printed and bound by CPI Group (UK) Ltd, Croydon, CR0 4YY

A CIP record for this book is available from the British Library

ISBN 978 1 4744 4663 1 (hardback)
ISBN 978 1 4744 4664 8 (paperback)
ISBN 978 1 4744 4665 5 (webready PDF)
ISBN 978 1 4744 4666 2 (epub)

The right of Louise A. Jackson to be identified as author of this work has been asserted in accordance with the Copyright, Designs and Patents Act 1988 and the Copyright and Related Rights Regulations 2003 (SI No. 2498).

CONTENTS

List of Figures and Tables	vi
Acknowledgements	vii
List of Abbreviations	ix
1 Introduction	1
2 Governance	14
3 The Glasgow Beat Man	53
4 Specialist and Plainclothes Policing	99
5 Policing the Rural	137
6 Women in Scottish Policing	175
7 Concluding the Twentieth Century	209
Appendix	218
Bibliography	225
Index	235

FIGURES AND TABLES

FIGURES

2.1 Map of Police Forces of Scotland, 1962 — 20

TABLES

3.1	Breach of the peace proceedings	84
A.1	Birthplace of recruits to Glasgow City Police	218
A.2	Former trades of recruits to Glasgow City Police	219
A.3	Social class of recruits to Glasgow City Police	220
A.4	Religion stated by recruits to Glasgow City Police	221
A.5	Birthplace of recruits to Ayr Burgh Police	221
A.6	Former trades of recruits to Ayr Burgh Police	222
A.7	Birthplace of recruits to Inverness County Police	222
A.8	Former trades of recruits to Inverness County Police	223
A.9	Social class of recruits to Inverness County Police	223
A.10	Religion stated by recruits to Inverness County Police	223
A.11	Birthplace of recruits to Inverness Burgh Police	224
A.12	Former trades of recruits to Inverness Burgh Police	224

ACKNOWLEDGEMENTS

Much of the research for this book was undertaken during a two-year project funded by the Leverhulme Trust (RPG-387) in 2012–14. This enabled the appointment of Neil Davidson, Linda Fleming and David M. Smale as researchers to join Louise Jackson (School of History, Classics & Archaeology) and Richard Sparks (School of Law) at the University of Edinburgh. In 2012–13 Neil Davidson conducted interviews with members of the Retired Police Officers Association Scotland (RPOAS), to whom we are extremely grateful. Where appropriate, transcriptions and recordings were deposited in the School of Scottish Studies Archives, University of Edinburgh, whom we thank (as the current owners of the material) for permission to quote brief extracts. Archival research in Fort William, Glasgow, Inverness and Wick (including analysis of occurrence books and anonymised personnel records) was carried out by Linda Fleming and David Smale. We are grateful to Police Scotland (previously Northern Constabulary and Strathclyde Police) for permission to access select archival materials beyond the usual 75-year closure period (until 1950 for Strathclyde and 1970 for Northern) in accordance with data protection requirements. The book draws on research in numerous archives and libraries; we acknowledge in particular the generous help of the staff of the Highland Archives Service (HAS), Glasgow City Archives (GCA), National Records of Scotland (NRS), and the Glasgow Police Museum (especially Alastair Dinsmor). We are grateful to the Scottish Institute of Police Research (SIPR) for its support during the Leverhulme Trust-funded stage of the project. The writing up of this book in 2017–19 (and the further research this entailed) was supported by the School of History, Classics & Archaeology through their awarding of research leave to Louise Jackson. There is not space to acknowledge the input of all with whom we have had conversations about this work over the years. Nevertheless, very special thanks are due to Angela Bartie, Ewen Cameron, Viviene Cree, Roger Davidson, Andy Davies, Gordon Johnston and Anna Souhami for their generosity in reading and commenting on draft chapters.

ABBREVIATIONS

ACPOS	Association of Chief Police Officers in Scotland
AR	Annual Report
BoP	Breach of the peace
CC	Chief Constable
CC(S)A	Chief Constables (Scotland) Association
CID	Criminal Investigation Department
CIS	Community Improvement Scheme
GCA	Glasgow City Archives
GH	*Glasgow Herald*
HAS	Highland Archives Service
HC	House of Commons
HL	House of Lords
HMIC	His/Her Majesty's Inspector of Constabulary (England and Wales)
HMICS	His/Her Majesty's Inspector of Constabulary for Scotland
ILP	Independent Labour Party
IRA	Irish Republican Army
IWM	Imperial War Museum
NLS	National Library of Scotland
NRS	National Records of Scotland
NUWW	National Union of Women Workers
NVA	National Vigilance Association
PF	Procurator Fiscal
PP	Parliamentary Papers (UK)

RIC	Royal Irish Constabulary
RPOAS	Retired Police Officers Association Scotland
SHRG	Scottish Homosexual Reform Group
SIPR	Scottish Institute for Policing Research
SMG	Scottish Minorities Group
SNP	Scottish National Party
SPF	Scottish Police Federation
SUWW	Scottish Unions of Women Workers
TNA	The National Archives
WAPC	Women's Auxiliary Police Corps
WPS	Women Police Service

I

INTRODUCTION

In 1981 Scotland's most senior civil servant Sir William Fraser commented that:

> There are those, inside the police service and outside, who reflect nostalgically on the constables of their youth – the picture is generally one of big men from the Highlands and Islands who maintained law and order in city and village by judicious use of the kind word, the frown and the back of the hand. Of course such men existed, although they were not so widely recognised as we are sometimes told.[1]

Our aim is to unpack and interrogate this characterisation, which has been sustained through collective memory and popular culture. Who were the officers who policed Scotland's diverse communities across the twentieth century? How and in what ways was law and order 'maintained', with what effects and on whose behalf? How were officers regarded in terms of trust, legitimacy and respect? To what extent was gender (embodied in the image of the 'big men') crucial to the construction of the police role? If this was an ideal that was lost, when and how did that come about and with what transformative effects?

This book is a social history in that it is concerned with the 'everyday'. More specifically it traces the sets of practices, identities and relationships through which polic*ing* was constituted as a result of encounters between individuals and social groups (including amongst the police themselves) since around 1900. It examines the factors that enabled co-operation, consensus and thus the building of trust between police officers and communities, as well as identifying and analysing points of tension and conflict. It considers both the formal rhetoric (and sets of structures) that defined and prescribed the policing ideal as well as the experience of policing from a range of grassroots perspectives, entailing consideration of the micro-politics of particular social environments. Moreover, the book seeks to contribute to the broader comparative history of policing by demonstrating the hybridity of police identities, which were constructed across time through intersecting geographies of nation, place and belonging: as 'British' and/or 'Scottish', as city/burgh/county, and in relation to police division/shift (urban) or village (rural).[2] Whilst highlighting the ways in which police repertoire was shaped by Scots Law (most significantly the rule of corroboration) given Scotland's separate legal system, the book evidences the range and diversity of co-existing policing styles, which were a product of local cultures and demographic factors as well as the attributes of individual officers.

A historical study of Scotland provides a useful vantage point from which to view changes in policing more generally across the UK. In 2013 a new single (national) service, Police Scotland, was created from the eight regional police forces that had been in existence since 1975. It can be seen as the final step in a pull towards centralisation through which the number of separate forces and constabularies in Scotland had been reduced from the sixty-nine that existed in 1900. The move to a single service has not been without controversy, and public debate has focused on whether and to what extent a single force can respond effectively to different local needs and communities.[3] As a result of such scrutiny, in 2017 Police Scotland restated its commitment to 'localism', entailing the improvement of communication, accountability and thus confidence in local areas.[4] In England and Wales decisions about the organisation of policing have gone in diametrically opposite ways, with the continuation of forty-three separate forces. Questions thus remain about the relationship between the size and scale of organisations, their effectiveness and (particularly in the recent period of austerity) their efficiency.[5] In terms of personnel, Police Scotland is the second largest police force in the UK, employing approximately half the number of officers of London's Metropolitan Police. However, the geographical area it covers is by far the largest – nearly fifty times greater than that of the Met – and the diversity of settlement and terrain presents distinct challenges. By examining the pre-history of what has become Police Scotland, this book may also contribute a longitudinal perspective to current debates about the meaning and delivery of 'localism'.

It is important to stress that, in discussing the police, our focus is on those employed within the specific formal bureaucratic institutions which, by 1900, had come to be referred to under the umbrella term of the Scottish Police Service (initially a loose associational identity which nonetheless may be seen as, in part, a progenitor of Police Scotland). It is restricted to the civilian police, and to the (urban) forces and (county) constabularies that were organised and funded through local (and subsequently regional) government (although enabled through parliamentary statute and subject to increasingly centralised modes of governance). We do not examine the operation of the nationally constituted military police, UK Atomic Energy Authority Constabulary, railway police, or the police officers employed by industrial firms or private individuals across the century. The police function was of course shared with a range of other occupations and agencies – most obviously factors and gamekeepers on large rural estates, or store detectives in large urban retail emporia. We recognise the existence of a 'mixed economy of policing' across the nineteenth and twentieth centuries, in which police officers formed one agency amongst many through which 'law and order' was maintained.[6] Indeed, we touch on the relationship between police officers and other regulatory agencies, stakeholders, and figures of authority.

In urban areas of Scotland especially, the term 'police' had been used in the nineteenth century (as in the eighteenth) to refer to a broad range of regulatory functions associated with civic improvement to enhance 'security, peace and comfort'. This included water supply, sanitation, street cleansing, lighting, paving and the regulation of markets as well as the management of 'vagrancy' and the prevention of crime and disorder.[7] The historical scholarship of David Barrie, W. G. Carson, Alistair Goldsmith and David Smale (amongst others) has shown how distinctions were gradually made by 1900 between 'law and order' aspects of policing (involving use of the criminal law) and those pertaining to civil regulation.[8] The police function was, by 1900, clearly talked about in terms of crime prevention. Nevertheless, as this book will detail, there were significant continuities between the duties and responsibilities of police officers and those of their Victorian predecessors. The 1967 Police (Scotland) Act repeated rhetoric that had been a mainstay of police acts, regulations and training manuals for over 100 years in stating that the object of police officers was 'to guard, patrol, and watch ... to prevent the commission of offences [against the law] ... to preserve order and ... to protect life and property'.[9] Into the 1970s most charges brought to court in urban areas were for 'police offences': those relating to 'good conduct' within urban space, and disorderly or anti-social behaviour. Constables in towns and cities were still required to report problems relating to the urban fabric: such as faulty streetlights, loose paving, and gas or water leaks. In rural areas most police time was taken up with administrative matters, including those of a sanitary nature (attending the dipping of sheep or the destruction of diseased livestock); the police were also involved in mountain rescue. Preservation of 'life' and 'order' was widely conceived as relating to both the material world (including the natural world) and social relations.

It is important not to overstate claims for a distinctively 'Scottish' or 'English' interpretation of the policing function. Broader regulatory activities were undertaken by police officers across Great Britain in both nineteenth and twentieth centuries (and at some points in Ireland, too, outside of periods of political unrest), whilst there was considerable exchange of people, ideas and practices from the late eighteenth century.[10] A number of recent studies have suggested that relations between police officers and 'the community' have been more harmonious in Scotland because of a historical legacy of 'genuine concern for the public good and well-being' and 'a more cautious approach'.[11] Yet this is largely hypothetical given that the social history of policing in Scotland – for most of the twentieth century – has remained in large part a blank canvas in terms of academic study. There has been little attempt to probe within and beyond living memory and to move beyond the assumptions about a benign paternalism to which Sir William Fraser was referring in 1981. Moreover, the idea of a distinctively 'Scottish' approach to policing needs itself to be placed under the microscope and analysed as an important narrative trope that has been used to frame the terms of public debate.

Whilst the social history of policing in twentieth-century England (and to a lesser extent Wales) has been explored through the extensive work of Clive Emsley, Barbara Weinberger, Mike Brogden, Joanne Klein and David Jones (amongst others), Scotland has remained surprisingly uncharted terrain.[12] Historians have produced recent important studies of very particular topics related to twentieth-century Scottish criminal justice history (most obviously the criminalisation of 'prostitution' and 'homosexuality', and responses to youth offending), whilst Andrew Davies's pioneering work on the Glasgow 'gangs' of the 1920s and 1930s has illuminated the micro-politics of the city and the relationship between its police and poorer residents in these specific decades.[13] Yet the view that has emerged is highly partial, the police themselves have rarely been the focal point, and historical research on the policing of rural Scotland (and outside of Glasgow and Edinburgh) is almost non-existent.[14] Published in 1964, Michael Banton's *The Policeman in the Community* provided a snapshot of the preventive and social role of police in one Scottish city division (assumed to be Edinburgh), and is now seen as a foundational text in the development of police studies. Yet little work has been done to date to situate Banton's study historically (looking at earlier decades) or geographically (across Scotland). This book aims to contribute to a more extensive mapping of the contours, textures and dynamics of the multiplicity of relationships between communities and police officers across the twentieth century.

A further very extensive historiographical field relevant here relates to organised labour and industrial action in Scotland in the first quarter of the twentieth century (focused specifically on the epicentre of Glasgow's 'Red Clydeside'). Within this field, historians have considered the policing of strikes and public protest – including the surveillance of pacifist, socialist and communist activisms as well as crowd control tactics – as part of a broader set of debates about the left in Scotland.[15] Strikes had been legalised (subject to circumscriptions) since the 1870s and the Trades Dispersal Act 1906 enabled picketing for the first time if it constituted 'peaceful persuasion'. Yet what this meant in practice was subject to police interpretation. In an important study of the policing of strikes in Britain, Weinberger argued that in Glasgow 'relations between the police and the labour movement were usually peaceable' in contrast to Liverpool, Hull and South Wales. This was not because the police were 'soft' (far from it), but because of high levels of organisation and disciplined behaviour amongst strikers, as well as the prominent position locally of the Independent Labour Party (ILP), which provided an 'umbrella' political voice (across disparate campaigns) that commanded 'some respect' in the city.[16] Where 'dramatic events' occurred in Glasgow, these tended to be the result of mistakes by police on the ground and 'over-reaction' by central (rather than local) government.[17] Thus the events of 'Black Friday' on 31 January 1919, when police in Glasgow drew batons without apparent provocation to disperse strikers assembled in St George's Square, have been overwhelmingly interpreted as a 'police riot' as outnumbered officers 'went out of control'.[18] As a result of the intervention of the Westminster government, military troops and tanks were commandeered to prevent what was hyperbolically described as a 'bolshevist rising'.[19] In fact the first decades of the twentieth century saw the final transferral of responsibility for the policing of public order from (central) military to (local) civil authorities.[20] This was the last 'deployment of troops in the city in peacetime', since even during the General Strike of 1926 (when the Army was put on standby) incidents were henceforth dealt with by civil authorities.[21] We do not intend to rehearse once again, here, the history of the policing of protest in Scotland. Rather, we seek to integrate awareness of its effects into our broader discussion of the dynamics of police-community relationships, including its resonance within popular memory and oral tradition, often in highly localised ways and across time.

The term 'community' is, itself, a complicated conceptual tool, since it has multiple meanings, effects and applications which have shifted across time.[22] We use it in this book in three ways: relating to a) ideals; b) identities; and c) social geography. Firstly, in relation to ideals, it is important to recognise that the language of 'community' has often operated as an 'evocative symbol' conveying a benign sense of mutuality and reciprocity. It has a tendency to project a set of shared values onto people and places, and thus has an ideological, prescriptive or normative function.[23] We are attentive, therefore, to the ways in which the rhetoric of 'community' has been deployed with regard to policing in Scotland in newspapers, official reports, speeches, and other formal texts, and with what effect. We show, too, that the normative language of 'community' has been bound up with the idea of 'the public'. Both terms have been used across the twentieth century – sometimes interchangeably and at other points with differences of nuance and meaning – to discuss police accountability and legitimacy.

Secondly, we are interested in who is included and who is excluded from the collective identities and ideas of belonging that have accreted around social groups which choose to define themselves as 'community'. We ask how ideas of inclusion, exclusion and marginalisation have affected relationships with (and even amongst) police officers – because of gender, sexuality, age, religion, 'race', ethnicity, class, poverty and other markers of status or difference.[24] A major focus of the study, therefore, relates to questions regarding whose interests and values police officers have upheld, the relationship between the rule of law and use of police discretion, and the ways in which police officers acted as mediators within disputes between social groups. In rural as in urban areas, we show that 'communities' (in terms of sets of identities, experiences and values) need to be thought about as 'diverse and pluralistic settings with competing normative communities' rather than as 'homogeneous entities'.[25]

Thirdly, we use the term 'community' as a category of empirical sociological and geographical description: to refer to the spatial entities of neighbourhood (urban) and settlement (rural) and their associated socio-economic structures within the landscape/cityscape.[26] We examine where police officers themselves lived in relation to the neighbourhoods and settlements that they policed, as well as the effects of technology (including motorisation) on their geographical and social orbit. Existing studies suggest that police officers are likely to be located socially as both part of 'community' (as private individuals) and as separate from it or as 'outsiders' (because of their official role as representatives of the state).[27] To what extent did the geography of policing make a difference in terms of social integration? We consider, too, the relationship between geographically settled communities and diasporic communities, including those whose lives were migrant or itinerant (whether for cultural, social or economic reasons), as well as the role of the police within these relationships. Finally, we use the term in relation to professional and associational networks: to refer to the 'policy community' of those engaged in policing and/or criminal justice in Scotland specifically.

In the early 1970s a further term – 'community policing' – was coined as a label to describe a particular set of approaches, practices and models, and was rapidly incorporated into policy in the UK and USA as a 'new orthodoxy'.[28] Over the next thirty years and beyond it was commonly used to imply partnership with other agencies (public, private and voluntary); emphasis on community engagement; forms of decentralisation (including responsiveness to local need); a proactive role (rather than a reactive 'fire-brigade' style); and a shift away from the idea of 'law enforcement' to one of preventive 'service'. Indeed, current usage of the language of 'localism' is a further attempt to pin down the ideals and relationships that the rhetoric of 'community policing' sought to sustain. In Scotland, specific 'community policing' initiatives were deployed in 1971 (ahead of England and Wales) as a result of the recommendation of the Scottish Office that Community Involvement Branches should be established in all Scottish forces. This built on the experiments with multi-partner community-oriented projects developed in Greenock in the 1950s by David Gray when he was Chief Constable: ideas which he then took to the Scottish Office upon appointment to the inspectorate of constabulary. Thus there is considerable substance to the claim that 'community policing' was 'pioneered' in Scotland in the post-war period specifically through Gray's work.[29] This book will discuss these early experiments with 'community policing', analysing the reasons for their genesis and considering the light that they shed on the dynamics of Scottish policing (as a set of social relationships).

The concept of 'community policing' is also relevant for another reason. From its origins as a label, it was written about (within police studies as well as policy documents) in ways that involved the remembering and mythologising of a past 'golden age'.[30] In Scotland (as in England and Wales), it has often been presented as a return to the 'traditional policing' epitomised by the 'village constable' or urban 'beat man' ('bobby on the beat'), in opposition to motorised rapid response policing methods and as a reaction to erosion of public confidence in the 1970s (discerned more readily in England than in Scotland).[31] To what extent did the policing actually delivered by constables in the first half of the twentieth century measure up with the ideals of the later 'community policing' vision? This book contributes to the growing field that deconstructs the golden age 'myth', by demonstrating that relationships between police officers and Scotland's many communities were diverse and variegated, experiences far from uniform and trajectories non-linear.[32] Moments of conflict are apparent in the public record across the decades – as well as examples of co-operation and consensus. Moreover, the historical record provides us with a rich source base through which to identify the specific factors, practices and approaches that fostered collaborative and harmonious relationships (and which enhanced police legitimacy) and, concomitantly, those that generated, exacerbated or intensified tension and distrust.

The book is grounded in extensive original archival research and collection of personal testimony relating to the period c. 1900–75. Our starting point – at the turn of the twentieth century – is framed by the Burgh Police (Scotland) Act of 1892 and Town Council (Scotland) Act of 1900 which, together, standardised policing roles and police administration under local authorities (burghs and counties). Its end point reflects this replacement of burgh and county with regional structures. Our primary historical research also ends just after the roll-out of Community Involvement Branches, given that these (and subsequent 'Community Policing' initiatives) resulted in almost constant review, assessment and evaluation, contributing significantly towards the established field that is now contemporary Scottish policing studies.[33]

Whilst the book (and some of its chapters) covers the whole of Scotland at the macro level (citing examples across cities, burghs and counties), we also focus in on two distinct regions in order to develop sustained micro-analyses of local styles of policing. The first of these is the Highlands and Islands, the most northerly part of the UK, policed by small county constabularies until 1975 (when they were consolidated into the Northern Constabulary) and with very low levels of recorded crime. Its demographic categorisation as 'remote rural' and its association with crofting, fishing and wool should not conceal the significant development of the aluminium-smelting industry from the 1890s onwards, nuclear power in the 1950s, and then oil from the 1970s, as well as its military and naval importance.[34] Our second regional study is of Glasgow and its broader conurbation and industrial hinterland of west-central Scotland, associated with shipbuilding, iron, steel and coal-mining (prior to rapid de-industrialisation by the early 1970s).[35] In 1961 the Central Clydeside Conurbation (as it was known) accounted for 1.8 million people – over a third of Scotland's total population – and extended into Lanarkshire, Dunbartonshire and Renfrewshire (areas that we also consider).[36] Densely populated as well as intensively policed, Glasgow itself was associated with the highest rates for recorded crime in Scotland, and came under the auspices of the City of Glasgow Police[37], Scotland's largest force, until 1975 (when it merged with surrounding forces through the formation of Strathclyde Police).

The primary research for the book (which began in 2012 prior to the creation of Police Scotland) used a wide range of printed and manuscript sources, including police personnel records (which have been analysed as large datasets in order to guarantee full anonymity), police station occurrence books, official reports (including annual data series), civil servants' policy files, parliamentary papers, and newspapers (local, regional and national). In addition, forty semi-structured oral history interviews were conducted in 2012–13 with retired police officers who had served in these two regions. Participants had joined the police service between 1945 and 1972, and mostly served a full thirty years before retiring between 1975 and 2002, enabling them to reflect on changes across their service. These interviews have been supplemented by other published or archived testimonies of police personnel who served in Scottish forces across the twentieth century. This includes a small number of published memoirs or autobiographies (relating mostly to those who became senior detectives or chief constables).[38] We also make use of spoken evidence given by officers, civil servants and criminal justice professionals to various committees of enquiry, the minutes of which were published or archived.

Much of our account is constructed from and through the perspective of police personnel themselves – whether in the form of official published reports, the unpublished paperwork constitutive of the bureaucratic record-keeping process that was an integral part of police method, or the spoken word. The perspectives of the policed – the other side of the equation – are harder to come by, particularly in the historical archive. We have endeavoured to recover these from published autobiographical accounts, from complaints that led to legal or other public action, from (limited) social studies or surveys, and by reading official accounts 'against the grain' (of their deliberate or intended meaning). Nevertheless, the fragmentary nature of this material makes it extremely difficult to gauge how and in what ways it is representative of all experience. In working with all of our sources, we view them as effects of particular subjectivities, junctures, conventions and frameworks but which, interpreted alongside each other, enable us to build a larger composite picture of the permutations and likely contours of relationships with the police. Ultimately, this book can only offer a series of glimpses across the extensive chronology and terrain that it seeks to cover. We hope that it will act as a stimulus to further research on the social history of policing in Scotland, by raising questions for inquiry and suggesting areas worthy of scrutiny.

Chronologies and Contents

This book is structured as a set of thematic and geographical trajectories rather than one simple linear narrative. This allows us to consider the co-existence of different temporalities relating to the pace of change within the contours of multiple police-community relationships and in distinct settings. These include deep continuities, gradual change, and more sudden rupture.[39]

The First and Second World Wars (1914–18 and 1939–45) can undoubtedly be characterised in terms of very substantial disruption and turbulence.[40] Firstly, wartime saw extensive reconfiguration of police personnel. Older officers were refused retirement, police pensioners were brought back into the job, and men working in other 'reserved' occupations undertook additional voluntary police duties (including as special constables). Voluntary roles relating to police work were also created for women in the years 1914–18, whilst the Second World War led to significant expansion of the extent and nature of their paid employment in the police service. Secondly, the movement and dislocation of people for a wide variety of reasons created a great deal of additional work (including the tracing of deserters from the armed forces or the escorting of prisoners of war). Where Scottish cities were subject to aerial bombardment (in Edinburgh as a result of Zeppelin raids in April 1916 and on Clydebank, which was decimated in March 1941), the police were crucial in co-ordinating responses, working alongside other emergency services.[41] Thirdly, wartime regulations under the Defence of the Realm Acts added seismically to the breadth of police duties as well as overall workload. They included enforcing the blackout, protecting 'vulnerable points' (such as railway stations, lighthouses and harbours) and monitoring enemy 'aliens' (or 'foreigners'). Police powers were extended very significantly during the First World War, particularly in regard to covert monitoring and surveillance of dissidence and unrest, as industrial disputes were recast as 'subversion' (and thus categorised as a political threat) on account of the war effort.[42] This set the tone for the interwar period, when the Emergency Powers Act 1920 enabled regulations to be authorised without public scrutiny, including the banning of meetings and processions. As Edward Goodwin has pointed out, whilst intelligence duties were intensified during the Second World War (as in the First), they were analogous with practices across the first half of the twentieth century.[43]

Overall, despite the scale of these disruptions and the heightening of surveillance, Weinberger is correct in suggesting that the British wartime experience had 'surprisingly little effect on police routines' and that 'the underlying structure of policing, based on patrolling the beat, remained in place'.[44] The notable changes to personnel and duties were for the duration only, and the organisation and practice of police work remained largely intact.[45] Arguably, it was the use of women in police work that constituted the most radical long-term legacy of both wars for the police service.

Thus this book highlights very significant continuities – from the 1890s to the 1960s – in the everyday routine of urban beat officers and (to an even greater extent) rural village constables, although it argues that the meaning and effect of this routine was locally contingent. We suggest that the most significant ruptures to the mode of policing that was established in the late-Victorian era arose from technological change, including motorisation, but that this was felt first in relation to the work of specialist units within urban forces. Vast amounts of police time were increasingly consumed by road traffic offences from the 1930s onwards, whilst the introduction and spread of police vehicles enabled different tactics, methods and styles of policing. Technological innovation also propelled the professionalisation of policing (although its significance was mainly realised in the later twentieth century). In relation to changing attitudes and identities, we demonstrate incremental shifts in ideas about who (in terms of gender and, subsequently, ethnicity) should be a police officer, whilst the extension of the electoral franchise in the years after 1918 transformed understandings of to whom the police were accountable. We also highlight significant shifts in moral consensus regarding methods for disciplining children and young people – specifically against physical chastisement – which led to both controversy and transformation in the years 1945–70.

This introductory first chapter has outlined our guiding aims, concepts and approach to chronology. In Chapter 2 we examine the formal mechanisms, structures and cultures of governance through which policing has been organised in Scotland. This includes the relationship between the UK Home Office, Scottish Office and local police authorities (prior to the creation of the Scottish Executive in 1999) and the disciplinary mechanisms through which police officers were themselves regulated (from training manuals and drill through to the handling of complaints about officers' conduct). This chapter provides an important backdrop to the study by focusing on the forms of governance that underpinned the interactions between police officers and private citizens on which later chapters then focus.

The next three chapters turn to the grassroots experience of everyday policing, comparing rural and urban areas – in terms of policing roles, styles and repertoires – through analysis of oral history interviews and other ethnographic source material. Situations and encounters were negotiated in relation to the law, which was interpreted in action through the crucial application of police discretion. Sociological studies have highlighted the importance of the idea of 'common sense' policing for rank-and-file officers.[46] Yet, what 'common sense' and 'discretion' meant in practice was a result of local cultures and contexts, which were more significant in shaping repertoire than the drill and rote-learning of training school, leading to considerable differentiation in relation to place. Chapter 3 focuses specifically on the role of the uniformed Glasgow 'beat man' as well as the group identity and reputation that was forged in the city for 'robust and 'tough' policing, grounded in male physical prowess (as embodied masculinity). Chapter 4 analyses the effects of encounters generated by specialist plainclothes units in urban areas on relationships between police and communities. We examine the work of the Licensing Department (the 'Vice Squad') in relation to street betting, the sex industry, and the criminalisation of 'homosexuality', before turning to specialist units and programmes associated with the policing of young people. Whilst city policing moved rapidly towards segregation of police roles through specialisation, rural officers remained generalists. Chapter 5 discusses the role of the 'village constable' in the Highland and Islands, identifying an approach to policing that was mostly diffusive and conciliatory in terms of the settled population. More 'robust' tactics were used in relation to male migrant labour although officers also acted as mediators between the settled population and those constructed as 'outsiders' (including members of Gypsy/Traveller communities).

As most of the book demonstrates, policing styles and encounters were gendered performances through which competing masculinities were constructed and played out.[47] In Chapter 6 we move on to examine the gradual appointment of female officers in Scotland from 1915 onwards, largely in 'specialist' roles working with women and children, and we consider the implications of this work for police relationships with communities. We argue that, into the late twentieth century, the authority associated with policing was assumed to be derived from physical strength and, concomitantly, the male body. Chapter 7 concludes our thematic study of the twentieth century by drawing together the book's main arguments and linking them to key events and trends of its last two decades. We return, again, to our central questions regarding who is entitled to be a police officer, whose interests and needs are met through policing, and how policing is delivered.

Notes

1. Fraser, 'Post-war police' (James Smart Lecture).
2. Ugolini and Pattinson, 'Negotiating identities'.
3. Fyfe et al., 'Experiencing organizational change'.
4. Police Scotland and Scottish Police Authority, *2026: Serving a Changing Scotland – Our Ten Year Strategy for Policing in Scotland* (2017), SPA/2017/02.
5. Mendel et al., 'Does size matter?'.
6. Churchill, *Crime Control*.
7. Barrie, *Police*, 12–15, 92, 113 and *passim*; Dinsmor and Goldsmith, 'Scottish policing'.
8. Barrie, *Police*; Carson, 'Policing the periphery'; Carson and Idzikowska, 'Social production'; Goldsmith, 'City of Glasgow Police'; Smale, 'Alfred John List'.
9. For similar earlier statements see Anon., *Police Manual* (1910), 21 and Glasgow Police Regulations 1857, quoted in Goldsmith, 'City of Glasgow Police', 6.
10. Barrie, 'Typology'; Dodsworth, '"Civic" police'; Dodsworth, 'Review of Barrie'. On Ireland see Lowe and Malcolm, 'Domestication'.
11. Donnelly, *Municipal Policing*, 27; Dinsmor and Goldsmith, 'Scottish policing', 53; Donnelly and Scott, 'Policing in Scotland', 183.
12. Emsley, *English Police*; Weinberger, *Best Police*; Jones, *Crime and Policing*; Brogden, *Mersey Beat*; Klein, *Invisible Men*.
13. Settle, *Sex for Sale*; Meek, *Queer Voices*; Davidson, *Illicit and Unnatural*; Davidson and Davis, *Sexual State*; Bartie and Jackson, 'Youth crime'; Jackson with Bartie, *Policing Youth*; Bartie, 'Moral panics'; Bartie and Fraser, '"It wasnae just Easterhouse"'; Davies, *City of Gangs*; Davies, 'Street gangs'; Davies, '"Sillitoe's Cossacks"'; Davies, 'Police violence'.
14. Exceptions are Goodwin, 'Police in Edinburgh', Smale, 'The First World War and policing', and Smale, 'Impact on policing in the Scottish Borders' (on the Second World War). Goldsmith, 'City of Glasgow Police' takes an institutional approach.
15. For example, McLean, *Legend*; Duncan and McIvor, *Militant Workers*; Smyth, *Labour in Glasgow*. More recently, see, on gender, Hughes, *Gender and Political Identities*, and, on race, Jenkinson, 'Black sailors on Red Clydeside'.
16. Weinberger, *Keeping the Peace?*, 153–4.
17. Ibid., 156.
18. Weinberger, *Keeping the Peace?*, 156; McLean, *Legend*, 132.
19. Weinberger, 158.
20. Cameron, 'Internal policing', 439; Wood, 'Internal policing'.
21. Goldsmith, 'City of Glasgow Police', 256; see Wood, 'Internal policing', 544, for deployment of troops to deal with strikers in Fife and Midlothian in 1921–2.
22. Delanty, *Community*.
23. Calhoun, 'Community'; Bauman, *Community*.
24. Sibley, *Geographies*.

25. Mawby and Yarwood, *Rural Policing*, 3.
26. Tilley, 'Modern approaches'.
27. Banton, *Policeman*; Reiner, *Blue-Coated Worker*.
28. Rosenbaum, *Community Policing*; Mackenzie and Henry, *Community Police*; Brogden and Nijhar, *Community Policing*.
29. Schaffer, *Community Policing*, 'Preface' (n.p); Banton, *Policeman*; Monaghan, 'Crime prevention'.
30. Brogden and Nijhar, *Community Policing*, 24–5.
31. Schaffer, *Community Policing*; Alderson, *Policing Freedom*; Shanks, *Police Community Involvement*, 4.
32. Loader and Mulcahy, *Condition of England*; Reiner, *Politics of the Police*.
33. Mackenzie and Henry, *Community Police*.
34. Perchard and Mackenzie, '"Too much on the Highlands"'.
35. Pacione, *Glasgow*; Mavor, *Glasgow*.
36. Anderson, *Scotland's Populations*, 100–1.
37. The City of Glasgow Police (formal title) was also commonly referred to as Glasgow City Police and it is this short form that is used henceforth.
38. Stallion, *Life of Crime*.
39. Corfield, *Time*.
40. On the First World War: Fraser, *Home Front*; Englander, 'Police and public order'; Smale, 'First World War and policing'. On the Second World War: Weinberger, *Best Police*; Goodwin, 'Police in Edinburgh'; Smale, 'Impact on policing in the Scottish Borders'.
41. Weinberger, *Best Police*, 129; Royle, *Time of Tyrants*, 152–3.
42. Weinberger, *Keeping the Peace?*, 138.
43. Goodwin, 'Police in Edinburgh', 130–45 and Weinberger, *Best Police*, 123.
44. Weinberger, *Best Police*, 122.
45. See Goodwin, 'Police in Edinburgh', esp. 245–54.
46. Waddington, 'Police (canteen) sub-culture'.
47. Barrie and Broomhall, *Police and Masculinities*.

2

GOVERNANCE

Writing in July 1931, not long after his appointment as Inspector of Constabulary for Scotland, Brigadier-General Robert Maxwell Dudgeon enthusiastically stated that 'the police forces in Scotland enjoy the confidence and goodwill of the community'. To maintain this trust, he wrote, it was 'essential that every member of every force should, by his command of temper under all circumstances, his manliness of character, and his courtesy, be regarded as a model citizen'. A regime of discipline, training and education would inculcate qualities of virtue, self-control and civility enabling each constable to act as an 'influence for good'.[1] In Dudgeon's account, then, the moral force of the (male) police constable – projected through a chivalric masculinity – cemented state and civil society. His words were published initially in his annual report and then quoted further in the Scottish press, making them a very deliberate statement – designed for a broad general audience – that was at the same time an assertion, aspiration and speech act regarding police legitimacy.[2]

This chapter discusses the formal articulation of the relationship between the police and governance in Scotland across the twentieth century from two perspectives. On the one hand, it examines the mechanisms and apparatus through which police forces and police officers were organised and regulated. On the other, it explores official rhetoric that positioned the police within the polity. Indeed, the two were indelibly bound together as flipsides of the same coin – as Dudgeon's 1931 statement highlights. Whilst most of this book is concerned with the informal and practical negotiation of relationships at grassroots level, this chapter examines how the police role was formally conceptualised, ordered and explained: by local and national politicians, civil servants (including inspectors of constabulary such as Dudgeon), and senior police officers. It demonstrates how the idea of police legitimacy was forged, debated and maintained with reference to the rule of law, democracy, citizenship and 'the public' (a category used sometimes interchangeably with that of 'the community'). As elsewhere in the UK, the contours of who was included within these categories shifted across time, partly in response to changes in the electoral franchise.

The focus on formal rhetoric is important both methodologically and empirically. The narratives (or stories) that are told about policing have the capacity to act as galvanising 'myths' (that is, as symbolic 'truths' as much as literal ones) that underpin collective identities.[3] For historians it is important not only to chart the (re)production of these narratives across time but to unpick them and to highlight the process of meaning-making. It then becomes possible to juxtapose official rhetoric with points of critique or contestation that surfaced within the 'public' domain (including through complaints procedures, civil litigation or government inquiries). Furthermore, as other chapters will show, official narratives can also be compared to other materials that reveal informal cultures or provide access to 'hidden transcripts' – to highlight gaps between theory and practice.[4] Such a methodology is the only way to proceed given that there was no systematic attempt to measure levels of 'public' confidence or trust in the police in terms of an aggregate of all 'public opinion' until around 1960 – at the very point at which concerns were emerging in the broader UK context about loss of trust.[5] A qualitative approach that analyses the construction and use of terms such as 'the public', 'community' and 'citizenship' in relation to 'police' across time enables the charting of consensus and contention at moments when they became visible (even if the whole picture inevitably eludes us).

This chapter begins by examining the tripartite balancing of police governance between the Home Office, Scottish Office and local police authorities, exploring debates regarding localism versus centralism in the context of police amalgamation and reform. It then moves on to examine the internal systems of Scottish police forces through the lens of training and discipline, analysing instruction manuals as formal rhetoric and as prescriptive tools delineating a normative ideal. The chapter then telescopes outwards again to examine the structural position of police officers in relation to other institutions of Scots law and criminal justice before outlining complaints and appeals systems, identifying significant flashpoints in the scrutiny of Scottish policing. Our concern throughout is with the formal positioning of the police as an institution *vis-à-vis* 'the public' and 'community' and ultimately with ideas about accountability. As Rob Mawby and Alan Wright highlight, there is a constant 'paradox' at the heart of debates about police governance. Policing as law enforcement rests ultimately on 'coercive power' but this needs to be balanced 'by the police with enabling their effective operation'. In democratic states, the police 'strive for legitimacy to achieve the active cooperation and trust' of citizens. Accountability (being answerable for actions or behaviour in relation to the rule of law as well as public finance) thus 'contributes to the legitimacy of the police'.[6] As Anja Johansen observes, 'police legitimacy ultimately depends on how police and government authorities have handled the inherently asymmetrical relationship between police and the policed'.[7] In assessing accountability we also acknowledge the role of the newspaper press: as an important forum through which the police role was promoted, critiqued and debated across the twentieth century and thus integral to the construction of formal 'knowledge' of policing.

The Model of Local Policing

The first police forces and constabularies in Scotland had been established in the late eighteenth and early nineteenth centuries as a result of the 'local initiatives' of propertied 'local elites' who saw it as a continuation of their communal duty as 'citizens' to undertake 'warding and watching'.[8] In urban areas municipal government was seen as the protector of civic virtue, associational culture and civil society in line with entrenched opposition to the idea of a centralised authoritarian nation state. Yet centre and locale were bound together in a symbiotic relationship. Legislation enacted through the Westminster parliament enabled local government to exercise authority, whilst the centre was dependent on local government for the quotidian regulation of public order. Constabularies were established in Glasgow (in 1800), Edinburgh (1805), Paisley (1806), Perth (1811), Aberdeen (1818) and Dundee (1824) through acts of parliament.[9] Thus municipal government 'was suitably empowered by the central state to govern on its behalf and this maintained the legitimacy of each'.[10] The 1833 Burgh Police (Scotland) Act was important in creating a more uniform model of urban policing, with an elected police commission or the town council constituting the police authority and answerable to a property-owning electorate (of £10 householders). It was permissive only rather than compulsory (in contrast to the 1835 Municipal Corporations Act south of the border), thus maintaining the idea of policing as a locally autonomous initiative in Scotland.[11]

Centre and locale were rebalanced – with a centrifugal shift towards standardisation – as a result of the 1857 County and Burgh Police (Scotland) Act which effectively set in place a national system of local (civil) policing (not dissimilar to that which had been introduced in England and Wales). The 1857 act compelled the (longstanding) Commissioners of Supply in the counties (which consisted of prominent landowners) to form constabularies that would also cover any towns where no burgh provision had been separately established. It created the post of Her Majesty's Inspector of Constabulary for Scotland (HMICS) and introduced a (national) state grant amounting to a quarter of the costs of pay and clothing; this was less than the grant (of a half) south of the border where the central state had more leverage as a consequence. Local police authorities were permitted to appoint their own Chief Constable, although (in theory) subject to the approval of the Secretary of State. Moreover, the influence of landowners was maintained through the establishment of unelected police authorities that consisted of the Commissioners and other county officers (the Lord Lieutenant, sheriff and magistrates). Their role was diminished in 1890 with the setting up of county councils and standing joint committees (to act as police authorities), the latter consisting of elected councillors and nominated Commissioners.[12]

By the early twentieth century, therefore, a model of civil policing, tied to the concept of local democratic accountability (although still linked to a property qualification), was in place. Indeed, across most towns in Scotland, policing had been standardised through the 1892 Burgh Police (Scotland) Act, which was adopted in all royal burghs (except Greenock and the cities of Glasgow, Dundee, Edinburgh and Aberdeen who generated their own police acts but tended to follow the 1892 act in many regards). The 1900 Town Council (Scotland) Act replaced separate police commissions (which had survived in some burghs) with direct control through the town council, whose 'watching and lighting committee' made decisions about the resourcing of burgh police forces.[13] Moreover, in Scotland (unlike England and Wales where they were appointed by the Crown) the magistrates in urban areas/burghs ('bailies') were appointed by the town council from amongst their number, further cementing the role of local municipal government in the administration of criminal justice and policing. Indeed, Scottish political identity was increasingly framed in terms of pride in 'local self-government' across socio-economic groups as property and gender qualifications were gradually removed – to incorporate working-class voters and women.[14] Nevertheless, whilst the Labour Party made in-roads – significantly in Glasgow and towns in west-central Scotland by the 1930s – 'the small business classes' continued to dominate many burgh/city councils for much of the twentieth century. Lairds continued to exercise political influence in the counties (as elected representatives even after the role of Commissioners of Supply was abolished in 1930).[15]

As Weinberger has pointed out, Defence of the Realm Regulations during the First World War enabled the central Westminster government to give direct instruction to the police regarding duties and priorities, effectively taking decisions out of the hands of police authorities and chief constables.[16] Yet a further complexity had also been added to this 'national local government system' involving 'power interdependence' of centre and locale: through the creation of the Scottish Office in 1885.[17] At first this office mainly advised local government on statutory duties. In 1926, however, the role of the Secretary of State for Scotland (Scottish Secretary) was upgraded and relocated to Edinburgh, leading to further policy devolution; the Scottish Office civil service was expanded and a more interventionist role developed.[18] Whilst the Scottish Office was rarely a point of resistance to Westminster, it often negotiated significant compromises based on Scottish particularity and has been described as a 'powerful administrative apparatus' or 'semi-state' exercising 'a degree of decision-making'.[19] The position was significantly consolidated during the Second World War by Labour politician Tom Johnston who, as Scottish Secretary in Churchill's wartime 'national' (or 'coalition') government galvanised cross-party support and set up a Scottish 'Council of State' of all ex-Scottish secretaries. He later described this as an 'experiment in political co-operation for Scottish national ends' inculcating a notable 'spirit of independence' that could be sensed 'not least in the Civil Service'.[20] The stout defence of Scottish interests by Scottish Office civil servants was apparent in subsequent decades.

The role of HMICS (located within the civil service) developed across time but had a crucial influence. Those appointed were high-profile ambassadors for the police service in Scotland (although technically separate from it). They were, at various points in time, key actors, policy entrepreneurs and critical friends, performing a significant mediatory role. Appointed overwhelmingly from military backgrounds until after the Second World War, the inspectorate's expertise was initially concerned with logistics and resource management.[21] HMICS was required to visit all forces annually, with power to advise the Scottish Secretary that the state grant be refused if a force was deemed 'inefficient', and to guide chief constables on best practice. The inspectorate's leverage was enhanced somewhat by the increase in national state grant to a half by 1919 (in line with England and Wales).[22] From their beginnings, HMICSs used their arts of persuasion to promote standardisation and sharing of resources. Significantly, they were staunch advocates of 'consolidation' or 'amalgamation' of smaller police forces on grounds of efficiency, a view shared by Scottish Office civil servants.

However, there was considerable reluctance in Scotland to move to a model of central compulsion because of sensitivity to local political interests and the primacy accorded to local accountability. The number of Scottish police forces was reduced very slowly from 64 in 1900 to 58 in 1929, 48 in 1939, 36 in 1949, and 33 in 1959, and the model of local burgh and county policing was remarkably long-lived.[23] Wartime emergency powers which forced amalgamation for defence reasons were barely used in Scotland. A rare exception was the creation of the Gretna Special Police Area, which (from June 1917 to April 1920) consolidated the vast munitions factory under the control of the Ministry of Munitions, instead of being split between the county constabularies of Dumfries (Scotland) and Cumberland (England). This was, nevertheless, undertaken through memoranda of agreement with the police authorities concerned and for a limited period only.[24]

Drastic proposals were in fact made in 1933 when the Police Consolidation (Scotland) Committee (chaired by Lord Ormidale) proposed the reduction of Scottish forces to just fourteen: Glasgow City should amalgamate with Lanarkshire and adjacent burghs, and Edinburgh with the Lothians and Peebles.[25] Given that they were not obvious losers, the recommendations were supported by the cities (with county councils more equivocal). However, fifteen Scottish burghs (of the nineteen who still had their own police forces) vociferously objected to the proposals as 'quite unacceptable' in a deputation to the Scottish Office.[26] With origins predating the 1707 Act of Union, the Convention of Royal Burghs was an extremely influential lobby group, and the report was 'pigeon-holed' by civil servants.[27] Divergence from England and Wales was very apparent during the Second World War when, as a result of the Defence (Amalgamation) Regulations, twenty-six forces on the English south coast were amalgamated into six in 1943. A similar move in Scotland was deemed 'politically impossible' and contrary to 'public opinion'.[28] Although Johnston did not press for Scotland to be omitted altogether from the regulations, he made it clear they would be 'a dead letter' north of the border.[29] When, in 1942, the Scottish Office suggested that Inverness Burgh might unite with Inverness County Police, the *Inverness Courier* rushed to the defence of the status quo, arguing for 'increased vigilance by local authorities over their rights and powers' against 'the dictates of Edinburgh and Whitehall'.[30] Dudgeon complained that the press was rabble-rousing, but the Scottish Office quickly backed down and approved the town council's new appointment.[31]

In England and Wales, where smaller municipalities had already lost the argument, a further forty-seven borough forces were abolished in 1946, but Scottish legislation of the same year took a more equivocal tack.[32] The 1946 Police (Scotland) Act introduced a protracted process by which the Scottish Secretary could put forward a proposal for amalgamation which would then be considered by full public inquiry, requiring ultimate parliamentary approval. Certainly, some areas agreed to amalgamate voluntarily, including Dumfries and Galloway (1948), the counties of Berwick, Roxburgh and Selkirk (1948), the North-Eastern Counties (1949) and the Lothians and Peebles (1950) (see Figure 2.1).[33] Mergers tended to be accepted by counties, persuaded of significant advantages in terms of recruitment, the sharing of technologies, and improved systems of communication across large geographical areas. However, the burghs – notably Inverness (as we have seen), as well as Motherwell and Wishaw, and Ayr – came out fighting in defence of their police across mainstream political parties.

The case made by the Labour-controlled town council of Motherwell and Wishaw is illuminating here. In 1948 council members staunchly defended their

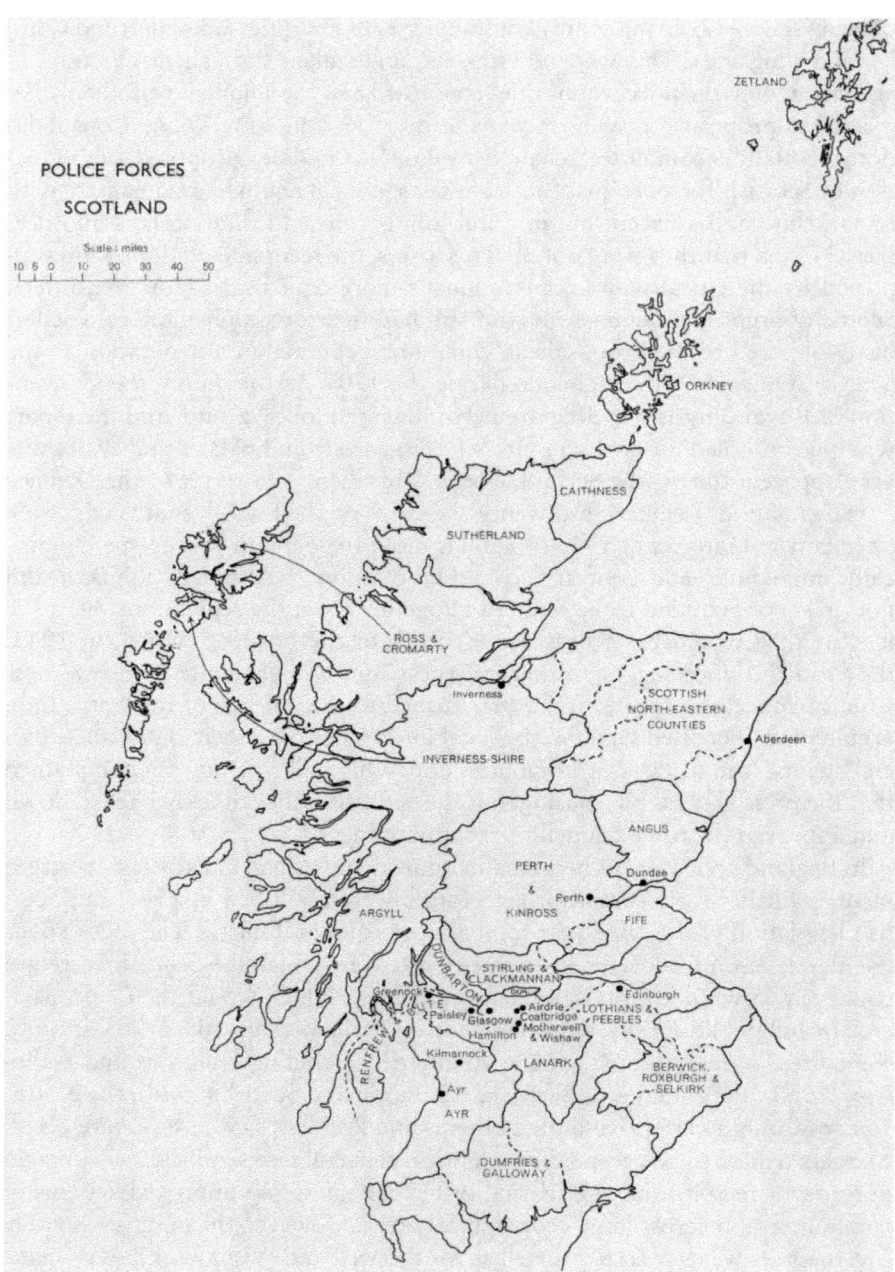

Figure 2.1 Map of Police Forces of Scotland, 1962. Source: (c) The British Library Board, PP, Final Report of the Royal Commission on Police Powers and Procedures (1962), Cmnd. 1728, Appendix IVc.

'local' control of the police force on behalf of the 'community they represent[ed]' in the face of pressure from the Scottish Office to amalgamate them into a much larger unit with Lanarkshire.[34] The defence was mounted in terms of local democracy and responsiveness to local need (through the 'close personal touch' forged between magistrates, councillors and senior police officers). Considerable emphasis was also given to the idea of tradition as they directly quoted the statement presented by their town's Lord Provost to the Ormidale Committee (15 years earlier) on behalf of the Convention of Royal Burghs:

> The burghs of Scotland have centuries experience of watching. The Police Force is a local service which most of the burghs possessing forces have maintained and controlled since the introduction of police [over] 75 years ago.[35]

They were referring to the 1857 act as a foundational narrative, sidestepping its original lack of an obviously democratic frame. Indeed, a letter to the *Motherwell Times* – in support of the local Labour administration and on the behalf of 'working men' – depicted the stand against police amalgamation as 'fighting for their democratic rights'.[36] Moreover, the campaign to save Motherwell and Wishaw police force was reported as uniting Labour Party, Scottish National Party (SNP) and Progressive Party candidates (the latter an anti-socialist alliance of conservatives/unionists and liberals) in the run-up to the local elections of 1949. The example of Motherwell and Wishaw, replicated in other Scottish towns, demonstrates the rhetorical emphasis that was placed locally on municipal control of policing for much of the twentieth century: as an expression of accountability as well as 'structures of feeling' relating to collective identity.[37] Indeed, its citizens claimed to speak from bitter experience. Motherwell and Wishaw had come under Lanark County Police from 1857 until 1930, during which, it was claimed, '[police officers] came and went frequently . . . [with] little or no interest in the affairs of the burgh'. This unhappiness had led Motherwell town council to pass a resolution in 1914 to separate from the county – but this had been prohibited by the Scottish Secretary on the ground of the wartime national emergency. The two burghs of Motherwell and Wishaw had in fact amalgamated in 1920 but it took them until 1929 to win the argument for a separate police force on the grounds of their increased population size. The popular memory of this struggle for autonomy galvanised them to defend their new burgh police force 'to the death' in the years after the Second World War, in fact remaining a separate force until 1967.[38]

Ayr Burgh Council used a range of tactics – including refusal to attend meetings – to sabotage the Scottish Office agenda. When the process finally resulted in a public enquiry in 1949, the town council objected that the procedure had been 'irregular', with their appeal upheld by Lord Birnam in the Court of Session, a highly embarrassing defeat for the Scottish Office.[39] Civil servant Charles Craik Cunningham advised his political bosses Arthur Woodburn (Labour) and then Charles Stuart (Conservative and Unionist) to put the matter on ice even though it was felt that the amalgamation of small forces was necessary from the perspective of efficiency. In the wake of the Ayr Burgh appeal, all other attempts at compulsory amalgamation were dropped since it was not considered 'politically feasible' to go 'against a very strongly held and vigorously voiced local opposition'.[40]

Yet the 'climate of opinion' was shifting. Galvanised by the 1962 Report of the Royal Commission on Police Powers and Procedures – which commented that something needed to be done about the 'extreme case of the multiplicity of small forces' in Scotland – Scottish civil servants had the political ammunition they had requested behind the scenes and they reopened the files.[41] The burghs of Inverness and Ayr were finally pushed into amalgamation with their respective counties through the ostensibly 'democratic' mechanism of consultative public inquiry and then act of parliament (rather than the straightforward imposition from above which was enabled in England and Wales by the 1964 Police Act).[42] By 1968 the Scottish Office had finally achieved its objective of reducing the number of forces to what it deemed an optimum level – twenty in total – with the system of direct local control by police committees (although now joint ones, uniting burgh and county) still in place, albeit weakened. Yet HMICS and Scottish Office civil servants remained unequivocally opposed to the idea of a 'national' police service for Scotland on the grounds of localism and affect: 'a constable ought to be feeling [that he was] a member of his own community' and 'have his feet . . . on local soil'. It was also seen as too controversial because of associations with the paramilitary model of the (national) Royal Irish Constabulary (RIC), an especially sensitive matter in the west of Scotland given affiliations with the island of Ireland.[43]

The final move towards regionalisation of the police service – and the creation of the eight forces that were to serve Scotland for the next 40 years from 1975 to 2013 – was the result of broader local government reform that created a new two-tier structure: of regional councils delivering major services, underpinned by multiple district councils delivering local planning and improvements.[44] Thus the burghs which had opposed police consolidation were themselves abolished. The only concerted opposition in 1974–5 was in the Scottish Borders, where a cross-party group of MPs attempted to fight regionalisation in parliament through an amendment to the Local Government (Scotland) Bill; but this was defeated when many members of the Conservative opposition voted with the Labour administration.[45] Across the twentieth century, the idea of shared interests grounded in 'community' and 'locality' tended to trump party political allegiances in resisting a centralising agenda in Scotland.

Sharing Resources – a Scottish Police 'Service'?

If there were clear centripetal pressures (most obviously from the burgh councils), there were other centrifugal forces, including the demands of rank-and-file police officers themselves. Indeed, it was the Scottish Police Federation (SPF) that became the most vocal in arguing for either one 'national' or a small number of 'regional' police forces in the 1960s, with a motion advocating the 'nationalisation' of Scottish policing passed at the annual conference in 1966.[46] The Federation's sudden rejection of the 'national' model some 10 years later was the result of the experience of regionalisation and the recognition (in the Strathclyde police area in particular) that one size did not fit all.[47]

Yet the ideas that lay behind distinct British and Scottish policing identities had been gradually nurtured from the early twentieth century, as this chapter will now show. That the 'British' police shared commonality as an occupational community was cultivated through the pages of *Police Review*, the trade magazine for the police service 'of Great Britain', which provided an important discussion forum for rank-and-file officers from 1893 (until publication ceased in 2011). In Scotland, as south of the border, the experience of the First World War intensified discontent regarding poor pay and gruelling working hours and encouraged membership of the Police Union (formed in September 1913). There had long been resentment of what was regarded as inferior treatment compared to colleagues in England and Wales. Although pensions had been introduced at the same time in 1890, Scottish officers had to serve 34 years to qualify for the maximum (compared to 26–30 years in England and Wales).[48] Yet officers in Scotland drew short of joining the 1919 police strike. Glasgow members of the Scottish Police Union stated that to strike was 'not in the spirit of the Glasgow police' since their desire was 'to act as a buffer between the two classes if possible'.[49] Elsewhere, lack of strike action may have been the result of intimidation: Norman Morrison's memoirs recall his dismissal for union membership (along with two other colleagues) by the Chief Constable of Argyll (as well as their subsequent reinstatement through the intervention of indignant 'ratepayers').[50] In March 1919 Home Secretary Edward Shortt appointed Lord Desborough to chair a Committee on the Police Service of England, Wales and Scotland to make recommendations on pay, pensions and conditions. Scottish police representatives were in agreement that they wanted 'equality with English police forces in every respect' – and chief constables concurred in the anticipation of improved recruitment (since it had long been felt that Scottish recruits were poached by English forces).[51] The police were in a strong negotiating position given levels of social unrest in many urban areas of Britain. That policing as a whole would benefit from standardisation of service was enshrined in the Desborough Report and, subsequently, the 1919 Police Act, which applied to all police forces across Great Britain.

The 1919 act created a consultative model, with parallel structures for Scotland and England/Wales. Whilst rank-and-file officers were prohibited from joining a trade union or striking, they were required to be a member of the Police Federation/SPF, which was accorded official recognition as representative of their views. The Home Secretary and Scottish Secretary were empowered to make regulations regarding pay, pensions, clothing, and conditions of service (including methods of discipline) – in consultation both with one another and, crucially, with representatives of all policing ranks. The Chief Constables (Scotland) Association (CC(S)A) was formed in 1919; so, too, was a Scottish Association of Superintendents and Lieutenants. Through the forum of the Scottish Police Council, representatives of all three police groupings met with the inspectorate, Secretary of State, and representatives of the local authorities to discuss changes to conditions. Whilst the consultative model fell woefully short of any model of national bargaining, Morrison (who attended the first meeting of the Scottish Police Council in October 1920) was impressed by the atmosphere of 'freedom and homeliness' in which discussions took place.[52] Moreover, the specific concept of 'the Scottish Police Service' – as an umbrella term for Scotland's separate police forces and constabularies – was increasingly and actively promoted through these new associational structures and cultures. Finally, as Weinberger suggests, the 1919 Act did not change the structure of policing but it did alter the 'distribution of effective power', giving chief constables (as a group), greater influence and detaching them somewhat from police authorities (whose authority was demoted), whilst bolstering the position of the Scottish Office.[53]

The CC(S)A was in fact a reconstitution of a mid-nineteenth-century organisation – the Chief Constables (Scotland) Club, whose purpose had been 'the cultivation of friendly intercourse and the consideration of subjects connected with the police service' and which had thought of itself as the voice of 'Scottish police'.[54] The atmosphere of the 'club' remained following the renaming: the CC(S)A met biannually in different locations, usually with a golfing competition as a focal point, lubricating the wheels of elite masculine sociability and camaraderie. Minutes of meetings had always been forwarded to the Scottish Office and good relationships long cultivated with the inspectorate (especially David Munro, himself a former Chief Constable of the Lothians). This was stepped up from 1923, when a Scottish Office representative was formally invited to attend.[55] It was the CC(S)A and Scottish Office who together commissioned the design of a generic badge for the Scottish Police Service (showing the thistle and motto *semper vigilo*) that was widely adopted in 1930, thus placing the concept on a symbolic footing.[56] Nevertheless, identity as a Scottish Police Service remained underdrawn either side of the Second World War and, as subsequent chapters will highlight, subservient in cities and burghs to localised and individualised force identities.

Desire for greater professionalisation (promoted avidly by sequential HMICSs) was also an important driver of Scottish centralisation. The Desborough Report had commented on the absence of any 'uniform system of training policemen' across Great Britain generally, recommending a standard two months for all new recruits (as well as the sharing of provision). In the interwar years the cities of Glasgow, Edinburgh and Aberdeen, who had their own training schools, began to train recruits from other forces across their regions. Dudgeon actively promoted 'improvement' (of both self and the police service) beyond the initial training, through 'knowledge and education' and the opportunity to 'qualify for promotion'.[57] Proposals for a national Scottish Training school were first mooted in 1943. The search for suitable premises began in 1946 and Tulliallan Castle (Kincardine, Stirlingshire) was acquired in 1948, although the building and conversion work that was required was a painstaking process lasting over a decade. In the meantime, keen to press ahead with a uniform Scottish police training, the Scottish Office opened Whitburn training centre in West Lothian as a fallback in March 1947. Its Nissan hut facilities were inadequate in relation to both quality and size of accommodation, and training had to be shared with Glasgow City Police Training School (Oxford Street) and (from 1952) Polkemmet House, West Lothian. In 1955 the first training courses (for senior officers rather than new recruits) were offered at Tulliallan. In October 1960 its vital new wing was opened and the Police College was finally available for a new intake of recruits.[58]

Analysis of the instruction manuals issued to recruits enables us to chart the values, principles and ethos that underpinned policing at the official rhetorical level. In 1893 around 3,000 copies of a generic *Police Manual*, the brain-child of Munro and prepared by a committee of the Chief Constables (Scotland) Club, was distributed for the first time.[59] Its aim was to guide 'members of Police Forces in Scotland' regarding 'common law and statutory offences', and to complement the separate 'Orders and Regulations' issued by each chief constable 'for the government of his own force'.[60] Further editions were produced (including those of 1910 and 1931), although the revision process fell behind during the Second World War. Aberdeen City Police had compiled its own comprehensive instruction book in 1936, and in 1943 this was made available to other forces. In 1952 the Chief Constables (Scotland) Association decided that the Aberdeen instruction book (renamed *Scottish Criminal Law, Police Duties and Procedures*) would officially be adopted by all Scottish forces as the definitive text.[61] Nevertheless, Glasgow City Police insisted on retaining its own *Instruction Book* into the 1960s, as it had long done so.[62]

In her analysis of instruction books used by English police forces, Joanna Klein argues that, by the early twentieth century, they 'presented a clear image of the ideal police officer as the epitome of a masculine worker' and as 'a kind of modern knight with all of his chivalrous qualities'.[63] They also provided a foundational or originating 'myth' that connected the role of police officer to 'a heroic English history of public service', grounded in Anglo-Saxon and medieval traditions of 'chivalry and honour'.[64] It is notable that the 1952 edition of *Scottish Criminal Law* depicted the Scottish police as a fairly recent rather than medieval project. The forward to the volume described 'the police force as we know it' as 'a modern development' that had established 'a great tradition of public service' in a 'comparatively short period'. Its origins were presented as lying in the Police (Scotland) Act of 1857 which led to the establishment of police forces throughout Scotland.[65] This was a partial version of Scottish police history that emphasised the centrality of the uniform national project (and of modern democratic forms of governance rather than feudalism), choosing not to mention the much earlier municipal model grounded in elites and in particularity.

Like its English equivalents, however, the Scottish text grounded the police role – and thus legitimacy – in the duty to uphold the rule of law, depicting officers as 'the protectors of the common weal, the guarantors of public order and liberty'. Whilst police officers in England and Wales swore an oath to serve the monarch as subjects, the Scottish constable was definitely 'not a servant of the crown' but 'a public servant appointed to preserve law and order for and on behalf of the citizens'.[66] The principles of equality and democracy were explicitly enshrined in the declaration (or speech act) that every officer in Scotland made on appointment to 'discharge the duties of the office of constable . . . according to the law, without fear, favour, affection, malice or ill-will'.[67] Nevertheless, despite the difference between the oath (England and Wales) and declaration (Scotland), the distinctions between the Scottish and English polity were of subtle nuance and both reflected common foundational texts that had shaped the construction of a British model of civilian police.[68] In 1919 the Desborough Report had further equated this with the new post-war democratic citizenship (in the wake of the 1918 Representation of the People Act) stating that across Britain:

> The constable . . . acts not as an agent of the Government, exercising powers derived from that fact, but as a citizen, representing the rest of the community, and exercising powers which, at any rate in their elements, are possessed by all citizens alike . . . [I]n this country the whole power of the constable rests on the support, both moral and physical, of his fellow citizens. We desire to emphasize this point as, in our opinion, it has an important bearing in the relation between the Police and the public – as to the consideration to which the Police are entitled on the one hand, and their obligation to the public on the other.[69]

Whilst mid-nineteenth-century 'citizenship' had been restricted through the franchise to male property-owners, the rhetoric of Desborough emphasised the idea that police officers (despite or even because of their working-class origins) were themselves both 'fellow citizens' and part of 'the community'. A conceptual distinction was set up, however, between 'the police' on the one hand and 'the public' on the other: as discrete entities implying reciprocal responsibilities and obligations. Moreover, 'the public' was implicitly defined as those who accepted the rule of law and who, as the 'law-abiding', sought to maintain it. Thus 'the public' was not simply 'the people' nor equated with popular opinion. Neither, and most crucially, did it include those viewed as 'the criminal' or the politically subversive (pacifists and communists/socialists who opposed the war effort of 1914–18), or those who for whatever reason were not recognised as 'citizens'. Nevertheless, as Johansen has argued, use of the terminology of 'the public' and 'democratic policing' as 'key legitimising concepts in official rhetoric' reached a 'highpoint' in Britain in the 1930s to 1950s.[70]

In addition to statements regarding the polity, Scottish instruction manuals outlined the type of person that a constable should aspire to be. Avoiding the romantic flourishes of some English instruction books, they similarly emphasised the qualities of obedience, neatness, civility and tact. Nevertheless, slight changes in emphasis are apparent across time. In 1910 'obedience to orders' was emphasised as the 'fundamental principle' – although it was stressed that this was not simply a 'will to obey' but 'aptitude and intelligence to give practical effect to the order of a superior'.[71] In 1910, too, the police constable was instructed on politeness and good manners: he 'must be civil, obliging and respectful in speech and in manner to all classes, of whatever degree or rank'.[72] By 1952 this statement had been expanded to incorporate principles of equality and democracy: 'All classes, rich and poor alike, are entitled to his services; and he must not be actuated by sectarian prejudices, class distinctions, or desire for personal reward.'[73] Moreover, from the 1950s to the 1980s the instruction book delineated 'personal character' (rather than obedience *per se*) as the building block of policing, which was depicted as a uniform set of attributes. Its 'mainspring' was 'self-control' (including 'even temper' and 'sobriety'), which was intrinsically connected to 'courage', 'honesty and truthfulness', 'tact', 'fairness', 'obedience', 'health' and an aptitude for 'study' and 'improvement'. Embodiment was depicted in classical terms – as in *mens sana in corpore sano* – with officers encouraged to participate in 'clean habits and wholesome pastimes'.[74] The archetype was that of dutiful, self-disciplined, self-effacing citizenship, which underpinned most educative and penal-welfare initiatives from the 1880s to the early 1960s.[75] Moreover, the continued use of the gendered pronouns he/his (long after women had been formerly admitted to the service albeit in small numbers) equated police legitimacy with virtuous masculinity – the 'manliness of character' laid out by Dudgeon in 1931.

As Klein has highlighted, physical force was barely mentioned at all in these manuals as an aspect of policing, other than to refer to 'the avoidance of unnecessary force' and restraint in using the baton.[76] The discursive emphasis was on personal character, civility and moderation and thus on moral force through exemplary conduct. Yet the importance of physical robustness, endurance and bodily deportment was rigorously enforced elsewhere: particularly through the ritual, practice and curriculum of the training school, which included military-style drill, parade and inspection, the latter necessitating the need to 'stand to attention' for sustained periods. Swimming lessons were requisite given the need to save lives (along with self-defence, including judo by mid-century). The presence of military models (most obviously drill) in police induction was grounded in nineteenth-century practices in which uniformed organisations adopted broadly similar models relating to physical deportment. Given that military models were further normalised and standardised as a result of the near ubiquitous experience of war (or national service) from 1914 to 1960, most training school recruits adapted with relative ease in this period.[77] Yet for those sent to Tulliallan from the 1960s onwards but who had never served in the military, police training school was certainly something of a sharp shock.[78]

In some regards the years after the Second World War saw the interchangeability of military and policing careers challenged. In 1946 Sydney Kinnear became the first career police officer to be appointed as HMICS (a move that was welcomed by serving chief constables), and this shift was consolidated in the subsequent appointment of Thomas Renfrew in 1958, Andrew Meldrum in 1966 and David Gray in 1970.[79] Whilst positioned as an independent intermediary between chief constables and the Secretary of State, they were very much part of a 'close-knit policy community' within Scotland from whose ranks they were drawn and they increasingly commented on strategic and operational aspects of policing.[80] Gray in particular played an important role as a 'policy entrepreneur' as subsequent chapters will show. The idea of the police as a professional occupation was increasingly encouraged.

Yet the complementary relationship between professionalisation (education of the mind), athleticism (physical fitness) and militarism (drill, deportment and physical obedience) continued to be articulated together through the textbook emphasis on self-discipline and the training school routine. Across time, official induction combined the physical training of the body with the theory of civility and character. As subsequent chapters will show, however, there were sometimes significant and even stark gaps between the official theory and formal deportment of Scottish policing (on the one hand), and local practices, adaptations and identities that (on the other) developed at the grassroots level when officers returned to division. Before these differences are examined in separate chapters on urban and rural policing, it is essential to consider the formal position of the police in relation to the other institutions and practitioners that constituted the broader architecture of Scottish criminal justice.

Police, Prosecution and Justice

The role (both formal and informal) played by Scottish police officers in making, shaping and framing legal decisions cannot be overstated. Within recent discourse, emphasis has often been placed on the prominent role accorded to an independent public prosecutor – separate from police and judiciary – as a distinctive historical feature of the Scottish legal system compared to England and Wales.[81] This role was (and is) overseen by the Lord Advocate as head of the Crown Office in Edinburgh, but operated at county level through the Procurator Fiscal (PF) and his depute or assistant. It was the job of the PF to take precognitions (statements) and to send papers on to the Crown Office for a decision as to whether to institute proceedings for serious 'crimes' (murder, rape and aggravated assault) under 'solemn process' (jury trial) in the High Court of Justiciary (in Edinburgh or on circuit). It was established by the late nineteenth century in urban areas that offences viewed as more minor and suitable for summary justice might be processed without jury before a bailie in a police court (or in some circumstances dealt with by the sheriff).[82] However, as Lindsay Farmer has demonstrated, 'the development of a system of public prosecution for the inferior courts occurred later and more gradually than is commonly supposed'.[83]

Whilst in many burghs legally trained officials were, increasingly, appointed to act as prosecutors, in some smaller ones the Chief Constable also acted as burgh PF into the twentieth century.[84] Most significantly, in the City of Glasgow, divisional police superintendents continued to be appointed by the Corporation in a dual role as burgh PF depute (assistant). Although theoretically answerable to the burgh PF – a legal professional who was responsible for advice and direction and brought cases in the central police court – the divisional superintendents acted as prosecutors on behalf of the Crown in the remaining divisional police courts (including the juvenile courts) on a daily basis. Explaining the system in 1907, Glasgow Chief Constable James V. Stevenson admitted that there was effectively 'a Police Fiscal' system in the city: 'the superintendent must decide a great many cases for himself as to whether he will take them up or not' and 'the great majority of cases are brought before the magistrates on the sole initiation of the superintendent of the division'.[85]

The elision of the roles of police and fiscal had staunch critics and defenders from the early nineteenth century when the first police courts were introduced.[86] For James Devon, reflecting in 1912 on his experience as Medical Officer for Glasgow's Duke Street Prison, the city's police court system (which dealt mainly with the urban poor) had little legitimacy:

> In Glasgow with all its police courts there is only one trained lawyer who prosecutes. The great mass of the charges are conducted by his deputes,

who are invariably police officers. The only witnesses in many cases are constables and the prosecutor is one of their superior officers. It is a state of affairs that does not impress an outsider by its wisdom, and it is not regarded by those who come within its scope as being fair.[87]

Yet these types of criticism did not unduly worry the Scottish Office (of which the Crown Office was part), even with the increased emphasis on democratic ideals in the years after the First World War.

In 1927 a senior civil servant admitted that the Glasgow system was 'not so unlike the case in England', although with the 'important distinction . . . that it is not the person who has arrested the alleged criminal who conducts the prosecution'. He stressed that the 'Police Fiscal' was solely answerable to the burgh PF (and not the Chief Constable) in his role as prosecutor, creating dual but not overlapping roles as 'prosecutor' and 'policeman'.[88] Writing from the police perspective, Charles Cameron Macdonald, who became police court officer for Glasgow's Marine Division around 1933, saw the system as highly efficient:

> The court was presided over by a lay magistrate who was guided by a solicitor called the Assessor . . . The system worked well and a tremendous amount of work was done. There was a staff of five, two [police] officers who delivered summons in the area, a constable in charge of the prisoners, the superintendent as the prosecutor, and myself responsible for the general running of the court.[89]

In 1961 the Sheriffs-Substitute Association stated categorically that 'in Scotland the police are investigators but never prosecutors' although 'in the lower courts there were exceptions to this rule in quite recent years', suggesting it lasted to mid-century.[90] Indeed, in its final report of 1962 the Royal Commission recommended that the term 'police court' should be discontinued in Scotland because of the 'mistaken impression' that it was not independent, hinting that memories of the system invoked by James Devon in 1912 were long-lived.[91] It is noteworthy, however, that the elision of police-prosecutorial functions attracted surprisingly little censure or criticism from those in municipal and central government (including those in political opposition roles) in the first half of the twentieth century, despite its use in Glasgow. Rather, the police courts – with their quick processing of 'a predominantly working-class clientele' for low-level offending and infringements of local byelaws regarding public order or nuisance – were presented as delivering an 'efficient and cheap form of justice'.[92] In Glasgow, police prosecution was justified and explained in terms of the volume of business, but, as we suggest elsewhere in this study, such a volume was itself sustained and enhanced by police tactics. Within the political economy of criminal justice, the supply of rapid judicial procedure facilitated and structured high-volume policing demand.[93]

Two key points are worth further emphasis. Firstly, this arrangement was broadly similar to modes of police prosecution south of the border at that time. Indeed, it has been suggested that the 'Scottish system' 'might have provided a template for police-led prosecutions in England from the mid-nineteenth century'.[94] Secondly, in Glasgow specifically discretion regarding prosecution for 'police offences' such as breach of the peace, drunkenness and street betting, as well as minor thefts and assaults, was mostly devolved to senior police officers within the locale in the first half of the twentieth century. This was statistically significant in the broader context of Scottish summary justice given that a very high proportion of cases – 32 per cent of all persons dealt with across Scotland in 1912, for example – were processed in Glasgow's lower courts.[95] As David Barrie and Susan Broomhall have demonstrated, 'from their inception [from the early nineteenth century], police courts dealt with more business, prosecuted more cases and punished more offenders than any other centre of justice in the country.'[96] By 1900, less than two per cent of all criminal proceedings in Scotland were conducted through the 'solemn process' of jury trial, whilst the overwhelming majority of cases arose from the regulation of urban public order and public space and were directed against the poor and working classes.[97] Indeed, into the early twentieth century, 'the whole proceedings' in the police court might last only 'a few minutes', with police officers sometimes acting as the sole witnesses.[98] Those who pleaded not guilty had the right to request an adjournment of 48 hours, but they were not necessarily advised of this right until 1908 (through the Summary Jurisdiction (Scotland) Act). Although free legal advice for the poorest could be requested for the higher courts through the 'Poor Agents' system, it was not routinely available in the police courts (other than in Edinburgh from 1910 and Dundee from 1926 through local government initiatives).[99]

Where there was a complaint about the police court (or other summary) proceedings, an appeal could be lodged through the High Court of Justiciary in Edinburgh to have the conviction suspended (in other words, quashed). Barrie and Broomhall have noted that although the number of appeals from the police court to the High Court of Justiciary increased across time, they remained 'fairly infrequent'.[100] Around forty such actions per year appear to have been brought in the first two decades of the twentieth-century across the whole of Scotland, declining to around thirty per year in the 1920s. A significant proportion of these appellants were business persons and traders (generally unrepresentative of the social class of the clientele of the police courts), often in relation to licensing byelaws.[101]

Moreover, data relating to the formal prosecution process conceal other aspects of police involvement in decision-making, which can often only be gleaned from ethnographic and qualitative evidence. Later in this book we show how policing in rural areas was not only largely administrative but also, when it came to conflict resolution, overwhelmingly delivered through informal mechanisms given the lack of either back-up or easy access to summary courts in remote areas (Chapter 5). Even in dense urban areas (as Chapters 3 and 4 show), a range of informal resolutions (as well as the use of discretion more broadly) can be tracked across the first half of the twentieth century. These include elements of 'khadi justice', defined by the influential sociologist Max Weber as 'informal judgements' based on 'concrete ethical or practical valuations' as opposed to the 'empirical justice' based on a technology of case precedent that clearly characterises Scots Law.[102] There are occasional glimpses, too, of 'rough justice', usually without official sanction and, increasingly, with very clear official condemnation. Finally, we also demonstrate – across the twentieth century – the regular use of semi-formal and sub-judicial processes, usually involving warnings but sometimes other forms of intervention, which sifted 'first-time' offenders out of criminal justice in line with the preventive aim of policing. These were systems initiated and run by the police although often in conjunction with other agencies.

Public Confidence, Discipline and Complaints

From the late nineteenth century onwards the official rhetoric of politicians, civil servants and senior police officers delineated a trajectory of ever-increasing confidence shared by 'the public' in 'the police' in Scotland. This narrative seam was established in the annual reports of HMICS David Munro who asserted at the end of 1890 that:

> The popularity of the constabulary and police appears to increase every year, which is very satisfactory, for nothing is more essential to peace and order than that relations between the public and police should be always of the most harmonious character.[103]

Dudgeon's later comments of July 1931, with which this chapter opened, were cut from a similar cloth. Yet the timing of these two statements is important since they came at the end of periods of significant unrest. Firstly, those of Munro must be situated in relation to the 'Crofters' Wars' of the 1880s when land raids and rent strikes on Skye and Lewis had led not only to attacks on the civil police by those resisting arrest for eviction (including the 'Battle of the Braes' of 1882 on Skye) but also to a series of military expeditions (in defence of landowners' interests) led by Inverness-shire sheriff William Ivory.[104] Secondly, the decade preceding Dudgeon's statement had included the General Strike of 1926 (and lengthier miners' lockout) in which there had been police baton charges in Aberdeen, Glasgow and Edinburgh, deemed disproportionate and unprovoked by those at the receiving end.[105] Moreover, only a year later, Dudgeon conceded in 1932 that 'the work of the police' had been of a 'strenuous nature' but of 'tactful manner' in relation to demonstrations by the National Unemployed Workers Movement (NUWM); these and other protests had led to the use of batons and mounted police in Glasgow in October 1931 and January 1932. Whilst those involved in the protests argued that the response had been indiscriminate, the police claimed that no order to draw batons had been given and that individual officers were simply defending themselves from armed rioters.[106] Such statements, therefore, need to be contextualised as interventions in a fraught set of political contexts.

The shared experience of the Second World War was ubiquitously presented as cause for trust in the police by lord provosts, including Glasgow's Patrick Dollan (Labour Party), who had himself previously been targeted for police surveillance given his pacifism and socialism during the First World War.[107] Dudgeon's successor as HIMCS, Sydney Kinnear, noted in 1952 that 'the relationship between the public and the police has never been better' and in 1955 that 'the public are increasingly willing and anxious to help the police'.[108] Yet allusion to a homogeneous 'public' concealed differentiated experiences. These constructions of current 'public' solidarity – in contrast to prior moments of dissent – aimed to establish and normalise co-operation in full recognition that it was never fixed or permanent. Thus sequential speech acts that referred to a momentum of approval concealed a more complex chronology in which opinion moved backwards and forwards. Moreover, as subsequent chapters will show, this rhetoric was a veneer that was layered over a complex range of fine-grained localised experiences that were also differentiated by age, socio-economic status, ethnicity, religion, gender, and political affiliations.

Nevertheless, it is significant that in Scotland there was no nationally articulated 'disquiet' regarding police legitimacy that traversed political affiliations and social classes in the first half of the twentieth century (although concerns were raised at local levels in relation to the policing of industrial disputes). This contrasts with experiences in England, where allegations about Metropolitan Police corruption (regarding night-clubs and bookmakers) were widely publicised in the late 1920s, as well as a complaint about the inappropriate treatment of female witness Irene Savidge (in relation to an 'indecency' case involving high-profile economist Sir Leo Chiozza Money). The latter led to a Tribunal of Inquiry in May 1928 to which Conservative Home Secretary William Joynson-Hicks conceded (under the terms of the Tribunal of Inquiry (Evidence) Act 1921 which required the resolution of both houses of parliament to proceed).

As John Carter Wood has demonstrated, significant concerns were raised in the UK national press (conservative as well as left-leaning) about the use of 'third degree'-style interrogation (in which psychological pressure was placed on suspects to draw confessions) across English police forces. Whilst Labour MPs played a prominent role in criticising police methods, there was some notable cross-party support.[109] This crisis of confidence led to the announcement in July 1928 that there would be a Royal Commission on Police Powers and Procedures which, it emerged, would cover England and Wales but not Scotland. The grounds that were given were that the role of the public prosecutor meant that conditions were different north of the border, implying, too, that the crisis was specific to England and Wales. That this was a flawed argument was highlighted in an anonymous contribution published in *The Scotsman*, which suggested that the arrangement in police courts 'where the superintendent acts as a Procurator Fiscal for his division' might warrant 'some inquiry'.[110] Women's groups in Scotland also expressed dissatisfaction, since they had hoped a Royal Commission would advance the employment of female officers as statement-takers (in the wake of the Savidge case). These points were not, however, taken up by Scottish politicians and the Royal Commission restricted its report of June 1929 to England and Wales. Indeed, only one tribunal of inquiry was held into policing matters in Scotland in the first half of the twentieth century (called for by the local police authority). It concerned a complaint of wrongful dismissal in 1925 made by two Kilmarnock police constables against their Chief Constable who, they claimed, had been motivated by hostility towards their police federation activity. Their grievance was not upheld, although it was found that the Chief had lacked 'tact and judgement' in dealing with events.[111]

The one major flashpoint that led to very significant national-level public scrutiny of police governance in Scotland was an official complaint that a 15-year-old boy had been assaulted in a back alley in Thurso by two Caithness constables in December 1957. The burgh prosecutor referred the case to the Crown Office, the Lord Advocate deciding not to prosecute.[112] However, the matter escalated when it was taken up by the newly independent (formerly Conservative and Unionist) MP for Caithness, Sir David Robertson, whose campaign, which involved a cross-party petition signed by over 200 members of Parliament, led to a Tribunal of Inquiry as a matter of 'urgent public importance' in February 1959.[113] The hearing in Inverness, covered extensively across the UK press, confirmed there were no grounds to prosecute since there was no corroboration of assault (although it was likely to have taken place), whilst its detailed investigation and examination of witnesses led to the officers being reprimanded for other behaviour. The case of the 'Thurso Boy' was one of a 'number of unrelated incidents' that led to the setting up of the 1960 Royal Commission on Police Powers and Procedures which examined the 'constitutional position of the police throughout Great Britain'. This included (amongst other matters) the 'relationship [of the police] with the public and the means of ensuring that complaints by the public against the police are effectively dealt with'.[114]

The 1959 Thurso tribunal was a watershed moment for police officers across Scotland as well as Great Britain. The two Caithness officers, as well as the 15-year-old complainant, were subjected to intrusive national press scrutiny which would have been viewed as 'contempt of court' in relation to ordinary criminal justice process.[115] Without doubt this placed a strain on social and political relationships locally, not least between Caithness County Council, the police committee and their local MP; but the ripples were felt widely.[116] For the police (whose views were represented in the *Police Review*) as well as some criminal justice practitioners, the Tribunal was a disproportionate and unfair response to a matter that should have been resolved through the police discipline and complaints system.[117] Even for critics of the police, as Paul Gordon has argued, the allegation 'was quite trivial by comparison with what was alleged elsewhere at the same time'.[118] The SPF used its annual conference in May 1959 to raise 'grave concerns' about damage to police morale and 'the status of the police in the community', echoed by Labour MP James Callaghan as Police Federation consultant and adviser. An SPF deputation (including Callaghan) to Scottish Secretary John Maclay (Conservative) in July 1959 sought reassurances that the police would be protected from 'the effects of malicious allegations' (assumed likely to increase) and that 'the interests of the police would not be disregarded'.[119] Thus the fallout of the Thurso tribunal included the erosion of confidence in public trust amongst rank-and-file police (as much as public confidence in police), although the police were quick to use professional networks to defend their position. It was also a wake-up call to any officers who were still using forms of physical chastisement to discipline errant youth.

The resulting Royal Commission was itself a significant – but ultimately complacent – intervention within national debates regarding police organisation and accountability. However, the sheer volume of evidence it collected (including comments 'in private' as well as those for official public record) renders it an important source for police historians. Set alongside other archival materials, it provides glimpses, albeit partial ones, of policy and practice relating to police discipline and complaints in Scotland. There were in effect three primary mechanisms that might be invoked, which we outline next – the Discipline Code, public prosecution, and civil law (although the processes that led to the first two were intricately bound together) – with a Tribunal of Inquiry the ultimate resort.

Since the nineteenth century the Discipline Code had been used to regulate the conduct of officers in British police forces through internal procedures. It covered all behavioural aspects that might bring the police into disrepute (and thus challenge the legitimacy that was grounded in moral force), including drunkenness or taking a drink on duty, 'gossiping' or neglect of duty, lack of punctuality and cleanliness, absence without leave, disobedience and insubordination, the taking of bribes and incivility, and, of course conviction for a criminal offence.[120] Policing was one of the most highly regulated of all occupations, particularly given that these prescripts extended into personal and private life. Well into the second half of the twentieth century officers had to apply for permission to marry or to live in accommodation that was not police-owned, and spouses were subject to similar levels of scrutiny.[121]

Penalties under the Discipline Code included (in order of perceived leniency) reprimands and cautions, fines, reduction in pay or rank, requirement to resign, and dismissal. Archival material relating to Glasgow City Police ('C' Division) for the years 1900–10 and for Greenock Police for the years 1910–20 shows that by far the most common default of the Discipline Code was for drunkenness or drinking on duty (half of all Glasgow cases and a third of Greenock ones).[122] Neglect of duty – including sleeping or idleness – also constituted a sizeable proportion of cases, dealt with by a range of penalties. 'Immorality', whilst representing a small number of cases, was dealt with severely. If male officers in the first decades of the twentieth century were found in 'disorderly houses' or consorting with 'prostitutes' or to have fathered children outside of wedlock they were likely to be dismissed immediately; they were also dismissed for keeping inappropriate company or other forms of inappropriate behaviour. Official national data collated by HMICS later in the century suggest that drunkenness had declined to 15 per cent of disciplinary offences in 1953 (although anecdotal evidence from interviews suggests that alcohol problems were persistent across many police areas both urban and rural), whilst neglect of duty remained a significant component of offences at 40 per cent of the total.[123]

Across the twentieth century HMICS published the annual numbers of police officers in Scotland who were dismissed or required to resign for disciplinary offences. This data series shows that comparatively high numbers left police forces under a cloud in the early part of the century (over 100 per year in the Edwardian period), dropping to 68 in 1919, 39 in 1927, and 21 in 1930, remaining thereafter remarkably constant – at less than 20 per year – into the late 1970s.[124] These figures should be set against the doubling in size of the Scottish police establishment (actual strength) from 4,868 in 1900 to 10,459 by 1970.[125] Whilst any simple interpretation of the data is subject to question, it seems likely that the comparably high numbers of dismissals around 1900 were linked to poor pay and poor conditions, resulting in high turnover. It may also reflect an attitude that was 'strict, and at times bordering on brutal' in the years when officers had no right to representation.[126] The data for the years after 1930 is suggestive of a well-oiled machine that, at a superficial level at least, had successfully inducted officers in skills of self-discipline (although it may also reflect a loosening of some prescripts and increasing recognition for the SPF). Equivalent information is not available for convictions of police officers for criminal offences across time, although these were published from 1952 onwards and demonstrated a three-fold increase even before the Thurso case: from 7 in 1954 and 15 in 1956 to 22 in 1958 (although numbers remained very small). Through the 1960s to 1970s convictions varied but were generally less than 40 per year (and sometimes less than 20). HMICS pointed out that these were invariably for 'motoring offences', a grey area that many did not see as 'proper' crime, and which did not necessarily result in dismissal nor result from public complaints.[127]

Although the majority of disciplinary cases were brought by superior officers (to discipline their workforce), a small proportion were the result of complaints lodged by 'members of the public', either directly at a police station or by letter to the Chief Constable.[128] In a tiny number of instances relating to the most serious allegations – particularly in the wake of the Thurso incident but also earlier in the century – complainants instead contacted the PF, approached their MP or wrote directly to the Scottish Secretary. Of the seventy-nine 'public' complaints processed by Edinburgh City Police in the 12 months between August 1959 and July 1960 (summarised for the Royal Commission), only fourteen (less than 20 per cent) were substantiated following investigation. Where allegations of minor assaults by officers on members of the public were made (12 per cent of cases), there was either no corroboration, the complainant withdrew the allegation, or the officer was deemed to have used reasonable force in the course of an arrest and no further action was taken.[129] The enforcement of legislation relating to motor offences brought the police (across Britain) into contact with a new group of 'offenders' – the middle-classes – who had previously escaped scrutiny.[130] It is no surprise, then, that in Edinburgh, incidents relating to motoring and parking offences formed the most common scenario that led to complaint (19 per cent) in 1959–60, as older and more affluent drivers (who did not think of themselves as 'criminals' to be stopped by the police) were initially affronted by officers whom they deemed rude and lacking in civility and later retracted the complaint.[131]

If charges against a police officer were of a serious criminal nature, precognitions would be taken from scratch by the PF who would refer them to the Crown Office. Yet for more 'minor' allegations, investigation was initiated by an inspector who might also take precognitions that were then handed over to the prosecutor. Once the PF (or Crown Office) was in possession of precognitions they would consider whether there was a case for prosecution in the criminal court (with conviction leading to automatic dismissal). If there was no evidence (including no corroboration) and thus no criminal proceeding, the case might be handed back to the police to pursue through the Discipline Code. However, a Scottish Office circular of 1952 inadvertently led to a change of practice – by instructing chief constables that if there was no public prosecution (as emerged in the Thurso case), then a Chief Constable could not pursue action for the same offence under the Discipline Code. The 1952 circular was even interpreted by some police forces to mean that the corroboration rule should apply to disciplinary cases as well as to criminal complaints. There were thus clear gaps in the resolution of complaints generally – exposed in the Thurso case – and problems also seem to have arisen because complainants were often left uninformed as to how a complaint had been dealt with.[132]

A further mechanism of redress for complainants – that was independent of the police and PF – was to sue individual officers for the costs of damages arising from 'over-zealous' policing or inappropriate behaviour in the civil courts. Indeed, there was some discussion in the aftermath of the Thurso tribunal as to whether the two officers concerned might have been sued under civil law, although it was unclear whether this would have been successful. In Scotland, unlike England, officers were individually liable for their actions as having 'no master', since they were not held in law to be employees of either the Chief Constable or the police authority.[133] Nevertheless, police authorities gave considerable support to any officer facing such action by covering costs.[134] Moreover, officers were also accorded very significant protection under Scots Law which affirmed that 'civil liability did not attach to a public official for an act done in the pursuance of his official duty, unless the act was done maliciously' (and with a presumption in their favour).[135] Indeed, the initial precedent for this was a legal judgement of 1888 when crofter John Beaton unsuccessfully brought a case against Sheriff Ivory alleging the wrongful arrest of the residents of Herbista, Skye.[136] One further tool, that of private prosecution (involving the use of 'criminal letters'), was extremely rare in Scotland and was unlikely to have been successful in the case of the Thurso Boy given lack of corroboration.[137]

Thus there were a variety of ways in which complaints could be made against the police and redress sought. Yet they were not necessarily transparent and not necessarily seen as fair – either by officers on the one hand, or complainants on the other. Appearing before the Desborough Committee back in 1919, Glasgow representatives of the Scottish Police Union were anxious that 'the power of a Chief Constable to dismiss a man without any reason be abolished'. Referring to James V. Stevenson, they explained that 'We have a splendid Chief Constable right now but he will shortly be retiring and we do not know who will be coming afterwards, so we want to be prepared'.[138] With the creation of the SPF, officers were accorded rights to representation and due process in disciplinary cases, but concerns were nevertheless raised in evidence to the Royal Commission in 1960–1 that in small close-knit burgh forces this was extremely difficult to put into practice internally because 'no member of the force is prepared to say anything on behalf of the accused in case of victimisation'.[139]

If officers themselves were concerned about intimidation, discrimination and partiality, the issue was just as pressing for civilian complainants. The Faculty of Advocates noted in its official statement to the Royal Commission that 'police officers in making instigations are always impartial and do listen to complaints from members of the public'. Nevertheless, their representatives requested a confidential hearing with members of the committee when the latter visited Edinburgh in May 1961, in which leading QC Manuel Kissen spoke of his personal feeling of 'an unconscious attitude' in which 'the inspector is sometimes a little too much behind the individual constable and not as impartial as one would like to see him'. He attributed this to 'the "we" attitude and "our side" attitude' that was 'subconsciously' there.[140] That both police and lawyers, from disparate perspectives, suggested different forms of unconscious bias were in operation served to highlight the need for an investigation system that was more independent.

Nevertheless, the Royal Commission expressed confidence in the Scottish system generally, in the role of the public prosecutor in acting as an independent investigator, and thus in the impartiality of the complaints system. Cases involving abuse of police powers in England, Wales and also Scotland were ascribed to isolated individuals or 'black sheep' in an otherwise highly disciplined police service (reiterating words also used by the 1929 Royal Commission), whilst the publication of 'news' that a police officer faced criminal charges was 'evidence of a Chief Constable's determination to deal properly with his men'.[141]

As part of the Royal Commission's investigations, a quantitative survey was undertaken by the Central Office of Information on the popular opinion of the police across Great Britain (the first of its kind). It concluded that, at a national level, 83 per cent had 'great respect for the police', although a more critical stance (of 'apathy') was taken by young people aged 18–25, as well as by motorists (resentful of the policing of motoring and parking offences) and those living 'in urban areas'.[142] A mere 1 per cent of those interviewed had registered a complaint at some time, and half of those were happy with how it had been resolved (which was deemed to indicate there was no cause for concern). The findings were not disaggregated for Scotland, although the anecdotal evidence given by senior Scottish police officers concurred with their view. The CC(S)A asserted (as HMICSs had across the century) that 'the relationship between the public and the police has never been better' and that there had been 'no serious deterioration in public-police relationships' (although rank-and-file officers spoke of loss of confidence).[143] In its final report the Royal Commission acknowledged but downplayed submissions for England and Wales that were made by the Law Society (referring to a decline in public confidence because of the 'malpractices of the police themselves') and by the National Council for Civil Liberties (NCCL) (on the use of 'irregular means of obtaining evidence', 'unnecessary violence', and of 'ineptitude' in 'dealing with political and industrial demonstration').[144] For Scotland there were no equivalent submissions and the Faculty of Advocates' official statement was (as we have seen) one of unqualified endorsement.

The Royal Commission concluded that it was unnecessary to introduce any radical overhaul of the system across Great Britain or to establish a separate body to investigate or oversee criminal complaints in any of the nations.[145] Nevertheless, it strongly recommended that the Scottish rule of corroboration should not apply to proceedings under the Discipline Code and that the investigation of a complaint should be taken out of the hands of a shift inspector and placed with a more senior officer external to the unit under investigation.[146] The Discipline Code was amended subsequently and a right to appeal was introduced for police officers.[147] Under the 1967 Police (Scotland) Act, HMICS and local police authorities were accorded statutory responsibility for ensuing that they were informed about the handling of complaints by chief constables. Moreover, chief constables were finally made liable for the actions of their officers (extending master and servant law to this employment relationship). Indeed, annual data regarding the number of complaints received across Scotland was officially published (for the first time) from 1965 onwards, demonstrating a doubling from 721 in this first year to 1530 in 1973.[148] Clearly the increase reflects knowledge and uptake of the complaints system, but also tensions between the police and some social groups that were very visible by the late 1960s. Yet the Scottish policy community (of police representatives, civil servants, HMICS and local government) maintained that most complaints were 'trivial or malicious or both' whilst ability to complain demonstrated a robust accountability.[149]

The Scottish Council for Civil Liberties (SCCL) and the Campaign for Reform

South of the border, the NCCL had been founded by leftist politicians, lawyers and journalists in 1934 in response to the police treatment of NUWM hunger marchers in Hyde Park and Trafalgar Square, rapidly becoming '*the* point of contact for complaints against the police'.[150] However, its image had remained metropolitan and London-centric.[151] An Edinburgh 'branch' was active in 1940 and 1941, highlighting the threat to civil liberties occasioned by wartime Defence Regulations (which, amongst other aspects, enabled the detention of those believed to be a threat to national security); but it appears to have been short lived.[152]

The SCCL was not founded until 1969, with its Executive Committee meeting for the first time in February 1970.[153] From the very beginning concerns about police complaints procedures were top of the agenda and, through its case work, the SCCL monitored their effectiveness, as well as becoming a conduit for complaints about the police generally. In the early 1970s there was a focus on police treatment of political campaigners and of white working-class youth in Scotland's central belt.[154] The SCCL continued to highlight the problem of unconscious bias in the treatment of complaints, arguing that the PF tended to rely on police reports (rather than precognising witnesses independently) and thus the police were still investigating themselves (often within their own force). Given that most complainants were themselves charged with an offence, there were concerns, too, that a finding of guilt was being used 'as a reason for not proceeding with the complaint'.[155] Yet the SCCL's ability to shift the terms of debate remained limited because of 'lack of direction and of resources' (including paid staff) in its early years.[156]

In England and Wales the very significant deterioration in the relationship between police officers and black communities – and in particular the controversial use of stop and search powers in relation to black youth – pushed the matter of police complaints procedures forward as a 'crisis' of civil rights and police legitimacy. In September 1972 the Select Committee on Race Relations and Immigration recommended that 'urgent steps' be taken to introduce an independent element into the complaints system to remedy the 'lack of confidence' in the system amongst Black and Asian communities.[157] At Westminster this was taken forward by Labour MP Philip Whitehead through a private member's bill. In February 1973 he agreed to withdraw his bill when Edward Heath's Conservative administration announced they would consult police representatives (in Scotland as well as England and Wales) on the introduction of an independent ombudsman as part of a new complaints system.[158]

Yet any hopes that this would lead to change in Scotland were soon dissipated. Alick Buchanan-Smith MP, Scottish Under-Secretary for Home Affairs, defended the *status quo* on account of Scottish particularity, arguing that 'the Scottish system already ensured that complaints of criminal conduct against police officers were investigated by a PF who was independent of the police'.[159] In the second half of 1973, Glasgow Labour councillor Bill Hatton pursued the campaign for independent commissioners to investigate police complaints in Scotland – having published his own report on police harassment of young people in the city, much to the chagrin of the Labour chair of the city's police committee Agnes (Nancy) Ballantyne. Yet this (and the work of the SCCL) was insufficient to mobilise public pressure, and procrastination became the order of the day.[160] In 1974 a Joint Working Party chaired by Sir William Fraser, consisting of HMICS David Gray and representatives of the Scottish policing associations, police authorities and Crown Office, recommended that an independent review procedure was not needed.[161] Whilst the independent Police Complaints Board was introduced in England and Wales in 1976, the suggestion that it should be extended to Scotland remained on ice, initially until discontent around police pay was resolved.[162] The 1979 Conservative Manifesto for Scotland (which resulted in the May election of the Thatcher government) proposed 'no change in police disciplinary proceedings' and, in his annual inspection review (published in October of that year), Gray defended the existing system as 'working very well' 'with sufficient independent oversight'.[163] Indeed, it was not until 2007 that the office of the Police Complaints Commissioner for Scotland (PCCS) was created, in a very different landscape by a devolved Scottish Executive.

Thus in England and Wales there had been a remarkable *volte face* towards the view that independent scrutiny of police complaints was an essential guarantor of police accountability and hence legitimacy.[164] In Scotland, in contrast, arguments about Scottish exceptionalism were used to ensure continuity of structures, personnel and procedures across the twentieth century – concealing the replacement of the local state as the primary locus of accountability with that of regional and central bureaucracy following regionalisation in 1975. As a number of commentators have argued, a 'benign narrative' was increasingly advanced – from the late 1960s onwards – which asserted that the practice and experience of policing in Scotland was different or 'other' to that in England and that its relationship to community was less conflictual.[165]

If the idea of the 'Scottish police' as a distinct 'system' had been residual in the 1930s, it was rapidly promoted in the last decades of the twentieth century – in response to the corruption scandals, leaching of public trust, and 'catastrophic deterioration of relations with the black community' that appeared to dog the police service in England.[166] These were exemplified by the 1981 riots in Brixton and Toxteth (which led to the Scarman Inquiry) and the conclusion of the Macpherson Inquiry into the murder of black teenager Stephen Lawrence in 1991 that the investigation had been marred by 'institutional racism'.[167] The rhetoric of Scottish particularity served to create a distancing effect in which Scottish policing was portrayed as 'untouched by race issues' or as 'no racism here'.[168] When questions were raised about the police investigation of the murder of Sunjit Singh Chhokar in Lanarkshire in 1998 – a case described in the press as 'Scotland's Stephen Lawrence' – the Lord Advocate sought to downplay the suggestion that it had been affected by 'institutional racism'.[169] This narrative of particularity was further elaborated in the context of post-1998 devolution and in response to the riots of summer 2011 – which began in London and were imitated in other English cities but not in Scotland.[170] Thus questions relating to policing were not politicised in terms of race and ethnicity as they were in England in the late twentieth century.[171]

Writing in 1980, Paul Gordon (researcher and civil liberties campaigner) suggested that there was 'little serious scrutiny' of police governance within either the press or broader 'public' debate in Scotland, with statements produced by HMICSs (such as those cited throughout this chapter) never seriously challenged.¹⁷² The late arrival of the SCCL undoubtedly meant there was no concerted defence of civil liberties – or sustained scrutiny of policing – for its own sake in Scotland for much of the twentieth century. Yet the story is in fact a more complex one. It was certainly the case that there was no one organisation that promoted civil liberties as its *raison d'être*, and thus complaints were brought on an individualised basis. However, as other chapters will also show, marginalised social and political groups used tools such as civil law, the news press and calls for public inquiry to highlight incidents of police misconduct and abuse of powers (often with the help of their MPs), although with mixed and inconsistent results.

Examples of the ways in which prominent feminist and socialist campaigners used these tools have been well charted for the early years of the twentieth century (and for Glasgow especially). In March 1914 militant suffrage campaigner Emmeline Pankhurst was arrested in Glasgow under the so-called 'Cat and Mouse Act' (which had enabled her temporary release from prison) as she addressed an audience at St Andrew's Hall. A large contingency of Glasgow City Police had entered the hall with batons drawn, storming the platform; in the resulting affray members of the audience as well as police officers were injured. A campaign of letter-writing was orchestrated to local newspapers, highlighting the 'brutal, unmanly and cowardly' behaviour of police and calling for a public inquiry. One correspondent reminded readers that 'the policemen are our servants, paid for by women as well as men'.¹⁷³ Yet the *Glasgow Herald*, ever critical of all forms of militancy, opined in an editorial that 'the police could not be held responsible for the use of force'; and inquiry calls were not pursued by any broader lobby.¹⁷⁴

From the Edwardian period to the 1920s, the radical and left-wing independent press (including the socialist weekly, *Forward*, founded in 1906 by future Scottish Secretary Tom Johnston) was an important counterpoint to official narratives of the policing of strikes and public rallies. In the wake of the General Strike of May 1926, *Forward* recorded that in Glasgow, where 300 arrests had been effected, 'numerous complaints have been made against the provocative conduct of certain policemen', calling for an independent inquiry – which was rejected by the city's magistrates who claimed police conduct was 'beyond reproach'. The article's author, socialist councillor Patrick Dollan, stated:

> The police are, presumably, the servants of the ratepayers, and should not be used for partisan or factional interests. But if the impression becomes current that the police are the servants of a faction and not the servants of the community, then police confidence in the community will be undermined.¹⁷⁵

The criticisms made here by strikers (echoing that of the suffrage campaigners) concerned both police methods (as disproportionate and provocative) and the use of the police for overtly political purposes (despite their supposed impartiality), issues around which the SCCL was to galvanise in the last decades of the twentieth century. Comments regarding the normative role of police officers as the 'servants of the community' are, nevertheless, highly suggestive of a dominant consensus that had been achieved regarding the conceptual place of the police within the polity.

Many of the socialist politicians who had been forthright in condemning police methods in 1926 went on to become bailies, lord provosts, and chairs of local police authorities with responsibility for law and order (and distanced themselves from the activities of the NUWM in the 1930s). Nevertheless, a small number continued to campaign consistently around police misconduct and miscarriage of justice – most obviously Independent Labour Party (ILP) politician John McGovern who, as MP for Glasgow (Shettleston) from 1930 to 1959, acted as spokesperson in parliament for complaints of this nature from across Scotland (alongside other ILP MPs). For over half of this period he did so external to the Labour Party machine (finally joining in 1947), which meant that his views were all too easily dismissed as lacking in credibility.[176] As we have seen, it was David Robertson, an independent unionist, who pushed for the Thurso tribunal in 1958, with cross-party support. The narrative of a more 'benign' relationship between police and 'community' in Scotland conceals a far more chequered picture – in which historical source materials relating to those on the social or political margins or denied the protections accorded by the law delineate a different set of experiences as well as resistances.

Scotland's four large cities all had vibrant press industries, producing daily papers (as well as weekly ones) that profiled locally and regionally generated news as well as covering national (Scotland and UK) and international content.[177] Yet with the decline of radical and independent titles (from the 1930s until the emergence of the *West Highland Free Press* in 1972), there was little evidence of the cultivation of a critical independent viewpoint, as even local news titles 'found themselves bought up by acquisition-hungry chains' and none subscribed to 'avowedly political objectives' as they had in an earlier epoch.[178] Nevertheless, across most of the twentieth century, the press was a crucial public space through which the rule of law was ostensibly upheld and rendered visible (in coverage of trial outcomes most obviously) and through which matters of governance more broadly became 'public' discourse.[179] The press was an important forum through which the activities of municipal government, including policing matters, were publicised. Scrutiny of policing was apparent, but was often played out in terms of local politics (including the dynamics of local government elections, or tensions between the central and local state). For the most part, the controversies covered were those generated by politicians (whether councillors and bailies, or MPs) as 'gatekeepers' of the polity and to which the press then responded. As the first part of this chapter has demonstrated, the local defence of burgh police forces was the most significant policing issue around which local newspapers galvanised in the first half of the twentieth century, unsurprising given that they, too, were closely associated with local (municipal) identity. In doing so, local press and politicians staunchly defended their policing 'tradition' from reformers.

Conclusions

This chapter has centred on the official structures, dominant narratives and prescriptive literatures through which the relationship between 'police' and 'public' was articulated and inscribed at a formal level. It has shown that police governance in twentieth-century Scotland (as in England and Wales) can be characterised in terms of the tension between centralisation and localism that sustained ideas of liberal democratic accountability. Yet this tension played out somewhat differently north of the border. At a formal level policing was discussed through a tripartite set of narratives (regarding shared identity, values and geo-political allegiances) best seen as concentric circles: from an outer (and more amorphous) Britishness, through an expanding seam of Scottish particularity, to an inner focus on the idea of local autonomy (presented as a quintessential historical legacy and core). The power dynamics shifted across time: from the heavy weighting accorded to local and municipal government in 1900, to a more evenly distributed spread across the three domains around 1950, and – particularly from 1980 onwards – towards a convergence on Scottish particularity (cemented by the setting up of the Scottish executive in 1999 and subsequently confirmed in the creation of Police Scotland in 2013).

It has also demonstrated that the policy community associated with Scottish policing was, for the most part, a small and closely knit personal and professional network. This enabled the tracing, for most of the century, of a loose 'umbrella' identity for Scottish policing – which connected down into strong and pervasive individual police force identities and allegiances that were also connected to a local sense of place. The variegated effects of this on policing styles and everyday practices at a grassroots level will be explored in subsequent chapters. Chief constables – particularly in cities and burghs – remained profoundly influential in shaping the culture of their forces; not only were they increasingly appointed from within Scottish policing (Percy Sillitoe, recruited to Glasgow from Sheffield City Police, was a notable exception by the 1930s) but the inspectorate, too, was increasingly drawn from their number. As an occupation, policing was amongst the most highly disciplined in terms of internal formal rules of conduct, reinforcing the training manual's depiction of the police officer as a model of civility, fairness and virtuous masculinity. Yet its critics have argued that the Scottish police and the criminal justice system have been subject to surprisingly little public scrutiny. The Thurso tribunal of 1959 can be viewed as the untoward, anomalous and even hyperbolic culmination of a very ordinary set of events that should have been dealt with through the usual disciplinary framework. Others might highlight its symbolic importance – in reinforcing training manual injunctions to behave with 'civility' and 'respect' to all, and in drawing a line of zero tolerance under the use of physical chastisement as part of everyday policing. In its wake, however, the narrative regarding the particularity of the Scottish legal system – including the separation of the policing function from prosecution – was marshalled to demonstrate a 'tradition' of police impartiality – even though there had been a significant overlapping of these functions in the first half of the twentieth century. Indeed, this was the *raison d'être* for sidestepping the introduction of an independent review process until very recently. Moreover, as other chapters will show, police officers – by the very nature of their job – continued to make decisions about the processing of criminal charges as well as the use of semi-formal and sub-judicial processes.

Finally, this chapter has shown how politicians, officials and senior police officers asserted a narrative of ever-increasing 'public' trust in the Scottish police across most of the twentieth century. Whilst this was subject to self-questioning in the last quarter, it was replaced with an argument that the absence of the politics of race in Scotland meant that policing 'here' did not face the crisis that engulfed English cities. As other chapters will go on to suggest, however, the rhetoric of a growing and undifferentiated 'public' trust conceals the differential experiences of more marginalised groups, neighbourhoods and communities in Scotland. Indeed, this book now turns its attentions to the informal practices, identities and relationships through which the everyday experience of policing was negotiated and constituted. The view from above is replaced with one from below as we explore a range of grassroots perspectives in specific geographical settings: firstly, in Glasgow (compared with other urban areas) and subsequently in Scotland's Highlands and Islands (as one of the most remote and rural areas of the UK).

Notes

1. PP, *HMICS AR*, 1930, Cmd. 3912, 6.
2. *Scotsman*, 1 August 1931.
3. Loader and Mulcahy, *Condition of England*.
4. Scott, *Arts of Resistance*. Oral history interviews, memoirs or formal complaints hint at, or give access to, informal and hidden narratives ('transcripts') that were either not publicly aired in an earlier time period or were recessive and thus partially hidden in comparison to dominant 'public discourse'.
5. Calhoun, 'Civil society/public sphere'.
6. Mawby and Wright, 'Police accountability'.

7. Johansen, 'Police-public relations'.
8. Barrie, *Police*, 265; Carson and Idzikowska, 'Social production'.
9. Dinsmor and Goldsmith, 'Scottish policing', 49; Carson, 'Policing the periphery I', 210; Barrie, *Police*, 92–145.
10. Morton, 'Civil society', 367.
11. Barrie, *Police*, 173.
12. Ibid.; Smale, 'New police'; Smale, 'Alfred John List'.
13. Barrie, *Police*, 178.
14. Morton, 'Civil society'; Pugh, 'Centralism versus localism?'
15. McCrone, *Understanding Scotland*, 131–2.
16. Weinberger, *Keeping the Peace?*, 134.
17. Ewen, 'Power and Administration'; Goodwin, 'Police in Edinburgh'.
18. Morton, 'Civil society', 363.
19. McCrone, *Understanding Scotland*, 163.
20. Johnston, *Memories*, 164.
21. Sir David Munro (HMICS 1880–1904) was a career soldier in the Indian (Madras) Army before appointment to a series of Chief Constable roles (including in the Lothians). Lieut-Col Sir Arthur George Ferguson (HMICS 1904–27) served previously in the First Boer War. Lieut-Col David Allan (HMICS 1927–30) served in the Black Watch before appointment as a Chief Constable (in Bootle and then Argyle). Brig-Gen R. M. Dudgeon (HMICS 1930–45), formerly of the Queens Own Cameron Highlanders, was governor of HM Prison, Edinburgh, 1920–30.
22. Goodwin, 'Police in Edinburgh', 65.
23. Figures exclude Orkney (until 1938) and Shetland (until 1940) as outwith the provisions of the 1857 Police (Scotland) Act.
24. TNA, HO45/10959/328532.
25. PP, *Police Consolidation (Scotland) Committee Report* (1933–4), Cd. 4463, 8.
26. NRS, HH55/360, F. O. Stewart to Charles C. Cunningham, 11 March 1942.
27. NRS, HH55/361, Cunningham to F. Newsome, 14 November 1944.
28. Emsley, *English Police*, 160. NRS, HH55/360, Cunningham to D. Milne, 16 March 1942.
29. NRS, HH55/260, file note, 14 October 1942.
30. *Inverness Courier and Advertiser*, 20 November 1942.
31. NRS, HH55/504, R. M. Dudgeon to Stewart, 16 December 1942.
32. Emsley, *English Police*, 169.
33. NRS, HH555/935.
34. NRS, HH55/951, Memorandum, Town Council of Motherwell and Wishaw, 26 June 1948.
35. NRS, HH55/951, letter, Town Clerk, Motherwell and Wishaw, to the Scottish Secretary.
36. *Motherwell Times*, 29 April 1949.
37. McLaughlin, '"Last one out"'.
38. NRS, HH55/951, Memorandum, CC John A. R. Murray, 1 May 1947; file note, 20 October 1948.
39. *Scotsman*, 14 January 1950; *Scots Law Times*, 4 October 1952, 193–9.
40. TNA, HO 272/42, Thomas Renfrew and Sir John Anderson, 25 July 1961, 29.

41. PP, *Royal Commission on the Police, Final Report* (1962), Cmnd 1728, paragraph 281. TNA, HO 272/42, Thomas Renfrew and Sir John Anderson, 25 July 1961, 32.
42. Fraser, 'Post-war police'.
43. NRS, HH55/959; TNA, HO272/42, Thomas Renfrew and Sir John Anderson, 25 July 1961, 24. Similar arguments about the RIC were made in 1919: see PP, *Committee on the Police Service* (Desborough), *Minutes of Evidence* (1920), Cmd. 874, Q. 8110, Roderick Ross, and Q. 8867, Sir Kenneth Mackenzie.
44. Pugh, 'Centralism versus localism?'.
45. *Southern Reporter*, 24 October 1974; 21 November 1974; 27 February 1975.
46. TNA, HO272/41, evidence of the SPF; NRS, HH55/959.
47. *GH*, 30 April 1976.
48. Morrison, *My Story*, 83; Klein, *Invisible Men*, 140.
49. PP, Cmd. 874, Q. 7159 and 7160. City of Glasgow Police, *Instruction Book* (1912), 119, stressed 'perfect impartiality' in handling strikes with the police role that of 'maintaining the public peace'.
50. Morrison, *My Story*, 109; on the SPF, see Goodwin, 'Police in Edinburgh', 93–126.
51. PP, Cmd. 874, Q. 7819 and Q. 8820.
52. Morrison, *My Story*, 123.
53. Weinberger, *Keeping the Peace?*, 166.
54. *Scotsman*, 20 February 1903. The CC(S)A was replaced in the late 1960s with the Association of Chief Police Officers in Scotland (ACPOS) for chief, deputy and assistant chief constables.
55. HAS, R91/1/5, minutes, 21 June 1923.
56. *Scotsman*, 6 June 1930.
57. PP, *HMICS AR*, 1930, Cmd. 3912, 6.
58. HAS, R91/1/6, minutes 15 July 1943; PP, *HMICS ARs* (1949) Cmd. 7965, (1955) Cmd. 9771, (1960) Cmnd. 1390.
59. Anon., *Police Manual* (1893); PP, *HMICS AR*, 1894, C. 7143; *Scotsman*, 20 February 1903.
60. Anon., *Police Manual*, 'Introduction', and 'Preface to the First Edition' (1893).
61. HAS, R9/1/7, minutes, 9 November 1951.
62. Ibid.
63. Klein, 'Quiet and determined', 201, 212.
64. Ibid., 204.
65. Anon., *Scottish Criminal Law* (1952), 'Foreword', n.p.
66. PP, *Committee on the Police Service, Report, Part I* (1919), Cmd. 253, s. 6.
67. Anon., *Scottish Criminal Law* (1952), 'Introduction', n.p.
68. Smale, 'Alfred John List'; Emsley, *English Police*; Johansen, 'Police-public relations'.
69. PP, Cmd. 253, s. 6.
70. Johansen, 'Police-public relations', 502.
71. Anon., *Police Manual* (1910), 12.
72. Ibid. Similar statements can be found in City of Glasgow Police, *Instruction Books*.
73. Anon., *Scottish Criminal Law* (1952), 2.
74. Ibid., 'Introduction'; n.p., and Anon., *Scottish Criminal Law* (1980), 'Introduction', n.p.

75. White and Hunt, 'Citizenship'.
76. Klein, 'Quiet and determined', 209–10.
77. Interview with Michael (pseudonym), conducted by Neil Davidson.
78. Interview with Brian (pseudonym), conducted by Davidson.
79. From 1965 this lead role was elevated to Chief HMICS. Sydney Kinnear (1946–57) joined Edinburgh City Police in 1924, rising to Superintendent before secondment as Assistant to HMICS in 1942; Thomas Renfrew (1958–66), former Chief Constable of Lanarkshire, joined Glasgow City Police in 1919; Andrew Meldrum (1966–70), former Chief Constable of Inverness Burgh, joined Stirlingshire in 1927; David Gray (1970–9), former Chief Constable of Stirling and Clackmannan, joined Renfrew and Bute.
80. McCrone, *Understanding Scotland*, 137.
81. Scott, 'Police', 357–9. In England and Wales the police brought their own prosecutions in most cases until the setting up of the Crown Prosecution Service in 1985.
82. Barrie and Broomhall, *Police Courts*; Farmer, *Criminal Law*. The sheriff also heard cases through 'solemn process' (jury trial).
83. Farmer, *Criminal Law*, 85.
84. NRS, HH60/263, Marshall Millar Craig, Crown Office, and R. N. Duke, Scottish Office, 1 December 1927. By this stage the prosecutor in Edinburgh's police court was a legal professional.
85. PP, *Royal Commission on the Duties of the Metropolitan Police, Minutes of Evidence*, vol. III (1908), Cd. 4260, Q. 4019, 40195 and 40199, James Stevenson, April 1907.
86. Barrie and Broomhall, 'Public men', 101–2.
87. Devon, *Criminal & Community*, 198. See also Barrie and Broomhall, *Police Courts*, vol. 1, 219 on the nineteenth century: 'many believed that they did not get a fair trial at the police court'.
88. NRS, HH60/263, Duke, 1 December 1927.
89. Van Slingelandt and Macdonald, *Long Way*, 67.
90. TNA, HO 272/57, Scottish Sheriffs' Substitute Association, 3.
91. PP, Cmnd. 1728, paragraph 375.
92. Barrie and Broomhall, 'Public men', 107.
93. Taylor, 'Rationing crime'.
94. Barrie and Broomhall, *Police Courts*, vol. 1, 202, citing the 1854 Select Committee on Public Prosecutions, which 'praised Scottish practice'.
95. PP, Judicial Statistics of Scotland, 1912, Cd. 7164: 50,615 persons were disposed of summarily in Glasgow out of 161,353 for the whole nation. Sheriff and burgh police court disposals are counted together here; figures are not given solely for police courts.
96. Barrie and Broomhall, 'Public men', 84.
97. Farmer, *Criminal Law*, esp. 73 and 109.
98. For example, NRS, JC31/1909/41, Jessie Brown v. George Neilsen.
99. PP, *Legal Aid in Criminal Proceedings* (1960), Cmnd. 1015, 41–2.
100. Barrie and Broomhall, *Police Courts*, vol. 1, 376.

101. NRS, JC30/2–3, High Court of Justiciary Appeals Books, 1900–28. In 1917–18 a third of appeals related to convictions of hoteliers, butchers, dairy operators and other businesspersons for infringements of the Defence of the Realm Regulations.
102. Weber, 'Bureaucracy and law'.
103. PP, *HMICS AR*, 1890, C. 6383, 11.
104. Cameron, 'Internal policing' Carson, 'Policing the periphery Part II'.
105. Wood, 'Internal policing', 545; Hughes, *Gender and Political Identities*, 187.
106. PP, *HMICS AR*, 1931, Cmd. 4118, 8; NRS, HH55/664.
107. *Scotsman*, 23 February 1940 (see also Chapter 4).
108. PP, *HMICS AR*, 1951, Cmd. 8552, 9; and 1955, Cmd. 9771, 9.
109. Wood, 'Press, politics' and '"Third degree"'.
110. *Scotsman*, 25 September 1928.
111. PP, *Dismissal of Constables Hill and Moore from Kilmarnock Police Force* (1926), Cmd. 2659.
112. NRS, AD 65/53.
113. NRS, AD 65/54; PP, *Hansard* [HC], 12 February 1959, col. 1360. Robertson resigned the Tory whip a week before the petition was presented because of 'the government's handling of Scottish affairs' especially the economic development of the highlands: *Caithness Courier*, 4 February 1959 and 25 February 1959.
114. PP, Cmnd. 1728, 1.
115. *Police Review*, 20 February 1959, 135.
116. *Caithness Courier*, 13 May 1959 and 3 June 1959. Robertson was re-elected later in 1959 as an independent unionist with an increased majority.
117. *Police Review*, 27 February 1959, 153.
118. Gordon, *Policing Scotland*.
119. *Police Review*, 22 May 1959, 382, and 23 October 1959, 714.
120. See, for example, Anon., *Police Manual* (1910), 8–9.
121. See also Klein, *Invisible Men*, 33.
122. GCA, SR/22/84/06/01, Greenock Police, Complaints: of 123 entries analysed for the years 1910–20, 40 related directly to drunkenness. GCA, SR/22/46/6, Glasgow Police: Reports against Officers, C Division: 30–40 reports were filed each year under the Discipline Code (samples for 1900, 1905 and 1910 analysed here).
123. PP, *HMICS AR*, 1953, Cmd. 9148. See Klein, *Invisible Men*, for similar findings for English urban forces.
124. Dataset compiled from *HMICS AR*s, 1900–78.
125. PP, *HMICS AR*, 1900, Cd. 548, and 1970, Cmnd. 4754.
126. Van Slingelandt and Macdonald, *Long Way*, on Glasgow in the 1920s.
127. PP, *HMICS AR*, 1973, Cmnd. 5734, 15.
128. Thirteen per cent of cases under the Discipline Code in Glasgow's 'C' Division for the sample years 1900, 1905 and 1910 resulted from public complaints (GCA, SR22/46/6).
129. TNA, HO 272/149 contains summaries of 79 complaints submitted to Edinburgh City Police in the 12 months after the Thurso tribunal: 49 per cent were made by letter to the Chief Constable, 21 per cent in person at a police station, and 10 per cent

by telephone to a police station. Four complainants contacted the PF, four contacted the Scottish Secretary, and one went to the press.
130. Emsley, "'Mother, what *did* policemen do?"
131. TNA, HO 272/149.
132. Summary drawn from PP, Cmnd. 1728; TNA, HO 272/41, HO 272/42 and HO 272//57; and NRS, AD 65/55.
133. Muir v. Magistrates of Hamilton (1910), *SLT*, 164; PP, Cmnd. 1728, paragraph 64.
134. TNA, HO 272/42, Sir John Anderson, 25 July 1961, 25.
135. Robertson v. Keith (1936), SC 29.
136. Beaton v. Ivory (1888), 14 R. 1057.
137. *Scotsman*, 9 October 1909, reporting on J.&.P. Coates (Ltd) v. Brown, the first 'private' prosecution for 'two or three centuries'.
138. PP, Cmd. 874, Q. 7202, PC Magill.
139. TNA, HO 272/41, meeting with SPF representatives, 31 May 1961, 12.
140. TNA, HO 272/41, confidential meeting, 29 May 1961, Mr Kissen, 1–2.
141. PP, Cmnd. 1728, paragraph 399.
142. Ibid., paragraph 335.
143. TNA, HO 272/41, CC(S)A, 30 May 1961, 17–18.
144. PP, Cmnd. 1728, paragraph 335.
145. Ibid., paragraph 478.
146. Ibid., paragraph 462.
147. PP, *The Handling of Complaints Against the Police* (Scotland)(1974), Cmd. 5583, paragraph 4.
148. PP, *HMICS AR*s: 1965 Cmnd. 3032; and 1973, Cmnd. 5734.
149. PP, Cmd. 5583, paragraph 20.
150. Clarke, 'Sincere and reasonable men', 536; also Clarke, *National Council for Civil Liberties*.
151. Moores, 'Progressive professionals', 552.
152. *Scotsman*, 6 April 1940; *Scotsman*, 7 April 1941; Goodwin, 'Police in Edinburgh', 136.
153. NLS, Executive Committee of the SCCL, Acc.12971/10, 19 February 1971.
154. NLS, Acc.12971/10–15. In 1975 the SCCL was amongst those (unsuccessfully) calling for a local inquiry into police treatment of those protesting against a National Front meeting at Glasgow's Kingston Halls: NRS, HH55/150.
155. NLS, Acc.12971/14, 17 January 1974.
156. NLS, Acc.12971/13, 12 September 1973.
157. PP, Select Committee Report, *Police/Immigrant Relations* (1971–2), Paper 471-I, paragraph 333.
158. *Guardian*, 24 February 1973.
159. *GH*, 24 February 1973.
160. NLS, B. Hatton, 'Complaints against the Police' (Glasgow: privately printed pamphlet, 1973–4).
161. PP, Cmd. 5583.
162. Gordon, *Policing Scotland*, 88.
163. Ibid.; PP, *HMICS AR*, 1978, Cmnd. 7686, 15.

164. Goldsmith (ed.), *Complaints*. There were significant teething problems with the PCB, leading to its replacement with the Police Complaints Authority in 1985 (also explaining continued reluctance in Scotland to follow such a model).
165. Murray, 'Proactive turn', 114; Gorringe and Rosie, 'Scottish approach?'.
166. Reiner, *Politics*, 81.
167. PP, *The Brixton Riots* (1981), Cmnd 8427; PP. *The Stephen Lawrence Inquiry* (1999). Cm 4262-I, 46.1.
168. Murray, 'Proactive turn', 114; Schaffer, *Community Policing*; Fraser, 'Post-war police'.
169. Murray, 'Proactive turn', 117.
170. Gorringe and Rosie, 'Scottish approach?'.
171. Murray, 'Proactive turn', 117.
172. Gordon, *Policing Scotland*, 1 and 94.
173. *GH*, 11 March 1914.
174. *GH*, 12 March 1914.
175. *Forward*, 26 May 1926.
176. The ILP had disaffiliated from the Labour Party in 1932. The extent of McGovern's questions regarding scrutiny of policing and judicial decisions can be followed through *Hansard*, https://api.parliament.uk/historic-hansard/people/mr-john-mcgovern/index.html (last accessed 29 October 2019). McGovern was most active in this regard in the 1930s and early 1950s, moving rapidly to the right towards the end of his career as MP. See Knox, *Labour Leaders*, 175–9.
177. Hutchison, 'History of the press'.
178. Ibid., 61–2. Early-twentieth-century socialist titles included the *Vanguard*, the *Worker*, and *Forward* (all of which were suppressed in 1916) as well as the daily *Strike Bulletin*.
179. On the nineteenth-century press, crime and policing: Barrie and Broomhall, *Police Courts* vol. 1.

3

THE GLASGOW BEAT MAN

'The beat man, plodding the pavement at night, the rain running down the back of his neck, formed the first line of defence against crime.' These comments, published in 1962 in Robert Colquhoun's memoir of a career in Glasgow City Police, were already nostalgic given the increasing use of cars and motor scooters for police duties.[1] Yet the 'beat man' was the quintessential building block of urban policing across the first two-thirds of the twentieth century: as an everyday and highly visible uniformed presence amongst local neighbourhoods, but also as the role that almost all officers undertook in the early days of their service. Becoming a 'beat man' was a rite of passage into the ethos, values, custom and practice of localised police culture. Focusing on the role of the 'beat man' at the grassroots level, this chapter shows how police identities were forged in relation to the specific urban and industrial communities of Glasgow and, more broadly, west-central Scotland, and how these in turn shaped repertoires and styles of policing.

On account of its sheer size, density and complexity, as well as the challenges it presented for policing, Glasgow provides a useful lens through which to focus any study of urban policing. Following an incremental rise in its population across the nineteenth century with the development of the shipbuilding and steel industries, Glasgow was the second largest city in Great Britain according to the 1911 census, with over a million inhabitants.[2] Yet its working-class population was severely overcrowded within inner-city 'slum' areas where many experienced profound poverty given the low-wage economy; these conditions have been described as necessitating 'a culture of survival'.[3] In the first three decades of the twentieth-century the most significant challenges for policing in Glasgow were related to the regulation of industrial disputes and public order. The depression of the 1930s led to significant male unemployment, which has been seen as an important factor in the emergence of the interwar territorial street gangs who were associated with 'collective violence and intimidation'.[4] Increasingly, too, there were concerns about the activities of organised criminal networks with involvement in housebreaking and protection rackets. Whilst both diminished with the onset of the Second World War as young males were conscripted, there was a swift resurgence in 'crimes against property with violence' in the city in the early to mid-1940s, leading to complaints about 'lawlessness' in the city.[5] The issue of 'gang culture' and violence was to come to public prominence again in the second half of the 1960s, this time in relation to the new peripheral housing schemes of Drumchapel and Easterhouse, to which the inner-city population had been decanted and dispersed, but which lacked social amenities for young people, leading to boredom and anomie.[6] That Glasgow was a 'violent' city was demonstrated in a very significant increase in murder cases across the twentieth century. The number of individuals prosecuted for murder in Glasgow rose from 10 in 1930, to 15 in 1960, 24 in 1965, and 30 in 1970, whilst remaining consistently at 2–4 per year for the cities of Aberdeen, Dundee and Edinburgh combined.[7]

Criminologists J. V. M. Shields and Judith A. Duncan ranked Glasgow as overwhelmingly the highest in Scotland for crime rates for the years 1961–2, which they calculated at 72 per 1,000 of population (in comparison to 60 for Edinburgh, 45 for Dundee and 44 for Aberdeen).[8] The west coast towns of Ayr, Hamilton, Paisley, Greenock and Dumbarton were also in the top third of the table for 1961–2 and Greenock had been the highest for 1954–5 (slightly outstripping Glasgow), with a rate of 44 in that year (when crime rates overall were lower). Shields and Duncan commented that 'the nucleus of the crimogenic Central Lowlands is Glasgow', calling for a broader 'ecological study' of crime that also took into account the 'relationship between police availability and recorded crime'.[9] This chapter embraces such an approach within its historical analysis, demonstrating that the styles and repertoires of policing that were generated in Glasgow – and implemented by the beat man (as well as other specialist teams and departments) – were one contributory factor (amongst others) in creating high levels of recorded 'crime' as well as being a concerted response to it.

Significantly, Glasgow was, consistently across time, the most intensively policed district of Scotland in statistical terms. In 1912 it had an authorised strength of 1,996 men (the largest force in Scotland by far), and an average of one police officer for every 10 acres or 506 residents. Fifty years' later, an authorised strength of 2,818 resulted in an average of one 'policeman' for every 372 residents or 14 acres, rendering it remarkably similar to Liverpool (statistically the most intensively policed district of England) and in stark contrast to the city of Aberdeen which averaged one 'policeman' for every 589 residents or 35 acres in 1962.[10] Indeed, Aberdeen's limited manpower had led it to become the first to experiment with motor patrol units from 1949 onwards; initially described as the 'Aberdeen system', this was developed into the system of Unit Beat Policing which was adopted more widely elsewhere in the UK in the 1960s. In Glasgow, Unit Beat Policing was rolled out from 1967 initially to the peripheral housing schemes. By 1969 it was estimated that the system covered 56 per cent of the population and 75 per cent of the city's area, although the Central Division was still wholly policed by foot using 'traditional methods' delivered by the beat man.[11] This chapter will investigate how these 'traditional methods' were constituted.

Oral history interviews with former officers who served in Glasgow and other industrial/urban areas of west-central Scotland form the backbone of this chapter's analysis of the ways in which police culture and identity – as dynamic and contingent – was constructed across time through social geography (the relationship between built environment and social interaction), generational difference (including military experience) and gendered ideas about the physical embodiment of authority. A specifically 'Glasgow' identity and style of policing is in evidence – at its apogee in the mid-twentieth century – that contrasted very markedly with those in rural and remote areas and, to a lesser extent, in other urban settings. The requirement for corroboration that was specific to Scots Law was negotiated in ways that were unique to local context. In Glasgow, given the high concentration of people and police officers (as well as crucial motor back-up from the 1930s onwards), it was incorporated into a police group identity as 'robust', 'tough' and 'no nonsense'. This was protective of those seen as 'law-abiding' – in relation to whom policing also involved a significant 'social work' element – and adversarial towards those seen as anti-social, embodied in the figure of the 'ned'. Interviews are suggestive of the repertoires – combining both formal and informal interventions – that were in operation from the 1940s to the 1960s and had been shaped in the 1930s. For some, particularly those viewed by others as 'old school', physical force was still dispensed as a form of 'rough justice' towards 'troublemakers' that kept matters well away from the courts – although this was usually done covertly and increasingly marginalised as unacceptable. For a far larger constituency, 'breach of the peace' (BoP) proceedings acted as a flexible catch-all that enabled work-around of the corroboration requirement, facilitated 'come-back' and enabled officers to assert, win and maintain authority within the area of their beat as part of a strongly defended territorialism.

Who Were the Police? Backgrounds and Origins

Between 1900 and 1950 the demographic profile of Glasgow's police officers shifted markedly – from that of immigrants to predominantly locally born, drawn from the communities of west-central Scotland. Glasgow's distinctive reputation for being policed by the Irish and by Highlanders – referred to in anecdote, memoir and popular culture – has been partly confirmed by previous historical research on the Victorian era. Those born in 'highland' counties formed a quarter of all recruits in the years 1852–71, rising to a third in 1872–91, whilst those of Irish birth constituted a fifth of Glasgow City Police personnel across the late nineteenth century.[12] Together they formed half of all officers in the 1880s. Our research shows that the trend to recruit 'outsiders' was even clearer in the years 1900–5, when those born in the north-east of Scotland, Highlands, and Ireland, together constituted around 70 per cent of those joining Glasgow City Police, each of these three groups forming roughly 20–25 per cent of all recruits (see Appendix, Table A.1). Those born in Glasgow or adjacent counties only constituted around 12 per cent of recruits at this time, which was significantly out of kilter with the city's population as whole.[13] The Glasgow trend for recruiting 'outsiders' – in part to avoid partisanship and conflict of interest – was distinctly different from Ayr Burgh Police, which recruited 60 per cent of its officers from the town or adjacent counties in 1900–10, as well as from the northern counties and Inverness Burgh (see Appendix). It was also at variance with Edinburgh which, like London, was more 'local' by this period.[14]

Personal networks facilitating highland recruitment continued after the First World War. A Gaelic speaker from Lochaber, Charles Cameron Macdonald joined Glasgow City Police in 1922 during a period of austerity in which many forces had ceased recruitment and Glasgow's lengthy waiting list prioritised ex-servicemen. As a reservist in the Lovat Scouts (a highland regiment that recruited mainly from rural areas), Macdonald's superior officers used regimental links to secure him an interview. His memoirs demonstrate how he 'enjoyed the friendship and camaraderie of many fellow Gaels', and record that he was later promoted to inspector in 1951 by Malcolm McCulloch, described as himself 'a native of Lochaber', who had joined in 1912 and was Chief Constable in 1943–60.[15] Indeed, in 1912 Govan Burgh Police – 45 per cent of whose officers were Highland-born – had been incorporated into Glasgow City, bringing with them their prestigious pipe band and thus reinforcing the association of a vibrant highland ethnic identity within Glasgow policing.[16] Against the backdrop of 'Red Clydeside' and the General Strike of 1926, Highland recruits were assumed to be unremittingly 'loyal subjects' of the British Crown, reflecting, too, their strong association with Scottish military ideals and identities.[17] As an inspector commented about one of his constables, 'He has no Socialistic or Bolshevist tendencies, but like a true Highlander, is quite the reverse.' This suggests an 'institutional bias' that was 'certainly anti-leftist' (in common with other British police forces) but was also specifically bound up with ideas about ethnicity in the Glasgow context.[18]

Nevertheless, Glasgow gradually grew to resemble other forces, with 63 per cent of recruits 'local' in terms of birth in 1930–1, rising to 69 per cent in 1946 and 80 per cent in 1948 (Appendix, Table A.1). It is important to bear in mind that these figures are for new recruits rather than all police force personnel. An individual police career could stretch for 30 years, and officers increasingly saw it as a job for life following the introduction (at a national level) of police pensions in 1890 and further improvement in pay and conditions in 1919.[19] Upon taking up his role as Chief Constable (1931–43), Sir Percy Sillitoe (an English-born 'outsider') introduced compulsory retirement for those who had reached pensionable service, shedding some 77 officers (recruited in the early 1900s) *en masse* to encourage 'new, fresh ideas' and a bottleneck in the promotions system.[20] Those recruited in the aftermath of the Second World War were predominantly Glaswegian (or from nearby counties) and it was this generation who were to shape the culture of the 1960s-70s. Nevertheless, Highland and north-eastern recruits continued to be highly valued and – keen to boost applications in 1958 – the force conducted a recruitment drive across the northern counties and outer Hebrides, sending senior officers who were 'native to these areas' out on the campaign.[21]

Like other UK forces, Glasgow recruits were drawn from the manual labour force. In the early 1900s a large proportion had worked in agriculture, peaking at 46 per cent just before the First World War (see Appendix, Table A.2). As Haia Shpayer-Makov has argued of the Metropolitan Police, rural recruits were assumed to be 'more physically robust' – as well as 'more steady' and compliant in following orders – than those raised in overcrowded and insanitary urban environments.[22] In 1907 Glasgow's James V. Stevenson (Irish-born) wrote to his fellow chief constables in northern and other rural parts of Scotland asking them to direct 'young men of good character and physique . . . who are desirous of joining the Police Service' to forward their applications to him.[23] The average height of Glasgow recruits in the 1880s to 1920s was consistently 5 feet 11 inches, some 5 inches more than estimates for the national male population as a whole.[24] Recruits were mostly semi-skilled or unskilled between 1900 and 1914, thus acquiring social status on joining (since policing was categorised alongside skilled occupations within the census classifications).[25] By the later 1920s those with skilled or semi-skilled industrial backgrounds were in the majority (64 per cent of recruits), and thus joined Glasgow City Police from equivalent status occupations, a trend shared across urban forces as industry replaced agriculture more generally as the major employer (see Appendix, Tables A.3 and A.6).[26]

For those who joined in the late 1940s, conscripted military service during the Second World War was a crucial defining experience. Recent research on men in reserved occupations on the home front has highlighted the fact that in 1945 – when membership of the military services was at its height – two-thirds of the male labour force were in fact in civilian employment.[27] For recruits to Glasgow City Police in the years 1945–8, however, there was a contrasting profile: our research suggests that only 20 per cent had been in civilian occupations in wartime compared to 80 per cent in the military.[28] Indeed, recruitment (as well as the retirement of older serving officers) had been put on ice during wartime with the effect that strength was extremely depleted when war finally ended (and those of pensionable age were finally allowed to retire). From December 1945 a huge recruitment drive took place, leading to the appointment of 377 men in 1946 alone (equivalent to 17 per cent of force strength).[29] The process of application, assessment and selection was organised through a west-central district recruiting board (one of five covering the whole of Scotland), with officers who met the basic requirements being allocated to their first choice of police force.[30] As servicemen were demobbed they may have turned to policing simply because it was recruiting (and an estimated 16 per cent left within two years), but for many there were pull factors: the attraction of secure pensionable service in a uniformed organisation (with over half going on to retire on full pension) in their local region.[31]

Finally, in terms of race, ethnicity and religion, Glasgow City Police was a white and Christian police force. It was also mainly Protestant, constituted mostly by those who identified either with the established (Calvinist) Church of Scotland or with one of the minority Scottish Presbyterian churches. Despite the presence of a Jewish community in the Gorbals, no records were sampled relating to Jewish officers. Diversity was restricted to the presence of Gaelic speakers from the Highlands or western isles and migrant Irish. The collapse of Irish recruitment (as well as the low level of Roman Catholic recruitment) in Glasgow can be linked to the effects of the Irish War of Independence of 1919–21, keenly felt in the west of Scotland given strong personal connections. In Ireland itself police officers in the RIC became a direct target for the Irish Republican Army (IRA) as representatives of the British state.[32] Indeed, Edward Stevenson, son of Glasgow's Chief Constable, was one of a group of RIC police officers killed in an IRA ambush in 1921.[33] In Glasgow such events were highly likely to have inflected police attitudes towards recruitment, as well as Catholic and Protestant attitudes towards police in the city.

Moreover, the Church of Scotland actively campaigned against Irish Catholic immigration in the 1920s, thereby promoting racism, and racist discrimination against Irish Catholics continued across industrial workplaces until the 1960s.[34] Data on religion is only included in police personnel files originating from the 1930s and 1940s. Between 1930 and 1948, the percentage of recruits who identified as Protestant in individual sample years ranged between 98 per cent and 87 per cent (Appendix, Table A.4). Nevertheless, there was a noteworthy rise in the number of Roman Catholic recruits overall: from 5 per cent during 1930–1 (although declining to 2 per cent just before the outbreak of war), reaching a high of 13 per cent in 1946 (and settling at 10 per cent by 1948). Demographic information for the city as a whole suggests that Catholics were significantly under-represented in Glasgow City Police in this period.[35] Thus there is validity in the claim that policing was seen as a Protestant occupation, although it was by no means homogeneous.

The first Asian and Sikh officer in Glasgow City Police, Dilawer Singh, was appointed in 1970, after serving as a Special Constable since 1968 (and some 4 years after the appointment of the first BAME officer in the UK in Coventry in 1966). Born in the Punjab and familiar with Punjabi, Hindi and Urdu, he progressed to inspector, serving 31 years with the police and HMICS.[36] However, his profile was unique for much of his service. Settlers in Glasgow from the Indian sub-continent had grown in number from around thirty in the 1920s, with significant increases in the 1950s. By 1970 the size of Scotland's Asian population, including second generation, has been estimated as 16,000 (with the majority residents of Glasgow and its environs).[37] Yet the number of black and Asian applicants and recruits in the 1970s remained tiny (as elsewhere).[38] It was argued at the time that attempts to recruit BAME officers to UK police forces would be unlikely to succeed if their communities were unresponsive to 'white definitions of status' or felt threatened by 'a hostile discriminatory white society'.[39] Nevertheless, the appointment in 1974 of Labour Councillor Bashir Maan as the first Asian and Muslim Chairman of a police committee anywhere in the UK was also an important signifier of social change in Glasgow.[40]

Culture and Identity

Generation and gender

More extensive analysis of personal testimony suggests that generational difference significantly shaped the perspectives of police officers. Interviews were conducted with seventeen men who served in Glasgow City Police, six who served in other forces in west-central Scotland (including Lanarkshire, Coatbridge, Dunbartonshire, Hamilton and Paisley) and one who served in both: all joined between 1947 and 1970. Whilst one interviewee had been in the Army during the Second World War, a further eight were part of a generation who had undertaken national service in the armed forces before the former finally ended in 1963.[41] Those with a commonality of military background and experience – either during or just after the war – might be contrasted with the cohort that joined in the 1960s, having, in the main, either undertaken apprenticeships or (in four cases) served as police cadets before joining as regulars at the age of 18 or 19. Wartime military identities were maintained as a significant reference point and were incorporated into the culture of policing: 'he used to have two rows of medals with the laurel leaf on one of them . . . they called him "Guns" . . . he was in the Parachute Regiment'.[42] Those who fought in the war were highly regarded by those who had been slightly too young to fight but had experienced military service. As Thomas, who joined Paisley Burgh Police in the early 1950s (having served in the RAF), put it: 'We had bomber pilots, fighter pilots, rear gunners, commandos, marines . . . they didnae stand the nonsense.'[43] A former Scots Guard who joined Glasgow City Police in the late 1950s explained:

> The majority of my shift, and all shifts, were all World War Two veterans. They were frightened of nobody, and that included the bosses. They were hard men, hard, hard men. Good officers, first class officers, [and I] learned a lot from them.[44]

A hyper-masculinity that emphasised toughness – in contrast to the softness that was associated with femininity and effeminacy – was accentuated in wartime and in relation to particular sections of the Army (with more chivalric and middle-class models deployed in relation to the RAF who were seen as 'the knights of the air').[45] Yet it had also become particularly influential across the traditionally male-dominated heavy industries (shipbuilding, steel and mining) of west-central Scotland epitomised in the idealisation of the 'hard man'.[46] As Juliette Pattinson, Arthur McIvor and Linsey Robb have identified, 'prevailing inter-war discourse stressed the tough, brutal struggle in the workplace to win coal, forge iron and make ships by men desensitized to danger and risk'.[47] In Glasgow in particular hyper-masculinity was aligned with a police reputation for 'toughness' (including recourse to physical force) that had been cultivated as a response to the problem of the city's street gangs in the 1930s and the depiction of Glasgow as Britain's 'most violent city' (including in the 1935 novel *No Mean City*).[48] The cultivation of 'toughness' as a key component of Glasgow police identity can be seen as an inevitable and necessary process for maintaining legitimacy and authority within a broader masculine street culture. This reputation was embellished through the emphasis on military prowess in subsequent decades by those returning to the city from war. It has also continued to shape accounts retrospectively – as retired officers who joined in the aftermath of war reflect back on their careers in dialogue with popular narratives of Glasgow policing in the 1950s, such as Joe Pieri's *The Big Men* (itself based on the memories of retired officers).[49]

A younger generation (who joined in the 1960s) similarly characterised ex-military colleagues – referred to by one as 'the '45 men' – as adopting a 'robust' style that might incorporate the informal use of violence: 'some of the older cops, I mean, they were hardy buggers . . . I've worked with some real hard men'.[50] Whilst distinguishing themselves from it, some were careful to depict this style as discriminating in its deployment:

> I've seen policemen deal fairly severely with the ungodly, but they were very kindly with those that are unfortunate or were in trouble . . . A lot of the officers that I served with had come through the war in various stages and they had seen far worse than they would ever see on the street. I think that had made them very much aware of their humanity, and what life is all about.[51]

Others offered a more critical evaluation of the military 'old school boys', dominant until the mid-1970s (given that many served 30 years), whom they saw as effecting a hierarchical and deferential culture that was resistant to change.[52] As John, who joined in Lanarkshire in the late 1960s, explained:

> They all had their war medals up from the Second World War. It was like they thought the world was fine the day they joined the police and nothing should have changed since then. There was a strong element of that.[53]

Donald, who served in both Dunbartonshire and Glasgow City Police in the 1960s, was very aware of generational difference (in both forces) between the ex-military cohort and those, like himself, who had missed national service:

> [For them] it was a case of 'your being the last command, if it moves you paint it' sort of thing. I think my generation of officers had come from an education system which taught you to ask questions. So you didn't accept that, you were prepared to say, 'Okay, Sergeant, but do you not think . . .?'[54]

The sixties' generation came of age in an era where there was increasing rhetorical emphasis on career and professional development as forms of self-realisation rather than on 'duty', citizenship or indeed, the exigencies of war.[55]

A relationship between drinking culture (including drinking on duty), wartime military background and the 'hard man' style of policing was also suggested by a younger generation joining in the sixties: 'You'd folk who'd been through hell and back; some of them took to heavy drinking'; 'it was a man culture when I joined – it was a drinking culture: politically incorrect would be an understatement'; 'I was part of the generation that said "no", but [for] the generation I joined it was a common thing'.[56] Some former soldiers, including those decorated for bravery, may well have had serious alcohol problems related to wartime experience, which colleagues purportedly tried to cover up:

'they used to hide him away if he got too drunk; some of his colleagues would bundle him into the car, take him home and report him sick'.[57] The rapid demise of the 'drink' problem was identified as, in part, a result of the retirement of 'the '45 men' by the mid-1970s,[58] but also a zero-tolerance approach that was associated with David McNee as last Chief Constable of Glasgow City (1971–5) and first Chief Constable of the newly created Strathclyde Police (1975–7): 'The first officer up before him for drink got sacked. The word went out that things were changing . . .'[59] The pressure to drink may have been exacerbated by wartime trauma, but it was also shaped by the policing imperative to build relationships of trust and confidence with publicans who might be a resource as informants or allies (if there was 'trouble'). For some, taking a drink from a landlord after 'clearing out' was an unspoken ritual that solidified a bond. Yet the line between confidence and complicity was a fine one, of which younger officers became aware if they refused a drink: 'the owner [of the pub] looked at me and they looked at the guy I was with and they said "Don't bring him by – I don't trust this policeman that can't drink"'.[60]

Thus at mid-century military masculinities were clearly mapped onto policing identities – and in Glasgow, especially, asserted in terms of physical toughness – although they ceased to be hegemonic as the 1960s generation moved up the ranks in the later twentieth century. Moreover, the association between authority and male physical prowess, an integral tool of British policing since the nineteenth century, remained unchallenged until the equalities legislation of the 1970s (see Chapter 6). Glasgow officers took pride in the height and build of colleagues:

> The officers from the Highlands, they got respect. I was going over to Ibrox one night to a football match, on duty. I was with . . . [two] fellow[s] . . . They were big men. We're sitting in the subway and the fellow [name] had his hands on his knees like this . . . Someone nudged him and said, 'Look at the paws. Take a look at the paws.' They fell into it, 'Never mind the paws, look at his trotters.' He had big feet.[61]

The physicality of individual officers was incorporated into a broader group identity that was integral to urban policing – and Glasgow policing in particular.

Habitus and the muster hall

'On the job' training – even more so than formal instruction – was formative in the transmission of an occupational identity and ethos.[62] Indeed, those who joined in early 1946 were put through an intensive training course of only four weeks' duration because of the need for men on the beat.[63] By the 1950s recruits spent a more leisurely 12 weeks at Whitburn Police Training College, followed by a three-week course on local byelaws at Glasgow's own training school at

Oxford Street.[64] However, acculturation into policing, including understanding of the use of police discretion and interaction with the 'public' – as well as one's place within the police hierarchy – occurred upon return through the practice of the beat and acceptance into 'the muster room'. It was a process that involved observation, imitation and iteration. The sociologist Pierre Bourdieu uses the term *habitus* to refer to 'systems of durable, transposable dispositions' through which group identities, values and social behaviours are acquired and embodied, enacted and transmitted across time.[65] The concept of *habitus* is useful here because it allows for transformation and adaptation. Individual officers adopted or shaped these dispositions to suit their own abilities, personalities and pre-existing philosophies.

The ways in which this active process operated in the specific context of mid-century Glasgow policing emerge in oral history interviews. Kenneth, who grew up in north-east Scotland, joined in the 1950s from an RAF background: 'When I came down here I was a pebble in the ocean and I very quickly learnt that the only way that I'm going to really make my mark here is do the same as the older boys are doing.'[66] When constables returned from the police college as probationers they were assigned to a divisional station, the focal point of which was the muster hall, in which a rigid but unspoken hierarchy was maintained:

> If you were a probationer and you went into the Muster Hall and you sat in the wrong seat, you got shunted: 'Get out of my seat.' That's all they would say to you.[67]

> You learned very quickly that you didn't sit down until the sergeant came, and you took an empty seat. But not a word was spoken, I kid you not. They didn't say, 'Who are you? What are you doing?' They would just treat you as if you weren't there. Did it do you any harm? It didn't, quite honestly, and they were the backbone of the service and they would go through hell and high water for you. But you had to know your place.[68]

Those who were probationers around 1960 recalled that officers were still drilled and marched out from the muster hall onto their beats (as in the Edwardian period). Probationers were described as 'flying' since they were not allocated a beat of their own but covered for others after shadowing an experienced officer: 'He takes you round for the first couple of nights and shows you, "This is what you do. You pull the padlock here, go down the back stairs, look up and check the windows at the back of the shop . . ."'[69] It was about learning a routine and timetable in relation to a mind map of the built environment, but also styles of communication and social interaction:

> There were a whole lot of other things [that you learnt] and the way they dealt with people – almost that you're a wee bit stand-backish, you're

friendly, cajole them, you know, didn't take any nonsense but weren't aggressive, weren't abusive, weren't sarcastic. One of the things that was said to me in the early stage in my service was, 'Son, never lose your place for anyone'.[70]

Being firm and holding your own was part of the collective approach that was integral to the Glasgow way of doing things. For a probationer, acceptance by police colleagues on the shift was slow and those interviewed estimated that it took around 8 months. In rural districts, where officers were often the only constable in a village, they negotiated their role and identity through others in key occupations, most obviously the doctor, nurse, teacher and minister as well as the broader settled population (see Chapter 5). In contrast, in urban areas policing was primarily constituted in relation to a distinct group identity and *modus operandi* (as 'we'): as local police (whether force, division or shift) defined in relation to the city or burgh.

Moreover, subtle distinctions between individual police forces – of character, ethos and approach – were instilled across the Scottish police service and were a point of reference but also self-identification from training college onwards: 'Aberdeen were always regarded as the cream . . . at the top of the exams list and stuff like that. Glasgow would always be at the bottom, and the county forces would fill in the other areas.'[71] Whilst Aberdeen City Police was regarded as 'academic' by the 1960s (with a requirement for 'highers' as entry qualification), Glasgow officers saw themselves as superior in terms of physical toughness: 'Glasgow city was a top force, there's no doubt about it. It was a hard force'.[72] Kenneth felt that 'it was seen as a city where, if you stepped out of line, you would be dealt with', whilst for Donald, Glasgow police had 'quite a hard reputation' for a 'no nonsense approach . . . [where] things were nipped in the bud'.[73] This was seen as a direct reflection of the extent and seriousness of criminal behaviour in the city: 'Glasgow at one time was the murder capital of Europe . . . I think the police response to that was "Don't take prisoners".'[74] As one officer, who moved to a northern constabulary later in his career, put it, Glasgow City Police was 'a bit rougher, to put it mildly, in dealing with hard cases' in contrast with the 'softly softy approach' of the county.[75] Physical restraint or force was never far from the surface in underpinning police authority in the city.

Glasgow's sense of superiority – 'We felt we were better than everybody else' – was thus also defined in comparison to small burgh or county forces who were looked down on because 'nothing ever happens there'.[76] Neighbouring burgh police forces such as Hamilton, Coatbridge, Airdrie, and Motherwell and Wishaw (surrounded by Lanarkshire) and, a little further south, Kilmarnock and Ayr (surrounded by Ayrshire), all had an authorised strength of less than 100. Yet local pride in policing ran high in the burghs.

In Hamilton it was articulated distinctly in terms of public service, civic duty and municipal history. David joined in the early 1960s: 'Your role, it is pressed on you, that you are there to serve the public. You are there to provide the best service you could for them.' Hamilton's town council had agreed to the force's informal amalgamation with Lanarkshire in 1949 through the sharing of a chief constable but decided to opt for independent status once again in 1958 (with the appointment of Robert B. Gordon) until final amalgamation with Lanarkshire (along with the other small burghs) in 1967. Purportedly appointed to improve discipline in the force, Gordon made his mark on force culture:

> We were expected to know the history of Hamilton because the Chief Constable's view was 'if one of my officers is stopped in the street and is asked a question I want him to be able to answer it'. So we had to learn about the Hamilton Mausoleum, where the old Hamilton Palace used to stand, all of these things.[77]

Whilst burgh policing had much in common with city policing in terms of role and function, strong shared identities that bound together the burgh police force and its municipality were entrenched, creating a differently inflected style and ethos to Glasgow's inner-city 'toughness'. Style, ethos and identity were forged in relation to highly specific localisms.

Religious identity

Looking back on the interwar years from the perspective of the early 1960s, Robert Colquhoun's memoir presented sectarian conflict between Catholic and Protestant as a community problem that was external to policing rather than having any internal manifestation:

> Like everyone born and bred in Glasgow, I knew the unspoken rules which are still adhered to by a woefully large section of the population: that you are born either a Rangers or a Celtic supporter, that religion and race can be matters of vital importance if you attempt to get a job with several large firms.[78]

As the Runnymede Trust highlighted in 1989, 'hostility towards Irish-Catholic migrants' is 'a form of racism'.[79] Yet its presence within policing in the west of Scotland does not appear to have been acknowledged in official police sources of earlier decades – despite its visibility amongst the local population from whom recruits were increasingly drawn. Officers who joined in the early 1960s offered a rough estimate, based on personal experience, that around 10 per cent of the force was Catholic at that stage, a continuation of the pattern of earlier decades.[80]

Interviews suggest that Protestant bias and anti-Catholic prejudice operated alongside ethno-religious stereotypes at the level of rumour and gossip – at the very least – in Glasgow and Lanarkshire police into the early 1970s. Notably, despite being surrounded by Lanarkshire Constabulary (described as '99.9 per cent Protestant'), Coatbridge Burgh Police was exceptional in Scotland as a distinctly Catholic force:

> Coatbridge [the town] is a 98 per cent to 2 per cent Catholic population, and the police service in Coatbridge was about 84 per cent Catholic and 16 per cent Protestant officers – that is the only way that we were able to police it.[81]

On amalgamation with Lanarkshire in 1967 former Coatbridge Burgh officers were retained in the town, and its distinctive profile only changed when the area became part of the Strathclyde Police district following regionalisation in 1975. The example of Coatbridge is significant in demonstrating that policing as an occupation was not necessarily associated with Protestantism. Rather, specific local political dynamics were crucial. In Coatbridge police legitimacy in relation to a homogeneous community could only be assured through high levels of Catholic recruitment. Elsewhere, however, there was implicit Protestant ascendancy, although the degree to which it was seen as a problem varied.[82]

A number of those interviewed felt that religion never 'came into it' and that 'police bonds' were much stronger than ethno-religious identities.[83] For others, anti-Catholic prejudice was residual but in retreat, shaped by a past legacy. Douglas, who joined Glasgow City Police in the 1950s and was 'technically Roman Catholic' on account of his father's denomination, felt that 'it didn't bother me because I had it right through my family'. His situation was complex given that his mother was Protestant and the family also had communist connections: 'Officially politics [and] religion were not supposed to be discussed by policemen. You were unbiased. You shouldn't discuss them. Unfortunately, higher up most did . . . but that was hushed up' and 'we never knew much about it'.[84] Working out on division, he found that officers 'were all mixed up – you didn't know who was who', whilst others suggested that by the 1960s Protestants and Catholics were distributed proportionately across divisions to avoid problems that had arisen in the past.[85] For a further group, ethno-religious prejudice was articulated through jokes, black humour, football banter (including support for Rangers, the Protestant team) and what was normalised as 'leg-pulling' (part of the *habitus* established in the muster room). James, who joined Paisley Burgh Police in the 1950s, felt that 'religion didnae come into it', but also recollected references to it from superior officers:

> I have been in the bar [at the front desk] and I would say to the inspector that someone wanted to join the police: 'Ask him what school he went

to . . . The only way a Catholic gets in here is a constable on either side of him'.[86]

Andrew Davies's work on the 1930s shows that physical force was used indiscriminately to police Protestant and Catholic street gangs alike, whilst insults that were overtly racist were only targeted (with impunity) by some police officers against Irish-Catholic working-class communities.[87] Meg Henderson's memoir of growing up in the Blackhill area of the city similarly recollects hearing anti-Irish/Catholic insults directly from the police (rather than others in her neighbourhood) as a child in the late 1950s.[88]

A number of interviews with officers who joined in the 1960s suggest that ethno-religious prejudice amongst some officers was a 'big issue' in Glasgow City Police that blighted both careers and claims to objectivity:

> They had whole departments where Catholics needn't bother applying, because you'll not get in. And you'll be asked, "What school did you go to, son?" You'd be asked quite openly, and in the traffic office, they actually had a sign on the wall: 'No Popery Here' . . . In one department, there was actually a tally for doing ministers and priests, it was as bad as that . . .[89]

The crucial turning point was associated with the 1971 appointment of McNee as Glasgow's Chief Constable, who encouraged the recruitment of Catholic officers; and, even more so, of Patrick Hammill (himself Catholic), who succeeded McNee as Chief Constable of Strathclyde in 1978. This led to the rapid promotion of other Catholic officers to senior ranks, ending the glass ceiling.[90] As Charles remarked,

> By the time I left [after 30 years' service], it was totally different. The culture in relation to religion: that changed. If anybody came in with that type of attitude [ethnic and religious bigotry], then they'd be ostracised, because that's something you wouldn't put up with.[91]

On the Beat: the Practice of Policing

The role of the constable had developed from that of the night watchman during the course of the nineteenth century with the city's division into individual beats.[92] In Glasgow, as in burgh police forces, it was a rite of passage to be given your 'own' beat and reputation was bound up with it metonymically:

> I had a great pride in my own beat, and if you came on my beat and you mucked me up or mucked up my beat, I'll go after you. That was one thing of it, you were very proud. (Glasgow City)[93]

You were given a beat, you took a pride in that beat. You took it as an insult if something happened in that beat because you were so closely connected to it. You were expected to know all the businesspeople and shop owners in the beat. You were expected to know them well. (Hamilton Burgh)[94]

'Owning' a beat was about knowing it inside out and ensuring good order and the protection of property, in line with the established role of the constable 'to guard, watch and patrol'. Brogden has commented that a great deal of beat duty in Merseyside between the wars was 'prophylactic': people who were out of place (such as 'vagrants' and 'drunks') were moved on to keep 'one's beat clean' of blockages and so enable passage.[95] But it also meant that the homeless were found shelter. In Govan in the 1950s 'there was nobody lying about in the streets . . . [because] we would take them into what they called a "doss house" or gave them a night in the cells, we did that often.'[96]

Ordering the streets included dispersal of children since play that was 'obstruction or annoyance' was also prohibited. As McNee himself remembered of growing up in the 1930s: '. . . the street in front of the tenements was our playground and it was there that I would play football with the other boys – and girls – until chased off by the local policeman'.[97] Because of the prohibition of 'obstruction', the older men who gathered on street corners were expected to give way to police officers: 'We walked down the street and, standing at the street corner, the men would just move to the edge of the pavement; you walked past along the wall; then, when you passed by, they'd return to it.'[98] This ritual, referred to in a number of interviews, was also an enactment of deference and respect towards police authority. If not performed, it was seen as a clear insult to police identity. Beat constables were also responsible for inspecting street furniture and the fabric of buildings: 'Not only did we need to look down, we had to look up and see if there was a chimney pot line at a dangerous angle . . . this all came under the protection of life and property.'[99] Thus the beat was as much about the ordering of the material world as the social one.

Glasgow was unusual amongst urban police forces because its officers were not given a specified route through their beat that they had to follow. In Liverpool in the 1930s, constables were required to reach fixed points at 15-minute intervals (where they might be met by a sergeant), which Brogden has described as 'the ultimate in disciplined, supervised, time-tabled work'.[100] In Edinburgh in the early 1960s, according to Banton, 'each beat had a number of "turns" or specified patrol routes', and a constable would make a note in the journal (kept in the police box) as to which he was taking before setting out.[101] Glasgow constables had more latitude and autonomy (although they, too, were required to make a note of where they were going). Various styles of police box had been used in Glasgow since the 1890s when the telephone was introduced, but the police box system was augmented and developed under Sillitoe in the 1930s.[102] Each beat had at least one red police box at mid-century, containing a telephone, the 'beat book', which included contact details for all property owners (in the event of break-ins or emergency), as well as a journal. When the lights flashed, the constable was expected to attend from whatever part of the beat he was on. Thus the Glasgow beat man was still subject to intensive surveillance mechanisms, although means of subversion were a little more easily found. He would be met by a supervising sergeant twice during the shift (for signing of his notebook), and the inspector once. As in the burghs, all locked or closed properties were checked to ensure they were secure twice in every shift (hence the use of the phrase 'pulling padlocks' to characterise night duty). Wealthier home-owners who were going on holiday notified the local police station (in Glasgow as in rural counties and burghs) so that property could be checked in their absence; this continued well into the early 1970s.[103]

The relationship of police officers to people, place, and thus both community and occupational identity was different in Glasgow and the large cities because officers were not permitted to live on their beat or division by the post-war years (although they were expected to live within the city boundary).[104] Unlike their peers in the counties or small burgh forces, Glasgow officers were able to leave their work identity behind them: 'you could be the most popular or unpopular policeman, and go back home and . . . how you performed your job didn't matter when you were back home'.[105] In Lanarkshire, in contrast, Robert recalls being told '"you have to live on your beat, you can't live elsewhere – you stay on your beat so you know what the problems are and speak to the local people"'.[106] The approach used in the cities was designed to create detachment, assuring impartiality, but its obverse effect was to enhance group solidarity as 'police'.

Married officers in Glasgow were offered police houses for their families which, in the post-war period, were built as part of the planning of the post-war housing schemes (often as a row or block together). They travelled in and out of work together on public transport buses, receiving free rides if wearing uniform:

> There must have been, within a very short radius, about 250 policemen staying in Drumchapel. When we came out for the nightshift you either got the 10 o'clock bus or the quarter past 10 bus. You would not get a seat on the top deck if you were a civilian – they were full with police officers . . . The conductresses were always pleased to see you on the buses, because then they knew there was going to be no trouble going into Drumchapel.[107]

Other officers chose to find private accommodation for their families because of concerns about the effects of this clustering on children.[108] Banton's study suggests that police officers and their families experienced victimisation at home in very particular areas: where there was 'smouldering hostility' in a small number of industrial towns and in housing schemes on Glasgow's outskirts.[109] Direct personal experiences of wives and children being stigmatised as a police family – of being seen as separate and different – were rare in our interviews but obliquely referred to in relation to Lanarkshire's industrial towns: 'my kids were always classed as the policeman's kids . . . [and] I've known bullying in relation with other policemen's kids'.[110] Where officers who lived in a cluster of police houses were targeted, through stone-throwing or minor vandalism, action by the group was usually effective in reasserting authority: 'four of us in the police houses got together and made an example of a couple of them; we waited for it to happen and went out and grabbed them, and it soon stopped'.[111]

Indeed, the social distancing that was encouraged in Glasgow when not on shift contrasted with the proximity that was prized by many of the small burgh forces. For John, who joined Lanarkshire around 1970, there were distinct advantages to the old burgh system – exemplified by towns such as Motherwell and Wishaw or Coatbridge – for police–community relations: 'You lived and worked in that town probably all your service, and stayed beside them in the same row of police houses. [It was a] much tighter community.'[112] For others such a model was considered too introspective, close-knit and cliquish, with amalgamation when it finally came bringing 'new police officers in with new ideas rather than old school and old timers saying "I have been here for 30 years" [who] . . . wouldn't allow themselves to go out their comfort zone'.[113] It is clear that accommodation arrangements (where police officers lived and next to whom) led to different dynamics between police and neighbourhoods.

Moreover, the work of the beat constable and the texture of his experience varied enormously in relation to the socio-economic profile of his beat. For Thomas, posted to cover Govan's commercial docks in the early 1950s, police work was mainly concerned with security (checking all those coming in and out of the gates in the context of continued wartime restrictions), the reporting of industrial accidents, dealing with workplace theft by dockers (seen as prevalent), and responding to drunken brawls and assaults involving merchant seamen (depicted as 'nothing we couldn't handle').[114] A keen piper, he found that the dockyard watchmen provided familiar company as well as information and comfort on a cold night: 'Some of them were from the Highlands and Skye and the Western Isles and I carried my chanter about with me in my baton pocket and I used to play them a tune . . . It was good to get a wee seat around the fire.'[115]

In Glasgow city centre, the protection of economic livelihoods was a significant concern given the concentration of shops, refreshment houses and businesses. The majority of the population was itinerant and mobile (shoppers and other clientele) compared to residential areas, so familiarity was built up with the proprietors of these establishments, particularly small retailers 'who were the ones who perhaps needed protection', given that the large chain and department stores employed their own security staff.[116] Where there were problems with restaurant clients leaving without settling up, it might be a matter of police presence around closing time rather than formal arrests.[117] Shopkeepers, restaurateurs and publicans (across the city and not just the commercial centre) were always potential allies of the police, since it was in their interests to ensure licences were renewed and 'trouble' minimised. When officers were on their own and got into difficulty, it was often proprietors who would telephone the station for back-up. 'Gossiping on duty' was technically a disciplinary offence, but accepting an invitation from a shopkeeper to go into the back-room for a cup of tea or spending time in a café with the owner might be 'an asset'.[118] Proprietors were an important source of police information (like the watchmen at the docks), which was more likely to be informally relayed rather than officially reported. Given that policing roles in Glasgow were highly segmented (unlike in rural areas), it was the job of the beat man to pass this on (again, often discretely) to a detective in the CID. This information circuit, with its tentacles down into the neighbourhood through the beat man, was crucial to the functioning of the CID in the years before regionalisation (and, subsequently, the information revolution of the late twentieth century): 'local knowledge . . . in my day . . . was how police worked'.[119]

Since 1857 the City of Glasgow Police Regulations had identified the object of policing as 'the prevention of crime, the protection of life and property, and the security, peace and comfort of all citizens'.[120] In practice, however, not everyone experienced or viewed police protection similarly. Norman Morrison, a teetotal Gaelic speaker from the island of Lewis who joined Glasgow City Police in 1889, professed profound cultural shock when he encountered the realities of Glasgow street life. He faced the open hostility of the labouring poor – 'my warnings were treated with scoffs, sneers and defiant contempt' – and the reluctance of 'citizens' to intervene to assist the police. In his memoirs he also describes 'overzealous' and 'questionable arrests' that were effected by some long-serving officers, including an incident that he refused to corroborate.[121] Disillusioned, he left Glasgow, finding employment in Argyll County Police which was more suited to his personality, values and style. Indeed, in 1907 Chief Constable James Stevenson, when questioned about 'the general attitude of the public' towards police officers in Glasgow, evidenced high levels of distrust between the police and entire neighbourhoods:

> The feeling towards the police is decidedly good in the better class localities, and amongst the shop-keeping classes. In the rougher localities the feeling is hostile and always in favour of the arrested person.[122]

This had hardly dissipated by the interwar period: cases were regularly reported of 'constables being mobbed and brutally assaulted while carrying out arrests' and of 'the usual crowd of would-be-rescuers' who dispensed 'rough handling and violence' to the police.[123]

For James Devon, Medical Officer at Duke Street Prison in 1908, the police faced an impossible task given that most 'offences' under the Glasgow Police Acts were caused by inequality, dense overcrowding, and lack of social responsibility amongst wealthier inhabitants:

> We take men of good physique and character, many of them country-bred and unacquainted with the complexities of city life. We pay them the wages of a labourer, and, with a uniform, invest them with powers and duties of the most varied kind . . . A complaint is made to the police of the bad language used by girls at a street corner in a certain slum district. It is certainly lurid; but where have they learnt it? . . . The girls are warned, but they persist in speaking their own language, and in bravado ornament it profusely and shout opprobrium at the policeman. One is caught . . . she is taken to the police station and again warned. The complaints persist. Again she is arrested. She is the bad one; she was taken in the act before . . . She is sent to prison in default of paying a fine. On examination it is quite clear that she is just an ordinary slum-bred girl, with no special vice.[124]

He was referring specifically here to the offence of 'using obscene, profane or indecent language' under the 1892 Glasgow Police Act.[125] The police acts were concerned with 'the rules of good conduct within the city' and the prevention of public 'annoyance'; but who, exactly, counted as 'the public' with the right to be annoyed was contentious.[126] Devon's polemical yet sympathetic account is worth quoting at length as illuminating the social interactions that might all too easily lead to escalation, penal intervention, and stigmatisation of individuals.

As Lindsay Farmer has suggested, in Scotland as in England, assessment of 'character, situation and history rather than responsibility for actions' had, by 1900, led to a preoccupation with the classification of individuals as 'law-abiding' or 'criminal' across social classes, replacing the broad concerns about the 'disorderly behaviour of the lower orders' that had driven mid-nineteenth-century policing.[127] Moreover, status as 'respectable' and 'law-abiding' had long been incorporated into the culture of the skilled working class. Yet well into the twentieth century whole neighbourhoods in Glasgow were still stereotyped as 'rough' (and thus crimogenic if not 'criminal') rather than 'respectable'. Davies's meticulous research has shown that, far from dissipating, the combative and unequal relationship between police and the city's poorest neighbourhoods continued, characterised by 'alienation from the law' amongst working people and the 'pervasive and routine' use of violence by the police in the 1930s.[128] This was not only deployed in relation to public protest – most significantly 'Bloody Friday' of 31 January 1919 and incidents during the General Strike of 1926 – but was a part of everyday experience in some neighbourhoods.[129]

Attitudes towards the police continued to be guarded in the years during and after the Second World War although some suggested there had been very significant improvement. Glasgow's first Lord Provost of Catholic origins, the socialist Patrick Dollan (elected to the office in 1938), reportedly told the SPF in 1940 that 'the attitude of the public' had changed over the last 15 years so that the police were now 'evolving into the counsellors and guides of the whole community' and that 'the public now regarded the police as their best friends'.[130] This tells us as much about his own personal trajectory and the complexity of socialist politics in Glasgow, where socialist parties had won the majority of Corporation seats (and, subsequently, Labour control of the police committee) for the first time in 1933, as it does about grassroots attitudes. Davies suggests that 'for the new socialist administration, demonstrating support for the police and judiciary' was a crucial concern.[131] Dollan's confidence – marshalled in relation to the need to maintain public morale in a war that he wholeheartedly supported this time (having been imprisoned for his opposition to the First World War), was consistent with the trope of the 'people's war' as a shared experience of pulling together.[132]

However, whilst street violence (involving predominantly young men) was perceived to have diminished in the early years of the Second World War, there was widespread comment on the 'growth of petty dishonesty' amongst a broader population (including children as well as older people) which casts doubt on the concept of 'the people's war'.[133] Colquhoun's memoirs luridly described the black-out regulations as turning 'Glasgow after dark into a shadowy cesspool of crime, thickened in violence and intensity by a constant addition of deserters and men on the run from military-service notices'.[134] Indeed, assaults and robberies using firearms were identified as significantly increasing across Scottish cities at war-end.[135] In 1946 Chief Constable McCulloch voiced disappointment in his Annual Report that 'the Police are entitled to expect a much greater measure of co-operation from the people whose interests they are endeavouring to protect', appealing for police assistance from 'all law-abiding members of the community' in reporting incidents using the new '999' telephone system.[136] Seán Damer suggests that, across the mid-twentieth-century, 'tenement dwellers called in the police as last resort, for they were the enemy; Glaswegians sorted out their own disagreements'.[137] Banton's group discussions with sergeants attending the Scottish Police College in 1960 suggested that there were greater feelings of resentment towards the police in

Glasgow and the industrial west of Scotland than elsewhere because of the continued legacy of the policing of the General Strike of 1926, still within living memory.[138]

A number of officers in our interviews characterised the dominant emotion that shaped working-class attitudes towards the police in the 1950s-60s as one of fearfulness: not necessarily of individual officers *per se*, but of the circumstances that led to significant interactions with them (including fear of intimidation and victimisation by others around them), and because of the circumstances of people's lives. It was police officers who delivered the 'bad news' of illnesses and deaths (given that few homes had telephones). Michael had grown up in an area of Glasgow associated with significant deprivation in the 1940s-50s before joining the police:

> I'd say that in the community I grew up in, the police were feared and, *to an extent*, revered. They were feared because nobody wanted them at their door. They were bad news at your doorstep . . . As someone who got caught by the police playing football in the street, twice, and ending up in juvenile court, I had a first-hand example of that side of it . . . I would say the word 'respect' might be overused. There was a respect but the police were feared because of the type of society I lived in.[139]

Kenneth was posted to a particular part of the Maryhill Division in the 1950s where he felt that 'the communication that you had with members of the public to a great extent were born from fear. They needed us'. When he first started, he encountered considerable aloofness: 'there was nobody ever come in and reported anything, unless it was somebody was lying dead in the street or something like that . . . they wouldn't go to the police, no, no.' Within the culture of the muster hall the area was seen as a 'hotbed' for violence, housebreaking and anti-social behaviour and its reputation was used to justify 'robust' policing: 'They used to put most of the younger, stronger, fitter cops down there and protect the old fellas.' Over time, however, Kenneth gradually sensed a growing confidence from the population: 'before I moved [posting] I could get them to come up and ask me all sorts of questions, intimate questions, domestic problems. I thought . . . "I must've done something right".'[140] Michael was a beat constable in the working-class areas of the Gallowgate and the Barras:

> Once you'd been around a wee while, people would speak to you and chat away. Invariably, they'd say, 'Can you no' do something about these weans that are running through the close at night?' . . . So they're looking for assistance, they're looking for reassurance . . . that there's somebody there to protect them.[141]

Any one officer had to work assiduously to build up a relationship of trust, and reticence towards the police remained a feature of many working-class neighbourhoods in the 1960s:

> In the Saracen area, and down around the George's Cross area, there was perhaps less appreciation of the police as a body than there would be in the West End, where people had really very little contact with the police . . . But again, to be fair, a lot of the – I won't say abuse, it didn't amount to that – but a lot of the ill-feeling [towards police] came from those that were involved in unlawful activities. The older generation, generally, would be appreciative of you, although they also had to remember their family connections. But it was usually the youngsters . . . It was mainly young males – young boxers, we used to say [who caused 'bother'].[142]

Chief Constable McCulloch also suggested in 1954 that reticence about using the '999' system was breaking down as it was used by 'a section of the public who in previous years, could never have been expected to co-operate' although 'even now some people are afraid to give us their names when they report a crime'.[143] Yet this co-operation should not be overstated. Working-class memoirs of growing up in specific areas such as the Gorbals and Blackhill in the 1950s-60s unremittingly depict the police as an 'enemy' to whom it was unacceptable to 'grass': 'to the police, who came from outside, everyone in Blackhill was scum, fit only to be raided and thrown into the back of Black Marias'.[144]

THE SOCIAL WORK ETHOS AND POPULAR MORALITY

Nevertheless, some interactions that officers had with local working-class residents in Glasgow neighbourhoods – as in other cities and burghs – were welcomed, particularly those characterised in Banton's study of Edinburgh as 'social work' rather than law enforcement. Assistance with burst pipes was ubiquitously requested and given in these examples relating to the early 1960s:

> Leaking taps that they brought to your attention weren't leaking taps – they were taps that they couldn't turn off because it was so bad. You would change the washer for them. I used to carry a bucket sometimes and a couple of washers.[145]

> [T]he old woman, she got a burst pipe, the police always knew where to go and find a key to turn the water off. She didn't call a plumber in the middle of the night, she would call the police.[146]

They acted as interlocutors with factors regarding tenants' problems concerning inferior accommodation. Undoubtedly some Glasgow officers (with a strong personal orientation towards the idea of policing as social service) associated their role and identity as beat man with a profound social responsibility that involved care for the vulnerable:

> When you had a beat of your own, that was your property. That was your area. These people were the people that relied on you. You had a sense of not only belonging, but a sense of responsibility to try and ensure that people – and the lives that they did have, and some were not all that great – had a better cut at life.[147]

> I saw the value of what I was doing as being 90 per cent social and 10 per cent enforcement. You knew who the vulnerable people on your beat were . . . and you would get to know somebody, an old woman who's left on her own.[148]

As the police instruction book specified, constables should be 'ready to afford assistance particularly to elderly and infirm persons and children'.[149] All officers had at least basic skills of literacy and numeracy that were higher than those of their more vulnerable clientele, whilst those who came through the 'cadet' scheme in the later 1950s were likely to have added 'highers' to their educational qualifications. This led – on some beats, and for some beat men – to clear respect for their knowledge and authority, and concomitant requests for assistance:

> That [police] box, I can picture it today . . . Late shift in particular, you'd come around there and there would be one, two or three people standing at the police box, knowing there was a change of shift . . . It would be for a variety of things, and I could recount several. Someone wanted me to read a letter to them because it came from their son who was in the armed services and they couldn't read. The regular used to be, 'Could you help me fill this form in?' . . . Again, not unusual, [but] not every day: 'My son's smoking and I told him not to, he won't take a telling from me, can you come and speak to him?' 'My boy's getting into trouble, he's with the wrong crowd, come and talk to him.' You would do that.[150]

The examples of police assistance given here mirror very closely those depicted by Banton in his ethnographic study of the work of beat men in the central division of Edinburgh City Police in the early 1960s. Banton argued that, in contrast to specialist departments, such as the CID and Traffic Department, the beat man was effectively a 'peace officer' who was 'operating within the moral consensus of the community'.[151] In the poorer neighbourhoods of Scottish cities, he suggested, beat men often established 'a protective relationship with law-abiding residents as well as more active enforcers of the peace' and were 'to a greater extent uniformed social workers' because informal methods of social control were weaker than in more prosperous districts.[152]

Banton also argued that police interventions were 'governed much more by public morality than by the letter of the law'.[153] In police memoirs and interviews relating to west-central Scotland, officers present themselves as sharing the values of the working-class tenement communities that they policed, in many cases through direct experience of growing up in similar surroundings. David McNee's autobiography comments on 'the indelible impression' that growing up amidst 'the rough and tumble of life in central Glasgow in the midst of the Depression' made upon him. His father, an active trade union member, had been a train driver before moving into a 'senior position in the locomotive sheds', so the family were amongst the better-off section of the working class. He describes how the Protestant work ethic, shaped through his family's evangelical non-conformist religion, created a guiding sense of 'right and wrong' that was embedded within a neighbourhood solidarity: 'We lived close by each other, we knew each other, and we helped each other.'[154]

Street football exemplifies the balancing of law and popular opinion. According to George, 'We could have filled our notebooks with groups of young boys playing street football. You didn't. You said, "Come on, boys. Go to the pictures." You didn't hammer them for it, because then you were just a baddie.'[155] In earlier decades some Glasgow officers adopted a more instrumental, although nevertheless informal, intervention. Douglas, who joined Glasgow City Police himself in the 1950s, had grown up in Springburn:

> If we played football in the street: "Here's the bobby" [and] everybody took off, grabbed the ball and ran for your life. In these days if the bobby got the ball he just took a knife out and shsss. Instead of booking anybody he just burst the ball . . . Part of it became the game: that you were expecting to get chased, or not chased but if he appeared . . . you all ran for your life.[156]

Thus the beat man was incorporated into the ritual of play as a 'bogey' figure. Moreover, despite accounts that highlight informal methods for dealing with street football, it was nevertheless the case that Glasgow youths were formally dealt with in large numbers across the period, leading either to police 'warnings' or proceedings in the juvenile court.[157] McNee explained his decision to 'book' a group of young men for playing football in the street in the early hours of a Sunday morning: '[I was] conscious that one of the city's more important bye-laws was being broken and, more relevantly, that those living nearby might want some sleep.'[158] The meaning of 'discretion', according to the *Instruction Book*, was that a constable 'should not be anxious to make arrests for trifling offences . . . unless the interests of public order make that course necessary'.[159]

Thus a social work imperative was an important element within the repertoire of policing in Glasgow as elsewhere and – for many officers and on some beats – it was a definitive one. Nevertheless, they actively used the law to enforce peace on behalf of those whom they saw as a moral majority in the neighbourhood. Moreover, former officers spoke of beats such as Garscube Road and Saracen Cross as extremely 'tough' because of the presence of 'troublemakers' who were disruptive to the 'law-abiding' and who consumed considerable police time.[160] Banton himself stated that his research on Edinburgh was concerned with a 'relatively law-abiding Scottish city', and that he had been unable to study 'what happens in situations where policemen are subject to strain and provocation' or how the police used the law more rigorously in relation to those known as 'criminals'.[161] Styles of policing quite clearly varied and fluctuated in Glasgow in relation to police assessment of the character and status of the individuals involved. For those considered 'law-abiding' – residents and shopkeepers who were polite and respectful – a conciliatory approach was deemed important in attaining respect:

> [You build respect] by being friendly to them. Don't come down hard on them. If there's somebody out there washing their kerb . . . they had to wash the pavement in front of their shop [so this should not be treated as obstruction] . . . You knew the ones you could say, 'Look, don't do that again', and you were respected. 'Thanks very much, Officer.' That was all you needed.[162]

Yet a very different set of tactics and approaches was reserved for those identified as the 'criminal', the 'nuisance' or 'troublemaker' – the 'ned' as he was called (the term was only applied to males) – and against whom the Glasgow reputation for 'toughness' was likely to be deployed, as this chapter will now demonstrate.

Dealing with the 'Ned'

This is how Joseph described Saracen Cross in the 1950s:

> It was a tough area to work. But you had to make your authority count. They would test you. When I went up there at first you were tested . . . The local neds up there would want to know how strong you were, how far you would go, how far they could push you. It always came down to an eye to eye with them to see who was going to blink first. You couldn't blink first.[163]

The methods that were used to assert this authority shifted across time as, in the years after the Second World War, informal physical coercion gave way to the assiduous use of arrest for breach of the peace, whilst Glasgow City police officers sought to maintain the city's reputation for 'robust' and 'no-nonsense' policing.

Clive Emsley has demonstrated that in some inner-city urban environments across the UK, police officers gained reputations as fighting men into the inter-war years and were expected to accept challenges issued to them in order to gain ascendancy within a ritualised culture of male pugilism.[164] Glasgow was no exception and Colquhoun's memoir highlights the symbolic importance of these performances in a stylised description of his first beat on the St Rollox Division, described as 'rough even for Glasgow' in 1923:

> Many of our fighting men didn't like cops. One character, an ex-soldier named Noble Dan, made a habit of approaching any uniform man who came his way and issuing him a solemn formally worded challenge to 'single mortal combat'. Every now and then some cop sighed, went with him into a tenement backyard and obliged. Noble Dan was invariably flattened.[165]

Within this story police reputation for physical toughness is depicted as effortlessly achieved and as a response to a broader aggressive masculine popular culture. The much-echoed trope that the police were the dominant gang amongst gangs also makes an appearance:[166] 'the thugs and petty thieves called us, at the politest, "snouts". Our name for them, then and still today, was "neds"'.[167] Within this territorial power struggle, individual officers were also defending group authority.

Davies has carefully evaluated the policing strategies that were developed in the 1930s to tackle the city's 'gang' culture. Chief Constable Percy Sillitoe was a great proponent of the latest scientific technologies, which he deployed alongside the more 'traditional' human resource. A mobile squad of police cars was introduced so that 'the police were able to get to any place where there was trouble as quickly as possible', acting as a crucial back-up for beat officers.[168] Motor patrols were also used to conduct spot-checks of gang members under 'stop and search' clauses in the Glasgow Police Acts; whilst fingerprinting was used to garner scientific evidence alongside the cultivation of informants, which continued to be an important mechanism for securing corroboration for convictions.[169] Perhaps most significantly, Sillitoe gave full endorsement to methods that were labelled 'brutality' by others, noting in his memoirs that this led to 'a general toughening' in police attitudes 'towards the gangsters'.[170] Moreover, Sillitoe's biographer suggested that a special squad that included 'ex-boxers' as well as 'regular police officers' was sent out to 'fight the gangs'.[171] Nevertheless, Davies shows that Sillitoe's claim that he had 'sounded the knell of gangsterdom in Glasgow' was significantly overstated to bolster personal reputation. Rather, it was most likely enlistment in the armed forces in 1939 that led to the demise of the activities of the notorious 'Beehive Boys', a group that had mutated from street gang into an organised criminal network of housebreakers – rather than 'any of the police strategies devised by Sillitoe'.[172] Prosecutions were ultimately limited because witnesses refused to testify (through fear and intimidation as much as defiance) and the police continued to be drawn into running battles, their ultimate tactics being physical resilience. Davies's work has shown 'that the police were ever ready to meet force with force' and that there was 'ready resort to violence on both sides'.[173]

These dynamics of territorial rivalry, forged in the earlier part of the century, had clear resonance in the mid-1960s, as Ian explained:

> If you spoke to guys in the street, hardened criminals – if they were loitering on a street corner, as a young bobby, you'd go up and said, 'Right pal, come on, you have to move.' They'd turn round and say, 'Look, young fella, I'm only moving because your gang's bigger than my gang.'[174]

Nevertheless, the personal testimony of former officers suggests that police tactics and behaviours shifted to reflect changing public attitudes towards the use of physical force to resolve disputes. This was ubiquitously referred to in terms of the decline of the 'clip round the ear' as a method of warning juveniles, with the 1959 Thurso Tribunal (see Chapter 2) a watershed moment across the UK. That a case emerging from a small town in Caithness captured public attention and led to a public inquiry may be somewhat ironic given Glasgow's reputation. In a culture in which teachers (as well as parents) legitimately used corporal punishment, the 'cuff' or 'clip round the ear' (with gloves or hand) had long been absorbed into informal styles of policing in working-class neighbourhoods across British cities, and it has often been presented as a harmless mechanism for disciplining naughty children. Yet in accounts of policing in Glasgow and other west of Scotland towns relating to the late 1940s and early 1950s, it seems to have been deployed equally in relation to teenagers and young adults who came into the category of 'ned' or 'troublemaker' as a standard mechanism of asserting authority:

> We'd belt his lugs [ears] and that would be the end of the story. If you were nae' going to lock him up and, just depending on the circumstances, just whack his lugs.[175]

> I got this kid who broke 18 streetlamps, I was by myself, no witnesses. I said 'I will give you a choice. You go to the police office or you get your backside skelped'. You know what he asked for, he got his backside skelped ... I just hit him a couple of times and went 'let's go see your mother and father' [and] they were quite happy with what

I had done . . . With young yins I saw their parents and quite often their parents gave me permission to do it.[176]

Such accounts may be shaped by a retrospective bravado. Forms of physical chastisement inhabited what was already by mid-century a twilight zone of police behaviour that was not officially condoned but neither was it condemned.

Police forces had very clear rules about the use of the baton, which could in theory only be drawn for self-defence (if 'likely to be overpowered') and not targeted at the head.[177] On every occasion it was used, an officer was officially required to submit a report, and officers took pride in stating that they had only drawn their baton once or twice in their entire police career in situations of considerable personal danger as well as bravery.[178] It was also stated as a matter of principle that the minimum of force should be exercised to make an arrest. As Davies work has shown, these principles were routinely flouted in the interwar years. Moreover, the minimum was flexible into the 1970s: 'The cops would never, they would always make sure that whatever happened, they weren't going to end up second best.'[179] Yet for the most part officers interviewed who joined around 1960 referred to physical coercion as something that was not used by themselves but by the older generation of 'hard men' with whom they served:

> They were trying to change the 'No Mean City' attitude – [that] you don't lift your hands to anybody. But that didn't bother the old school bobbies, the guys who had served during the war and all the rest of it. They would think nothing of taking a guy round the back court and giving him a hiding or giving the kids a clip around the ear.[180]

> [For] just normal bad behaviour, that's how they dealt with it . . . warn them in the back [close] and boot their behind and say, 'On you go' . . . A lot of them [neds] are thankful for that, because they never had convictions, they never went to court. But I remember the cops that did it, the old cops would do it, to warn them. Maybe go up to the house and see their parents.[181]

> A lot of the neds accepted it. Maybe got a slap on the back of the head and that was it, away up the road, never complained – very rarely.[182]

It is important to note that the persistence of 'rough-handling' into the post-war years was not restricted to Glasgow and is presented as a residue of 'old-fashioned' policing in sources relating to Edinburgh and Dundee too.[183] The quotations above suggest that police use of physical chastisement to discipline 'troublemakers' was accommodated – and thus given legitimacy – within a broader popular morality in which it was accepted by all without complaint as preferable to prosecution and formal sanction.[184] It was incorporated into a broader landscape of (informal) patriarchal social regulation, accompanying that exercised by fathers and teachers. It is presented, too, as an organic response to the problems of a dystopian society that police officers could only mirror or reflect. Alan, who joined in the late 1940s also described how he had on occasion organised and supervised fist fights to keep troublemakers out of the dance hall and thus regulate 'trouble' within the accepted parameters of local masculine street culture (although he acknowledged that this would not have been approved by senior officers).[185]

When the voices of those who were on the receiving end of this type of policing do surface, they tell a different story. Davies has recently drawn attention to the attempts of the inhabitants of the Garngad to protest, firstly, against the anti-Catholic insults and aggressive methods of a beat man they nicknamed 'Constable Hitler' and, subsequently, against a series of wrongful police arrests and convictions in 1933–5. He has highlighted how even 'the ratepayers and shopkeepers of the Garngad' described events in terms of '"the unwarranted assault by the police upon residents of this district"', and has demonstrated a clear miscarriage of justice.[186] In July 1935 ILP MP for Shettleston, John McGovern, called for a public inquiry (brushed off by Scottish Secretary Godfrey Collins) into the actions of police in both Glasgow City and Lanarkshire, referring in parliament to 'police terrorism in the Garngad' in which 'indiscriminate arrests' had been made for breaches of the peace, to police intimidation of witnesses who disagreed with their account of events, and to the complicity of the convicting sheriff. Whilst Collins was clearly supportive of Sillitoe's methods, McGovern drew attention to the way in which assumptions had been made about an entire neighbourhood, entailing (amongst other methods) the provocative deployment of a 'Black Maria' police van in the area 'before any disturbances of any kind had taken place'.[187]

There were reasons (both personal and political) as to why McGovern acted as the parliamentarian through whom complaints about corruption, judicial bias, and police methods were voiced. In July 1931 he had asked questions in parliament regarding both 'brutal' prison sentences given to lay preachers for speaking on Glasgow Green without a permit and (later in the month), the sentencing of seven Glasgow youths to 14 days' imprisonment for playing street football.[188] In October 1931 he was himself arrested and charged with 'mobbing and rioting', against the backdrop of the Glasgow Green free speech campaign and the broader actions of the NUWM. He successfully conducted his own defence in Glasgow Sheriff's court, arguing, too, that he had been brutally kicked in the spine by an officer during the course of his arrest.[189] Glasgow City Police had continued to label and monitor McGovern as a communist and anarchist activist – despite his own claims that he opposed violent methods of protest (which he contrasted with Communist Party methods of deliberately orchestrating 'clashes with the police' to stoke 'bitterness of the whole State machine').[190] Nevertheless, in 1933 he had been amongst those successfully calling for a Tribunal of Inquiry into bribery and corruption amongst members of Glasgow Corporation.[191]

Finally joining the Labour Party in 1947, McGovern continued to be a conduit for concerns about abuse of police powers in the years after the Second World War. In November 1950 (when the Progressive Party was in brief control of Glasgow Corporation) he called (unsuccessfully) for a public inquiry into the 'administration and discipline of the Glasgow police' on the grounds that the police were failing to tackle the post-war violent 'crimewave' (about which there was wide concern), but also because of instances of 'police brutality' towards 'civilians in the cells and on the streets'.[192] Labour members of the police committee had recently voiced protest at Chief Constable McCulloch's decision not to dismiss (from the force) a detective constable who had been convicted by jury of an assault on 'a Pakistani shopkeeper' in his own store on Garscube Road (for which he had been fined by the sheriff).[193] The call was also made against the backdrop of the highly publicised capital conviction of Glasgow policeman James Ronald Robertson for the murder of a 40-year-old Glasgow woman by running a stolen motor car over her.[194] Whilst the Lord Provost and Chief Constable viewed these instances as truly exceptional, McGovern implied a set of systemic problems. In his response, McCulloch rejected the allegations and stated that he had only received four complaints alleging 'assaults' by officers during the year, none of which had been upheld.[195] Yet as we highlighted in Chapter 2, lack of independent oversight meant that the complaints system was neither robust nor trusted by many in this period.

In other interviews with former Glasgow officers who joined in the late 1950s and early 1960s (in the wake of the Thurso Tribunal), informal physical coercion is described as outmoded by this period and restricted to an aberrant minority. Instead former officers emphasise a proactive law enforcement model as shaping the police stance towards 'gang members' and 'neds': '[there was] no summary justice – it was more satisfying to arrest them and detain them . . . pick them off one at a time for one misdemeanour or other'.[196] The retributive culture of 'come-back', which enabled officers to work around the Scots Law requirement of corroboration, was delivered through legitimate arrest for either breach of the peace ('riotous and disorderly conduct') or the fallback of 'using words or behaviour with intent to provoke breach of the peace'.[197] That this was a particularly localised 'Glasgow' solution is demonstrated in Table 3.1. In raw numerical terms people (mostly males) in Glasgow were the subject of BoP proceedings in exceptionally large numbers: over 9,000 in 1950 (doubling to over 18,000 in 1970), compared to 356 in Aberdeen, 420 in Dundee and 500 in Edinburgh. What is more significant, however, is the high percentage of all proceedings brought (and thus of police and court time) that BoP constituted: over

Table 3.1 Breach of the peace proceedings as a percentage of all crimes and offences in Scotland's four cities, five-yearly intervals. Source: Calculated from HMICS ARs, Cmd. 3007, Cmd. 3963, Cmd. 5299, Cmd. 8330, Cmd. 9750, Cmnd. 1343, Cmnd. 3050, Cmnd. 4707.

City	1925	1930	1935	1950	1955	1960	1965	1970
Aberdeen	8	22	15	14	12	11	10	13
Dundee	16	12	8	12	16	15	15	18
Edinburgh	14	10	9	8	9	11	11	13
Glasgow	26	28	21	37	21	16	24	27

a third in 1950 and over a quarter in 1970, in contrast to around a tenth in Edinburgh. In Dundee, where there were similar concerns to Glasgow about youth gangs in the late 1960s, proceedings reached 18 per cent by 1970.[198] BoP proceedings were by far and away the most widely used legal tools in the Glasgow City Police apparatus across the post-war period, outnumbered only in the data for 1960 by motor vehicle and betting/gambling offences (when the latter were particularly high); for all other years in these 5-yearly samples BoP significantly outnumbered all other proceedings. Thus in comparative terms (across time and place) the BoP charge was the primary instrument of official police intervention. Its widespread usage in Glasgow was not new but a continuum with the pattern established far earlier. Late-Victorian use had also been significant, and BoP had similarly constituted over a quarter of all crimes and offences in 1925 and 1930.[199]

Oral history interviews provide further insight into the use of BoP as a general tool for dealing with anti-social behaviour in the post-war years and as an option for offences for which other charges would not stick (because there was no corroboration to sustain them). In some cases officers were less concerned as to whether arrest would lead to successful prosecution. Rather, the action of 'booking' (reporting or charging someone), arrest and (overnight) jail (assuming the station duty officer accepted the initial charge) might be seen as sufficient punishment in itself and a mechanism for asserting authority on the beat:

> Neds, you can control them. You've just got to let them know who the boss is. You just give them . . . a friendly word [and] say, 'Listen, this is my area. You come in here and misbehave, you get the jail'; end of story. When you get them in a group, they're difficult. They're all playing and brass necked. But you get them one at a time, you say, 'Right, this is my beat; you're done. You'll keep getting done.'[200]

For most of the time Glasgow beat men were required to patrol on their own (to maximise efficiency), which made it difficult to make arrests on the spot, given the need for corroboration (unless a wider audience was present and assisted). However, there were some beats where constables were permitted to pair up regularly with their neighbour for night duty; they could also request assistance from a neighbour (by calling division and arranging to meet him at the police box) if they thought an arrest was possible or likely. Peter, who was a beat constable in the 1960s in a central area that he describes as being used as a meeting place for youth gangs coming in from the Castlemilk housing scheme, explains why BoP was an effective tool:

> If a guy is trying to be too smart with you and showing off in front of his pals, you ignore it. But the following day you come back with your neighbour and [the guy] says, 'How are you tonight?' 'Well, you're getting the jail for last night. Now you know what you're getting done for' ... By the time you get this guy the second night, and by the time you and your neighbour get hold of his hand, it's a breach of the peace because he'll start effing and blinding. It's a breach of the peace there and then, so he's going to jail for that.[201]

Other officers admitted that they experienced very significant personal danger on their beat but recovered from this by resolving to pursue retribution. Garscube Road was deemed a very tough beat in the early 1960s:

> At least half a dozen times I grabbed my hat, stuck it under my arm and run away from a situation knowing full well that if I stayed, big deal, I might take two of them out, but at the end of the day, I was going to get right hammered. I had a right good look at them first of all. Boy, there came a day of reckoning, they might get picked off a month later.[202]

As Brian (who joined around 1970) stated: 'That was always the big thing about the Glasgow police; if they meddled with you, they knew that you were coming for them, albeit at a later date. Total necessity, otherwise you wouldn't last two days.'[203]

The principle of knowing who you were dealing with so that you could come back afterwards for the 'reckoning' (which it was stressed was achieved through BoP proceedings in the post-war years) was ingrained as a first line of both defence and action:

> I always remember an old cop saying to me once, 'If you come up against a group like that and they come at you, stand your ground and if you know them say, "Willie Smith I'm getting you. Jones I'm getting you. You're

next."' He said, 'They'll suddenly realise wait a minute and they'll begin to slip away, and you're not left with as many in front of you.' He said, 'If anything happens to me I'm coming for you, I don't care what happens. I'm coming for you and I'm coming for you.' (Joined early 1950s)[204]

BoP charges were used to uphold the authority of individual police officers (who would return with back-up) in relation to groups through the threat and menace of 'come-back'. Yet, as Michael explains, BoP charges could also be seen as an ethical response (albeit often a work-around) to the needs of other residents and proprietors and a key example of the exercise of discretion:

> Will I make the situation better or worse by what I'm going to do? . . . That's what it boils down to. You can often, very often, especially if you're in communities that you're known in, know that you should be locking someone up because half of the community will rejoice. There are people that cause difficulties in communities and the fact that the policeman locked him up for a breach of the peace, shouting and balling and swearing in the street, put him to the court, will be a great sense of relief to many people . . . You don't always get comment but you can sense or sometimes they'll say 'Aye, you got the right one last night'.[205]

Some of those interviewed were frank that officers sometimes lied in court in the 1960s to provide corroboration (having been on the scene but not witnessed the offence committed) in order to get 'a genuine conviction'; this was allegedly known about by magistrates and lawyers.[206] Indeed, police criticism of Scots Law was apparent in comments reportedly made by Assistant Chief Constable William Ratcliff in 1969 that it was 'far more difficult to get convictions in Scotland in a system designed "specifically to defeat the ends of justice".[207] Thus anecdotal evidence suggests that discretion may have been used on occasion to administer 'justice' in line with an officer's own moral compass (if not the letter of the law), which was nevertheless justified by the officer concerned as aligned and in tune with those seen as the 'law-abiding community'.

Oral history interviews commonly cited domestic violence cases or 'wife assaults' as a key example of the malleability of BoP proceedings. Officers saw themselves as the chivalric protectors of vulnerable women whose fear of giving evidence against husbands was compounded by the rule of corroboration (where violence took place behind closed doors). This particular anecdote (relating to the mid-1960s) exemplifies many of the themes of this chapter, including the discrepancy between training and practice, the performance of masculine physical toughness as a trademark of Glasgow policing, and flexible use of the law to enable an outcome that (from the police perspective) was seen as socially just in relation to a wider popular morality (but which may also have contributed to the further stigmatisation of poor communities):

> I remember going to a domestic; I was straight out of the College. The senior bobby that was with me said 'What did they tell you at college to do in domestic incidents?' I gave him the standard input from the College. He said, 'Oh aye, well I'll show you how we do it in the wine alley.' So, first of all, we get to the door and we could hear the rammy behind the door. He said, 'You stand at that side of the door.' He stood at the other side of the door. He took his stick out and he knocked on the door with his baton. 'Who the eff is it?' 'The polis.' 'F- the polis', and a chain would come through the glass portion of the door . . . So the window was smashed; so he just leaned in, opened the door . . . and he said, 'The door's open. Are you coming to speak to me?' The wife and the family would be – the wife would be wanting to make a complaint and he would be telling her – he'd be full of drink and all the rest of it. But we knew, nine times out of ten, if we went into the house, took her complaint, by four o'clock in the morning, she'd be down at the office withdrawing the complaint. So, what he did, in this instance, was, 'We're not coming in; you come out to see us.' As soon as he stepped over the threshold, he grabbed him and locked him up on a breach of the peace on the stair end. That solved the problem.[208]

Other officers described the arrest of known wife-beaters for drunkenness as they left pubs as a protective measure (ensuring a cooling-off period in the cells overnight) as well as zealous enforcement of motor vehicle legislation as a *quid pro quo*: 'he bought a car, we made life hell with him with the car, particularly if she appeared in the street with a bruised face, just by stopping him [and] giving him tickets'.[209]

Looking back on these tactics, former officers now see them as the product of a 'different era' that cannot be justified in relation to present-day standards and expectations, but which enabled the achievement of an outcome that was fair at the time (in relation to wider community values) on occasions when the letter of the law militated against it. They argued that local 'neds' accepted these frameworks and that they were thus part of a broader shared culture and value system: 'I think by and large the neds knew the score.'[210] Yet in the late 1960s/early 1970s – as in the 1930s (as Davies's work has shown) – there were those who raised concern about Glasgow's police methods.[211] In June 1973 Labour councillor Bill Hatton accused the police very publicly of a 'deliberate policy of harassment' against young people in the city, arresting them for 'trumped up charges' – usually involving BoP – and of 'driving them off the streets'.[212] Although most of the allegations related to the work of the plain-clothes anti-violence squad (see Chapter 4), some uniform beat officers were implicated.[213] Dispensation of social justice to 'troublemakers' (according to the police perspective) was experienced as intimidation and harassment by some of the young working-class men who were its targets.[214]

The Special Constabulary

That the Glasgow style of policing was about a physical toughness learnt as part of a group culture and identity – and which saw the police as distinct and separate from the 'public' – is emphasised further in the poor relationship that regular officers had with members of the Special Constabulary (part-time volunteers) by 1960. In burghs such as Hamilton, as well as county police forces including Lanarkshire and Dunbartonshire, special constables were for the most part highly regarded by regular officers and seen as useful for corroboration and back-up. The contrast with prevalent attitudes in Glasgow was brought out for Charles when he transferred from Dunbartonshire in the first half of the 1970s:

> In Clydebank, we had a really good relationship with the Special Constabulary . . . Then I transferred into the City of Glasgow, and the attitude there was 'unpaid and unwanted'. They used to say to them . . . 'Where do you work?' They'd say, 'I work in a steelyard', or something like that. The next question would be, 'How would you like it if I came and did your job for nothing?'[215]

Accounts were overwhelmingly similar across interview material. Indeed, the inspectorate was very aware this was a systemic problem in Glasgow. In 1961 it was noted that the actual strength of 450 special constables lay well short of the authorised establishment of 2,000, and numbers continued to erode to only 92 in 1973 (less than 5 percent of establishment).[216] In 1974 David Gray described Glasgow's Special Constabulary as 'the poorest of any force in Scotland'.[217]

The uses that could be made of special constables had been more limited in Scotland than in England and Wales, with Orders of 1923 and 1940 (issued by the Scottish Secretary) restricting their use to 'occasions of emergency' and the prevention of 'tumult or riot'.[218] During the 'emergency' of the Second World War, the Special Constabulary in Glasgow had, however, gained significant recognition for its work, receiving praise for 'splendid work during the blitz on Clydeside'.[219] A total of 1,773 special constables had been serving in July 1942 and, at war-end (according to one of their number), were 'keen as mustard' to serve 'the somewhat scared public of Glasgow . . . to put down gang warfare and all serious crime'.[220] Chief Constable McCulloch saw a role for the Special Constabulary in responding to the 'high incidence of crime' stoking public pressure in 1951, and it was agreed that specials should go out on the beat to accompany a regular officer in the evenings or at weekends.[221] Yet the Police (Scotland) Act of 1956 not only maintained the restriction on their duties to 'emergency', 'suppressing riot' and the gaining of 'practical experience' (for training purposes only), it also cut their hours to one tour of duty a month. This was largely a result of the influence of the SPF, who saw any expansion in the role of specials as undermining the status of full-time rank and file. In the wake of the 1956 Act the Special Constabulary collapsed in Glasgow, as its members felt that 'their services are not really wanted' and 'some of the regulars have made it apparent to the specials that their presence was nether welcomed nor required'.[222]

Analysis of oral history interviews suggests it was not merely to do with resentment that specials were undertaking 'free' work or concern that they lacked commitment. As Gordon commented:

> They were seen as a liability to be honest, because you never knew whether you could trust them or not . . . An incident happens and you get involved and suddenly there's a stramash. You end up rolling about the ground, and it gets physical, you need to be sure that your . . . neighbour . . . would back you up. We were never quite sure with some of the specials.[223]

At the core of the problem was the idea that they were not 'proper' police, that 'the neds knew' they were 'not real police' and that they could not be relied upon to deliver the tough style of policing that was necessary in Glasgow.[224] Although some specials undoubtedly won trust individually by demonstrating physical bravery, as a group they tended to be viewed as 'outsiders' in relation to the close-knit culture of the regular shift.

Conclusions

It is interesting to note that the dominant representation projected of Glasgow City Police through the official documentation of the Chief Constables' Annual Report was that of a highly efficient scientific organisation deploying the latest in modern technologies: telecommunications, forensics and motor transport. Yet by far and away the dominant reputation of Glasgow police within the city's broader popular culture was of authority that was claimed through male physical prowess – of 'hardness' and 'toughness' – rather than status/position or specifically moral force. It was constructed through the *habitus* of the muster hall, inscribed into everyday life through the performance of police identities on the beat, and recognised by working-class communities (through resistance as much as acquiescence or deference). Its hegemony and longevity was a function of the shared valuing of hardness and toughness within male-dominated street culture, enhanced further by military identities configured during the Second World War. Within the repertoires of some police officers, 'toughness' tipped over into over-zealous use of physical force (beyond that sanctioned within the principle of that which was 'reasonable'). These moments are impossible to quantify because they were mostly hidden, although examples occasionally surface. Notably, Sillitoe gave this over-zealous use of physical force some sanction in the 1930s but it was formally proscribed in the years after the Second World War. For the most part – across the twentieth century – 'toughness' was exercised through the application of legal BoP proceedings, which can be clearly measured using the formal documentation of criminal justice statistics. The BoP charge contained considerable malleability and flexibility as a 'catch-all' through which those for whom other charges could not be proven might be detained (with provocative tactics sometimes used).

Glasgow officers were in large part drawn from the local white Protestant skilled industrial working-class population by mid-century, and police values, styles and repertoires are probably best seen as a refraction (rather than reflection or simulacrum) of this as officers forged a very distinct group identity that was passed on to new recruits through a process of accretion and as a form of resilience. A new generation joining in the 1960s (when ideas about gender difference were increasingly being challenged by the effects of de-industrialisation amongst other factors) were motivated by career, professionalism and service rather than military discipline; whilst aware of this cultural difference, they were unsure how to challenge the 'old school'. That Glasgow City Police (and the uniform branch in particular) had succumbed to elements of cultural atrophy was suggested in David Gray's inspection report of 1971, which expressed concerns about the quality of the leadership at divisional chief-superintendent and superintendent level, where there was a lack of 'imagination and progressive ideas'.[225] Most of these officers had joined in the 1930s-40s during the Sillitoe years or in the aftermath of the Second World War.[226] In 1975 Gray tellingly praised McNee for 'promoting men of ability' so that 'there is new life in the force' with 'ideas and initiative' in contrast to the previous regime in which 'for too long promotion in the Glasgow force was by seniority'.[227] However, any significant reconfiguration of police culture was, as Chapter 6 will demonstrate, a gradual response to sequential equalities legislation and the technological transformations of the later twentieth century rather than the initiatives of any one individual.

Finally, this chapter has shown that a further style of policing was widely deployed on the everyday beat which, whilst receiving much less emphasis within the reputation for 'toughness', was a significant element in the repertoire of the beat constable. These were the interventions associated with social responsibility and social service (referred to by Banton as 'social work') in relation to those the police deemed 'respectable' and 'law-abiding' (including the more vulnerable) within poor neighbourhoods. Nevertheless, these interventions could also be encapsulated within a chivalric and paternalistic model of masculinity that complemented the reputation for 'toughness' seen as so critical in relation to the criminal, the anti-social and the 'ned'. Styles of policing depended on context and on an assessment of the individuals involved. Police officers undoubtedly offered invaluable assistance: with housing problems relating to utilities such as water and electricity; with guidance on parenting, 'bullying' and other interpersonal difficulties; with the passing on of information about births, death and illnesses; and with advice about bureaucratic procedures. Shopkeepers and other proprietors depended on them and were their allies. Yet at best the relationship between police officers and the working-class communities that they served in Glasgow remained an uneasy one – in part because of their lack of embeddedness compared to the burgh police officer, who lived as well as worked on his patch, but also because of a deep historical legacy of mistrust, fear (of intimidation generally), and not 'grassing' on neighbours. The police distinction between 'law-abiding' and 'troublemakers' concealed a more complex set of relationships within those districts where resentment of the police was widespread.

Notes

1. Colquhoun, *Life Begins*, 19.
2. Anderson, *Scotland's Populations*, 99.
3. Pacione, *Glasgow*; Damer, *Glasgow*, 90.
4. Davies, 'Street gangs'; Davies, *City of Gangs*.
5. TNA, HH60/79.
6. Bartie, 'Moral panics'.
7. PP. *Judicial/Criminal Statistics, Scotland*: for 1930, Cmd. 3963; 1960, Cmnd. 1343; 1965, Cmnd. 3050; 1970, Cmnd. 4707.
8. Shields and Duncan, *State of Crime*, calculated data for eight crime groups only in order to generate crime rates that might be compared to similar data for England and Wales.
9. Ibid., 78.
10. PP, *HMICS ARs*: 1912, Cd. 6712; 1962, Cmnd. 2006; *HMIC ARs*, 1912, Paper 76; 1962, Paper 250. In 1962 Dundee's 331 policemen policed an average of 555 residents and 389 acres per officer, whilst in Edinburgh 1,123 policemen policed an average of 423 residents and 30 acres per officer. Figures for Liverpool were one policeman to every 387 residents and 14 acres and, for Manchester, one policeman to every 396 residents and 16 acres.
11. NRS, HH55/1727, inspection report, Glasgow, August 1969.
12. Withers. '"Long arm"'; Goldsmith, 'City of Glasgow Police', 116.
13. The Decennial Census suggests a decline in the proportion of Irish-born residents of Glasgow (from 9 per cent in 1901 to 5 per cent in 1931) and of Highland-born

residents (4 to 3 per cent), with a rise in residents born in the West Central area, including Glasgow (69 per cent in 1901 to 78 per cent in 1931).
14. Goodwin, 'Police in Edinburgh', 29. In the 1920s two-thirds of Edinburgh recruits were Edinburgh-born and 15 per cent of recruits were born in the Highlands and Islands. Neither Glasgow nor Edinburgh recruited much from each other's hinterland across the first half of the twentieth century or from England and Wales. In 1889 only 22 per cent of Metropolitan Police recruits were London-born, but this rose to 37 per cent in 1905: Shpayer-Makov, 'Appeal', 197, and *Making of a Policeman*, 59. A half of Manchester and Birmingham recruits originated from the cities themselves or adjacent counties in 1900–39: Klein, *Invisible Men*, 15.
15. Van Slingelandt and Macdonald, *Long Way*, 38, v, and 79.
16. GCA, SR22/55/24, personnel records of Govan Burgh recruits c. 1880–1912 who subsequently transferred to Glasgow.
17. Streets, 'Identity'.
18. GCA, SR22/63/18 letter to CC, 17 May 1927; Weinberger, *Best Police*, 183.
19. Goldsmith, 'City of Glasgow Police', 53.
20. Sillitoe, *Cloak without Dagger*, 125; Goldsmith, 'City of Glasgow Police', 140. Sillitoe's predecessors included James V. Stevenson (1902 to 1922) who moved from the RIC, and Andrew D. Smith (1923 to 1933), born in Wigtownshire and who joined Liverpool Police in 1901, transferring to Glasgow in 1902. Sillitoe (1931–43) and McCulloch (1943–60, Glasgow-born but raised in Lochaber) were succeeded by James A. Robertson (1960–71), the Glasgow-born son of a policeman who joined Glasgow City Police as a constable in 1926, and then David McNee, Glasgow-born and police-trained, who returned as Chief in 1971 following a stint as Deputy Chief Constable of Dunbartonshire.
21. GCA, SR22/40, Glasgow, *CC AR* for 1958, 22.
22. Shpayer-Makov, 'Appeal', 196.
23. GCA, E4/2/28, CC's letter book, 27 February 1907, letter to the CCs of Fife, Banff, Elgin, Wigton, Perth, and Inverness.
24. Goldsmith, 'City of Glasgow Police', 407; Floud et al., *Changing Body*, 144, cites regular recruits to the British army averaging 5 feet 6 inches amongst the age group 20–24 in the years 1905–9. By 1948 this had risen to 5 feet 7½ inches (average height of men aged 20–21 called up under Military Training Acts): cited in PP. *Report of the Committee on Police Conditions of Service Part II* (1948–9), Cmd. 7831, 8. The national minimum height requirement was 5 feet 8 inches according to Scottish Office Police Regulations; individual forces were permitted to set a higher one: 5 feet 9 inches according to City of Glasgow Police, *Instruction Book* (1912), 69. Many Scottish forces set a local requirement of 5 feet 10 inches and several required 5 feet 11 inches.
25. Goodwin, 'Police in Edinburgh', 32–3.
26. Ibid.
27. Pattinson, McIvor and Robb, *Men in Reserve*, 2.
28. Analysis of a sample of 490 personnel records for recruits to Glasgow City Police 1945–8.
29. GCA, SR22/40, Glasgow, *CC AR* for 1946.

30. NRS, HH55/615.
31. Percentage calculated for 200 recruits who joined in 1946.
32. Brewer, *Royal Irish Constabulary*.
33. *Irish Times*, 9 June 1921.
34. Armstrong, *People without Prejudice?*; Davies, '"Sing that song"'; Ritchie, '"They do not become good Scotsmen"'.
35. Cunnison and Gilfillan, *Third Statistical Account*, 725. In 1954, 27 per cent of Glasgow's population were described as regular Roman Catholic churchgoers and 29 per cent as regular Protestant churchgoers.
36. *Herald*, 20 September 2014, https://www.heraldscotland.com/news/13180973.glasgow-based-sports-campaigner-given-accolade-at-asian-achievers-awards/ (last accessed 3 January 2020); Sikhs in Scotland, http://www.sikhsinscotland.org/people/people-from-scotland/singh,-mr-dilawer/191.phtml (last accessed 3 January 2020).
37. Maan, *New Scots*, 103, 160 and 168.
38. NRS, HH 55/1727, Glasgow, annual inspection documents indicate four BAME applicants in 1974, all rejected (as under-age, incorrect nationality or under the height requirement).
39. J. Lambert, 'The police and community', *Race Today*, November 1970, 388–90.
40. Bashir Maan (2013 interview), Colourful Heritage Online Archive, https://www.colourfulheritage.com/portfolio/bashirmaan2013/ (last accessed 11 May 2020).
41. Vinven, *National Service*.
42. Interview with Andrew (pseudonym), conducted by Davidson.
43. Interview with James (pseudonym), conducted by Davidson.
44. Interview with Joseph (pseudonym), conducted by Davidson.
45. Francis, *Flyer*; Rose, *Which People's War?*.
46. Johnston and McIvor, 'Dangerous work'; Young, 'Hard man'; Damer, *Glasgow*, 150–3.
47. Pattinson et al., *Men in Reserve*, 14. Chand, *Masculinities on Clydeside*.
48. Davies, 'Street gangs'; Davies, *City of Gangs*. McArthur and Kingsley Long, *No Mean City*, told the story of Gorbals 'razor king' 'Johnnie Stark'.
49. Pieri, *Big Men*. Interview with James (pseudonym), conducted by Davidson: 'Have you ever read *The Big Men*? Well that was pretty much the way it was'. See Summerfield, 'Culture and composure' on the concept of 'the cultural circuit'.
50. Interview with Gordon (pseudonym), conducted by Davidson; interview with Andrew.
51. Interview with George (pseudonym), conducted by Davidson.
52. Interview with Ian (pseudonym), conducted by Davidson.
53. Interview with John (pseudonym), conducted by Davidson.
54. Interview with Donald (pseudonym), conducted by Davidson.
55. White and Hunt, 'Citizenship'.
56. Interview with Michael (pseudonym), conducted by Davidson; Interview with Charles (pseudonym), conducted by Davidson; interview with Donald.
57. Interview with Ian.
58. Interview with Gordon.

59. Interview with Michael; see also interview with Ronald (pseudonym), conducted by Davidson.
60. Interview with Donald.
61. Interview with Joseph.
62. Brogden, *Mersey Beat*, 19.
63. NRS, HH55/615.
64. NRS, HH55/1237.
65. Bourdieu, *Logic*, 53.
66. Interview with Kenneth (pseudonym), conducted by Davidson.
67. Interview with Ian.
68. Interview with Alexander (pseudonym), conducted by Davidson.
69. Interview with Peter (pseudonym), conducted by Davidson.
70. Interview with Alexander.
71. Interview with Robert (pseudonym), conducted by Davidson; see also interviews with Andrew and Gordon.
72. Interview with Joseph.
73. Interviews with Kenneth and Donald.
74. Interview with Donald.
75. Interview with Thomas (pseudonym), conducted by Davidson.
76. Interviews with Peter (pseudonym) and Douglas (pseudonym), conducted by Davidson.
77. Interview with David (pseudonym), conducted by Davidson.
78. Colquhoun, *Life Begins*, 38.
79. Armstrong, *People without Prejudice?*, 27.
80. Interview with Gordon.
81. Interview with William (pseudonym), conducted by Davidson. Personnel records are not extant for Coatbridge, so personal testimony is drawn on here.
82. Personnel records for Greenock Burgh Police 1900–45 were selectively retained in GCA SR 22/84/4/1. For 114 records where religion was stated, only three were Roman Catholic, the remainder Protestant.
83. Interviews with Ronald, Joseph and Gordon.
84. Interview with Douglas. Charles Macdonald was also raised as a Catholic within a mixed marriage: Van Slingelandt and Macdonald, *Long Way*, 3.
85. Interview with Michael.
86. Interview with James.
87. Davies, 'Street gangs'.
88. Henderson, *Finding Peggy*, 52.
89. Interview with Charles.
90. Interviews with Charles, Kenneth and Donald.
91. Interview with Charles.
92. Goldsmith, 'City of Glasgow Police'.
93. Interview with Kenneth.
94. Interview with David.
95. Brogden, *Mersey Beat*, 99.
96. Interview with Thomas.

97. McNee, *McNee's Law*, 21.
98. Interview with Joseph.
99. Interview with Gordon.
100. Brogden, *Mersey Beat*, 2.
101. Banton, *Policeman*, 16.
102. See Goldsmith, 'City of Glasgow Police', 98.
103. Interview with David.
104. In the first decades of the twentieth century they were required to live within their division: see City of Glasgow Police, *Instruction Book* (1912), 31.
105. Interview with Gordon.
106. Interview with Robert.
107. Interview with Joseph.
108. Interview with Donald.
109. Banton, *Policeman*, 212.
110. Interview with Colin (pseudonym), conducted by Davidson; see also interview with David.
111. Interview with David.
112. Interview with John.
113. Interview with William.
114. Interview with Thomas.
115. Ibid.
116. Interview with Donald.
117. Ibid.
118. Interview with Douglas.
119. Interview with Thomas.
120. City of Glasgow Police, *Instruction Book* (1912), 15.
121. Morrison, *My Story*, 21–2.
122. PP, Cd. 4260, Q. 40246–7, James V. Stevenson.
123. *GH*, 23 August 1922, 8 and 11 August 1920; see also 19 September 1930.
124. Devon, 'Causes of crime'.
125. City of Glasgow Police, *Instruction Book* (1912), 212.
126. Ibid., 125.
127. Farmer, *Criminal Law*, 118; Knox and McKinlay, 'Crime'.
128. Davies, 'Police violence'. See also Davies, '"Sillitoe's Cossacks"'.
129. Davies, 'Police violence'.
130. *Scotsman*, 23 February 1940.
131. Davies, 'Police violence', 69.
132. Knox, *Labour Leaders*, 92–9; Weinberger, *Best Police*, 130.
133. TNA, HH60/79.
134. Colquhoun, *Life Begins*, 58.
135. TNA, HH60/79.
136. GCA, SR22/40, Glasgow, *CC AR* for 1946.
137. Damer, *Glasgow*, 90.
138. Banton, *Policeman*, 211.
139. Interview with Michael.

140. Interview with Kenneth.
141. Interview with Michael.
142. Interview with George.
143. *News of the World*, 17 January 1954.
144. Macfarlane, *Gorbals Diehards*, 150; Henderson, *Finding Peggy*, 51 and 53.
145. Interview with Alexander.
146. Interview with Gordon.
147. Interview with Alexander.
148. Interview with Gordon.
149. City of Glasgow Police, *Instruction Book* (1912), 31 and (1923), 89.
150. Interview with Alexander.
151. Banton, *Policeman*, 7
152. Ibid., 180.
153. Ibid., 146.
154. McNee, *McNee's Law*, 19 and 21.
155. Interview with George.
156. Interview with Douglas.
157. NRS, HH60/905. In Glasgow's Eastern Division an annual average of 278 juveniles were 'booked' for 'street football' in the 1960s.
158. McNee, *McNee's Law*, 38.
159. City of Glasgow Police, *Instruction Book* (1912), 31 and (1923) 34.
160. Interview with George.
161. Banton, *Policeman*, xii and 131.
162. Interview with Peter.
163. Interview with Joseph.
164. Emsley, *Hard Men*.
165. Colquhoun, *Life Begins*, 18.
166. Damer, *Glasgow*, 149.
167. Colquhoun, *Life Begins*, 19.
168. Sillitoe, *Cloak without Dagger*, 127.
169. Davies, 'Street gangs', 262
170. Sillitoe, *Cloak without Dagger*, 149.
171. Cockerill, *Sillitoe*, 132–3, was based on interviews conducted by journalist James McGlinchy; also quoted in Davies, '"Sillitoe's Cossacks"', 48.
172. Davies, 'Street gangs', 267.
173. Davies, 'Street gangs', 253 and 266; Davies, '"Sillitoe's Cossacks"'.
174. Interview with Ian.
175. Interview with James.
176. Interview with Alan (pseudonym), conducted by Davidson.
177. City of Glasgow Police, *Instruction Book* (1912), 32; (1923), 75.
178. Interviews with David, Robert, Peter, Ronald and Gordon.
179. Interview with Charles.
180. Interview with Ian. 'Hiding' suggests a more severe beating.
181. Interview with Andrew.
182. Interview with Peter.

183. Banton, *Policeman*, 175; Jackson with Bartie, *Policing Youth*, 39–42.
184. See also McLaughlin, *Crimestopper*, 13.
185. Interview with Alan.
186. Davies, 'Police violence', 71, quoting *Evening Times*, 12 June 1934.
187. PP, *Hansard* [HC], 4 July 1935, cols 2019–64.
188. *GH*, 3 July 1931 and *Scotsman*, 21 July 1931.
189. NRS, HH55/664; McGovern, *Neither Fear nor Favour*, 74.
190. NRS, HH55/664, confidential letters: Mr Duke, Scottish Office, to Sillitoe, 30 January 1932, and Sillitoe to Duke, 3 February 1932; report of DS John Forbes to Sillitoe, 2 February 1932; McGovern, *Neither Fear nor Favour*, 81.
191. PP, *Glasgow Tribunal of Inquiry* (1933) Cmd. 4361.
192. PP, *Hansard* [HC], 21 November 1950, cols 181–3. For full press coverage see GCA, SR/22/62/13.
193. GCA, SR/22/62/13, news cuttings include *GH* 18 October 1950 and *Bulletin* 27 October 1950). Press reports did not consider whether this was racially motivated. For hostility generally towards Asian shopkeepers in Glasgow see Maan, *New Scots*, 166.
194. GCA, SR/22/62/13, news cuttings.
195. *GH*, 22 November 1950.
196. Interview with Joseph.
197. Glasgow Police Act 1892, s. 135.
198. Numerically BoP proceedings increased in 1960 compared to 1950 but represented a smaller percentage of all crimes/offences because of a significant hike in the number of betting and gambling cases.
199. Farmer, *Criminal Law*, 104, 113–14.
200. Interview with Peter.
201. Ibid.
202. Interview with Kenneth.
203. Interview with Brian (pseudonym), conducted by Davidson.
204. Interview with Douglas.
205. Interview with Michael.
206. Interview with Kenneth.
207. *GH*, 28 November 1969.
208. Interview with Ian. The 'wine alley' was a stigmatising term used to describe the Moorepark slum clearance scheme built in Govan in the 1930s; see Damer, *Moorepark*.
209. Interview with Alexander.
210. Interview with Gordon.
211. See, for example, *GH* 9 July 1970 and 3 August 1973.
212. *Evening Citizen*, 13 June 1973; 14 June 1973; 15 June 1973. *GH*, 3 August 1973; 11 August 1973.
213. NLS, B. Hatton, 'Complaints against the Police' (Glasgow: privately published/printed pamphlet, 1973–4).
214. See also Bartie, 'Moral panics'.
215. Interview with Charles.

216. NRS, HH55/1237, Glasgow, inspection report, August 1961.
217. NRS, HH55/1727, Glasgow, inspection report, August 1974.
218. NRS, HH55/804.
219. Ibid., extract from HMICS inspection reports, Glasgow, 24 and 25 June 1941.
220. Ibid., Special Constable Robert Sykes, letter to Joseph Westwood (Scottish Secretary), 17 December 1945.
221. Ibid., correspondence between McCulloch and the Scottish Home Department, 26 February 1951, 14 January and 30 January 1952.
222. Ibid., Commandant of the Special Constabulary, Glasgow, to McCulloch, 25 March 1958, Elliott Binns to T. A. Critchley, 23 March 1960.
223. Interview with Gordon.
224. Interview with Peter.
225. NRS, HH55/1727, inspection report, 1971.
226. NRS, HH55/1727, data for the 1973 inspection.
227. NRS, HH55/1727, inspection report, 14 July 1975.

4

SPECIALIST AND PLAINCLOTHES POLICING

As the twentieth century progressed, police roles in large city forces were increasingly compartmentalised into discrete areas of specialisation: defined in relation to forms of technology, types of offence or categories of person. An initial distinction between the beat constable's brief 'to guard, patrol and watch' and that of the detective to investigate 'serious' crime was established early in the nineteenth century but the number of detectives remained small before 1900. By 1821 Glasgow City Police had a 'Criminal Department' of six detectives, growing to 39 by 1900 and 137 by 1932, dispersed across divisions.[1] Whilst only half of Scotland's police forces employed detectives in 1900, the experience of the Second World War led to the setting up of criminal investigations branches in most remaining forces by 1946.[2] Furthermore, by the early twentieth century, additional teams of plainclothes officers in the cities (technically part of the 'uniform' branch rather than the CID) dealt with 'licensing, betting, gaming and vice laws'.[3] Officially described as the Licensing Department, they were referred to colloquially as the 'vice squad'. The 1930 Road Traffic Act created a panoply of new offences and all Scottish police districts were required to set up motor patrol teams as a result.[4] In Glasgow a specialist Traffic Department was created by Sillitoe to undertake the regulation associated with the new measures, increased car ownership, road traffic accidents and 'joy-riding'. In 1946 his successor, McCulloch, consolidated fingerprinting, photography, forensic science and criminal records into one 'Investigation Bureau' to serve not only Glasgow but the whole of Scotland.[5]

Yet despite its association with professionalisation, specialisation was not seen as overwhelmingly beneficial. In 1946 HMICS Sydney Kinnear warned that 'care must be taken to ensure that the beat constable . . . is not ignored' and that 'achievement and success' should be 'shared by all' to build morale around 'a common purpose'.[6] In 1974 it was claimed that until recently 'the Glasgow force was one where specialisation was carried out to a marked degree' so that 'the constable on the street' was 'denuded of responsibility', a trend that had been even more pronounced there than in than other cities.[7]

This chapter examines the effect of encounters generated by specialist units on police–community relations in urban Scotland across the twentieth century. Banton characterised specialist departments as consisting of 'law officers' who collected evidence to enable successful prosecution, in marked contrast to beat constables who were largely 'peace officers' and 'uniformed social workers'.[8] We suggest here a more complex set of contours. Rather, specialist departments that had strong connections with 'social work' can be found across the twentieth century, most obviously in the setting up of Policewomen's Departments (which will be dealt with separately in Chapter 6). In Glasgow, probation (criminal justice social work) was part of policing from 1905 until 1931. Moreover, from the mid-twentieth century onwards, experiments with specialist units that were entirely preventive in orientation (including Juvenile Liaison Schemes and subsequently Community Involvement Branches) began to emerge – although in Greenock initially rather than in Glasgow.

Our aim is not to provide a comprehensive or detailed chronological account of the development of specialisation, but to focus on a small number of key examples selected because they involved the social and moral regulation of often marginalised groups for behaviours that were the subject of shifting public attitudes or legal change across the twentieth century. Thus they have the potential to shed a very clear light on the relationship between the social construction of 'deviancy' and police methods, and thus on the relationship between policing and the moral values of wider communities. The first half of the chapter examines the repertoires, styles and approaches used by members of the 'vice squad' in relation to street betting, female 'prostitution' and homosexual offences, whilst the second considers specialist plainclothes responses to offending by children and young people. We emphasise throughout the centrality of gender (particularly ideas about masculinity) in forging police identities and dispositions and in shaping the daily encounters that constituted lived experience. We begin, however, by discussing the meaning of plainclothes and the importance of cultivating informants for both detectives and 'vice squad' officers, drawing attention to distinctive sub-cultural aspects that were developed within specialist policing units.

The CID and the 'Vice Squad'

The police uniform was itself a key component of the technology of urban panoptical surveillance, announcing police presence and visibility as a safeguard for the law-abiding and as a deterrent to the law-breaker.[9] Yet from the foundation of modern urban policing in Britain, it was recognised that there was an equivalent need for plainclothes officers to undertake more discrete surveillance, inquiry and investigation.[10] This was not necessarily to conceal police identity – in contrast to undercover work that involved disguise and impersonation – but to avoid advertising the fact. It had the capacity to generate greater levels of trust and confidence that might lead to disclosure – particularly from those on the edges of criminality. As a former Glasgow officer commented: 'you had the advantage of not being there in a uniform with a hat on . . . so you could get closer to situations and, of course, they [those with knowledge of criminality] very often brought you in'.[11] Donald, who joined Glasgow City Police in the mid-1960s, explained how plainclothes work helped build the relationships through which knowledge was passed on:

> You got to know people like pub owners and club owners . . . they themselves flew a bit close to the wind on a number of fronts, and they knew that, and they knew that you knew that. So they were good sources of information for 'a guy's out there whose been in, he's got a knife' or 'he's got a razor' or 'he's been trying to deal drugs'.[12]

Given this propinquity to criminality, the work could be especially dangerous: 'You had to learn to fight. If you didn't know how to do it, you had to learn it quickly.'[13]

As the previous chapter has shown, Glasgow's working-class population was long reluctant to 'grass' on neighbours and, especially, to be known to have done so. Archival documents suggest that the anonymous tip-off note, sent to divisional detectives, was a preferred method for informants in the first decades of the twentieth century. For example, in a study of abortion cases relating to fifty-four persons tried in the High Court of Justiciary between 1900 and 1930 (half of which were Glasgow cases), Roger Davidson found that 20 per cent were the result of anonymous tip-offs.[14] The memoirs of Glasgow detective Robert Colquhoun describe his cultivation of informants in the 1940s and 1950s, most of whom he had arrested at some point 'and sent off on the road to a prison sentence':

> Part of any success I've had is due to the efforts of gentleman [*sic*] with the unlikely names of Bolo, the Judge, and Tic-Tac, not forgetting two ladies known professionally as Sally and Bonnie Jean [who worked as 'prostitutes']. They constituted part of my private corps of underworld

informers – Grasses or squealers in gangland jargon – the course of indispensable flow of information to any detective, the quick phone call or unsigned note that lies behind the trite courtroom phrase: 'acting on information received'.[15]

The personal contact surrounding the arrest as well as informal interaction with informants through routine visits to the more marginal spaces and places within the city led to the role of confidante. Moreover, it was well known that prisons themselves were at the centre of 'an intelligence system', which detective and plainclothes police officers might tap into through the cultivation of informants.[16] Plainclothes and detective officers occupied a twilight zone where the borders of licit and illicit merged.

It has commonly been observed that police culture constructs typologies and stereotypes for those who are 'policed'.[17] Within detective memoirs of the first half of the twentieth century, the terms 'underworld', 'gangland' and 'criminal fraternity' are commonly evoked to talk about those involved in organised or 'full-time' crime, against whom the police pitted their courage, strength and intellect in what amounts to display of a 'heroic' masculinity.[18] The 'real criminal' was thus distinguished from the Scottish 'ned', a type that was more synonymous with the out-of-control and anti-social 'hooligan' or 'thug'. Yet as the criminologist John Anderson Mack demonstrated in his study of criminal networks in the west of Scotland – which was based on ethnographic fieldwork carried out between 1946 and 1958 – detectives tended to distinguish further in practice.[19] Individuals who were known to make a successful full-time living out of burglary and housebreaking (as highly skilled experts in safe-breaking, explosives or lock-picking) and who were not seen as violent might be viewed with respect by police officers: 'the police found him a friendly character, easy to get on with'; 'he is regarded by the police with a certain grudging respect, as a quiet, rational and able criminal'; and 'cheerful and companionable, always smiling, salutes his police friends in the street'.[20] In effect they mirrored all the attributes of respectable members of the community and, indeed, many of the values of the police themselves.[21] This contrasted with others who 'were regarded by the police as surly, unsociable, unpleasant characters' and who had, indeed, spent considerable amounts of time in prison. A key determinant here was the hostile attitude of this group towards the police: 'has been known to threaten the police for putting him in prison'; 'dour and uncooperative with police'; and 'described by the police as an evil and dangerous man – spat in direction of police at last sentence'.[22]

Mack's conclusions were also inspired by the various trials of the 1950s relating to murderer Peter Manuel (1956–8) and 'criminal tycoon' Samuel Mackay (1959–60) which he saw as lifting 'the curtain' on the criminal networks of the west of Scotland – to a very public audience given the extensive coverage of the trials in the press.[23] He noted in particular that the 'code of not talking to the police' that was common amongst 'habitual associates' did not extend 'to casual associates from a distance'. Those who were most likely to act as informants were those with 'connections in the gambling world' but also 'scrap merchants' who had connections through resetting to housebreakers and who would 'oblige the police from time to time by turning someone in'.[24] These individuals on the social margins – of the ordinary working-class community on the one hand and the networks of organised criminality on the other – were cultivated by detectives and plainclothes officers as informants.

Detectives had long claimed higher status in comparison to the uniform section of police forces on the assumption that they were undertaking the 'real policing' of 'thief-taking'. Within detective memoirs, prestige is claimed in relation to the seriousness of the 'crimes' that they solved.[25] Detective work was presented in terms of acumen and innate intelligence, often combined with physical durability and toughness. Thus the detective made claims to an elite masculinity, in comparison to the doggedness of the beat man. Yet there were significant changes in the sub-culture of both detective and other plainclothes work, most obviously in relation to styles of dress. Into the early 1960s, donning plainclothes as opposed to uniform invariably involved 'belted raincoats and trilbies' which was not only ubiquitously recognisable as police dress but was still incorporated within the sartorial codes of order, cleanliness and smartness that framed policing as a highly disciplined occupation. Those who moved into plainclothes in the late 1960s and early 1970s, however, sought to subvert these codes:

> The first thing I did was grow a beard, I grew my hair long, started wearing jeans and what today you would maybe call a bomber jacket . . . [so] we could easily mix in bookies' and clubs and pubs without drawing attention to ourselves.[26]

This was a tactic to enable easier blurring and thus traversing of social boundaries, recognised as increasingly necessary amidst heightened concerns about serious and violent crime, and the transformation of organised criminal networks as a result of the greater mobility associated with technological change. But it also involved the assertion of distinction by plainclothes officers attached to a uniformed 'shift', as a sub-culture within policing:

> As a uniformed officer, there was about 30-odd officers in my shift in the 'central' [district]. We'd all report for duty 15 minutes before time to be briefed according to what we needed to know before we went out. The plainers used to amble in 5 minutes after the briefing had started. They always sat in the front row, they always sort of slouched. If something

was called out that was on your beat, you called out your number and the duty officer who'd be reading the briefing to you would note against that item, '318 attends to this' sort of thing. But the plainers had a kind of lazy way of doing it. So there was always a wee bit of glamour attached to it.[27]

Status was claimed through reluctant or 'lazy' bodily compliance with the rules that underpinned the disciplinary regime.

Despite commonalities of not wearing police uniform, the CID and plainclothes teams were different entities. In Glasgow (until the setting up of a specialist public relations branch in 1974) CID detectives were the lynchpins of contact between the news press and the police, which meant they acquired a very prominent public role. The senior investigating detective dealt with all queries and put out his own press statements regarding 'serious cases'.[28] He was quoted by the specialist crime reporters of the city's multiple newspapers and, thus, according to true-crime writer Andrew Ralston, senior detectives 'were household names' accorded respect and fear.[29] Crime reporters were instrumental in constructing narratives and reputations for these figures, which undoubtedly bolstered police legitimacy in the 1950s and 1960s. Glasgow journalist Bill Knox (who started as a junior on the *Glasgow Evening News* in 1944) described in his own memoirs (published in 1968), how the specialist crime reporter was 'often on first-name terms with many of the local force, his face a passport to information about the day's happening.'[30] Indeed, Knox played an important role in the publication of the memoirs of Robert Colquhoun (former Chief Superintendent of Glasgow's CID) in 1962. Credited with making a 'great contribution' towards the 'preparation' of the book, it seems likely Knox acted as a ghostwriter given the similarities of syntax and expression.[31] As has been widely acknowledged, detective memoirs, detective fiction and crime journalism are interdependent genres and together constituted an important component of public knowledge of policing.[32]

In contrast, plainclothes officers dealing with 'vice' were more liminal. In the discussion that follows we focus on three aspects of their work – the regulation of street betting, female 'prostitution', and 'homosexual offences' – to unpack further the relationship between plainclothes policing, changing social attitudes, and ideas of 'community' and who constituted it. As in other areas of policing, decisions (by both police and public prosecutor) were influenced considerably by local concerns about what was in the public interest. The Scots Law requirement for corroboration was also a very significant factor that shaped procedure and hence outcome. Finally, as we shall see, ideas about gender roles – especially appropriate and acceptable masculinity – influenced the values, ethos, and thus social interventions, of the 'vice squad'.

Street betting

Police officers, like the working-class communities from which they were drawn, often saw the criminalisation of street betting (until the law changed in 1960) as unfair given that race-course betting, which privileged those with time and resources, was permitted. In 1950 the SPF stated (in evidence to the Royal Commission on Betting, Lotteries and Gaming) that 'the mass of people with whom they came into contact' were overwhelmingly of the view that 'there is class discrimination' and that there should be equalisation of the law.[33] Indeed, the Chief Constable of Ayr Burgh Police – where the discrepancy between street and track betting was particularly apparent given the presence of a prominent local racecourse – 'held the view that the betting laws were unpopular with the public, and the time of the police was better devoted to other more necessary duties'. As a consequence 'if [bookmakers] kept clear of trouble, if they did not allow people to gather about the premises, or there were no complaints, then we did not take action'.[34] Published criminal justice statistics show this approach continued; a mere handful of individuals were proceeded against each year for betting, gambling and lottery offences in Ayr across the 1950s, with none in 1950 or 1960 (on the eve of decriminalisation).

Yet the approach taken in Ayr differed from that in Glasgow, where the number of cases proceeded increased progressively from 2,581 in 1950 to 13,126 in 1960, and in Lanarkshire where it increased ten-fold – from 137 to 1,345 – in the same period.[35] In Glasgow arrests for street betting came squarely under the job description of the 'vice squad', which David McNee joined in 1948:

> Enforcement was generally tempered with discretion. Gambling was an integral part of Glasgow working-class life and the street bookmakers catered to a pretty wide social demand. Even to a man who did not bet, nor saw the need for it, it would plainly be only a matter of time before the law was changed; and enforcement of the gambling laws was rarely oppressive.[36]

If in Glasgow a middle line was struck that honoured the law but used it in moderation, a very significant number of cases were nevertheless brought (nearly a fifth of all proceedings in the city in 1960). Moreover, in the industrial town of Shotts in Lanarkshire in the years just before the Second World War, William Muncie was assiduous in his pursuit of street betting which, as county beat man, he was permitted to investigate:

> To many people it was a degrading sight, groups of ten to twenty men at a street corner, some pacing about nervously between glances at the racing papers . . . Complaints came frequently from the wives of these men.

There was cause for complaint too – for they and their children were, in the end, the losers. There was also cause for complaint from anyone who had to pass these groups as they blocked the footpath and spat all over it; and from anyone living in the vicinity, because the language was loud and, at its best, it was rough.[37]

William Merrilees, who undertook this work as a plainclothes officer in Edinburgh's 'vice squad' from 1926 to 1940, was of a similarly intolerant view when it came to street betting, referring to the 'menace of gambling schools' and the complaints made by 'harassed wives whose husbands had lost their pay-packets'. In December 1936 he used cine-film footage successfully to secure convictions for betting at a pitch-and-toss game in a back court off Bangor Road, Leith, and he went on to deploy the technology in Edinburgh's Waterloo Place.[38] It is clear that in these examples, police intervention was prompted by the high level of public complaint and the gender dynamics of street betting. Whilst gambling may have been part of masculine popular culture, it upset the precarious household economies of the 1930s as much-needed wages were gambled away; women and children were seen as innocent victims. In the case of street betting, policing strategies depended on specific local cultures and contexts, but they tended nevertheless to reflect a paternalist assessment of the social needs of working-class families and thus of the 'public good'.

Street soliciting and the sex trade

As with street betting, there is considerable evidence of a police approach that was sympathetic and protective rather than judgemental towards women caught up in the sex industry. In this, plainclothes officers not only reflected popular moral understanding but also drew on their everyday experience of street life. As Louise Settle has demonstrated in her study of the regulation of female 'prostitution' in Scotland in the years before the Second World War, Glasgow's Chief Constables James Stevenson (1902–22) and Andrew Smith (1922–31) both highlighted low wages, unemployment and poverty as the underlying causes, setting a paternalistic tone in advocating a rehabilitative agenda.[39] In theory the law criminalising street soliciting was more robust in Scotland compared to the situation south of the border. Yet as Settle also shows, semi-formal procedures helped to sift women away from the courts, and young women and first-time offenders were more likely to be seen within police culture as 'victims' – of economic circumstances or harsh treatment by abusive husbands or 'pimps' – than as the 'social evil' associated with more persistent offenders.[40]

Street soliciting in Scotland was mostly prosecuted with reference to the Burgh Police (Scotland) Act of 1892 which made it an offence for those labelled 'a common prostitute or streetwalker' to 'loiter about or importune for the purposes of prostitution', punishable by a fine of 40 shillings and the option of 30 days' imprisonment on a subsequent conviction.[41] In Edinburgh and Aberdeen the more severe penalty of a 10-pound fine or 60 days imprisonment was specified for a first conviction under local byelaws.[42] Unlike legislation in England and Wales, the Scottish equivalent did not require proof of 'annoyance' to the general public, in theory easing the path to successful prosecution in the burgh police courts (since men who had been accosted were extremely reluctant court witnesses).[43] Arguably, too, the Scottish penalties acted as a very significant deterrent. London magistrates were restricted to a 40 shilling fine only, whilst prison sentences that were permitted outside of the capital were limited to 14 days. It is notable that women were prosecuted for soliciting in comparatively large numbers in Scotland in the first decade of the twentieth century: a peak of 3,192 in 1909 compared to 11,727 in England and Wales (whose population was 10 times that of Scotland).[44] Yet figures declined starkly in subsequent decades: to 803 in 1920, 394 in 1930 and 91 in 1952. This contrasted markedly with England and Wales, where an interwar decline was reversed after the Second World War, with 10,319 prosecutions in 1952 (over a hundred times that of Scotland).[45] The Scottish decline may have resulted from a number of factors, including the effects of the blackout on street culture during the First World War and, subsequently, the wider availability of the telephone and motor car, which made street soliciting less necessary for some women involved in the sex industry.[46]

Yet it also reflected changes in the practice of policing, specifically the introduction of a multiple warnings system. This was an established practice in Glasgow by 1908 and Edinburgh by 1925, and was still standard procedure by the late 1950s when it attracted the interest of London's Metropolitan Police as a possible model for imitation south of the border.[47] Plainclothes officers conducted observations in pairs to ensure corroboration and were instructed (through police orders and with the approval of city magistrates and the public prosecutor) to make careful use of a warning system prior to any prosecution. In the first instance they were required to witness an individual woman accosting a man on at least three occasions, recording the details in their notebooks as evidence. On the third occasion they were to stop and 'warn' the woman on the street that, if she persisted, she would be 'liable to arrest'; this informal warning was then logged. On a reoccurrence, she could be arrested, taken to the police station and charged with importuning. On this first arrest, however, she would be given a 'formal warning' by the duty officer at the station. It was only if a subsequent offence was committed, the duty officer again accepted the charge, and the PF depute (who in Glasgow was likely to be the police superintendent) considered there to be a case to answer, that the woman would be brought before the burgh police court. The Edinburgh PF Charles Angus Macpherson gave the number of street cautions as 114 in 1925, 127 in 1926 and 225 in 1927 (with figures of 164, 393 and 202 respectively for 'formal cautions'), demonstrating how 'quasi-judicial' decision-making sifted offenders away from the courts and hence criminal justice statistics.[48]

Moreover, in both Glasgow and Edinburgh, the police referred women who had been warned to a moral welfare worker (a special branch of social work) whom, they hoped, would assist in their rehabilitation to a 'respectable' life. As the memoirs of Edinburgh policeman William Merrilees noted: 'I felt that in the case of many of the girls, and particularly the immature, reformation was possible, and infinitely to be preferred to sentence.'[49] Promoted to the role of sergeant in the Licensing Department, his memoirs state that he had responsibility for co-ordinating police responses to prostitution in Edinburgh and described liaising closely with Church of Scotland Police Court Missionary Christine Haldane, to whom cases were referred for reclamation (a role she continued for 30 years).[50] Thus, as Settle has argued, the warning system was largely preventive and welfarist in its orientation with regard to first-time 'offenders' who were viewed as vulnerable 'victims', whilst those who persisted were likely to be stereotyped through very different language as 'old pros' or 'hardened prostitutes' – 'habitual offenders' for whom imprisonment was seen as the only appropriate solution.[51]

It was argued that the development of the warning system prevented complaints of miscarriage of justice – which were rare – by providing 'safeguards against the possibility of a mistake'. Indeed, one such Glasgow complaint, dating to 1907, seems likely to have instituted the new mechanism for the recording of formal warnings at a police station on initial arrest. The case involved Jessie Brown, described as a 'spinster' aged 30–40 and living in a tenement flat comprising two rooms and a kitchen in Apsley Place, Gorbals, who claimed she had been wrongfully arrested by two plainclothes officers in South Portland Street on the evening of Saturday 28 December 1907.[52] Detained in a police cell for two nights, she was tried summarily at the Southern Police Court for loitering and importuning for the purposes of prostitution, for which she was convicted and admonished (despite her not-guilty plea). On legal advice, she later obtained medical certificates confirming she was *virgo intacta* and thus 'could never have earned her living by prostitution'. Her requests to the Chief Constable and magistrates that the conviction should be quashed were refused on the grounds that they had no powers to do so. A civil action in the sheriff's court against the two police officers for malicious arrest and perjury was also unsuccessful. Brown's case was taken up by her MP George Barnes (Labour), who brought it to public attention in the House of Commons in June 1909, asking the Solicitor-General for Scotland whether he was aware that 'this poor woman is absolutely innocent'.[53] The conviction was finally suspended on 10 December 1909 by judges in the High Court of Justiciary on legal grounds: that she had not been advised of her right of adjournment at the original summary trial.

The case is of interest not only for Brown's sheer persistence but for the contrasting accounts of her character and reputation – presented by her lawyers on the one hand, and by the police on the other. Brown's counsel stated that 'she was well-connected and of the utmost respectability . . . [that] she had never been in the hands of the police, nor was there the slightest ground for suspicion of her chastity and respectability'. Yet the two plainclothes officers maintained that she had been 'known to the police to be a prostitute for 12 months', that her house (which was visited by 'gaily dressed young women' sometimes with men) was under observation as a suspected brothel, and that 'neighbours frequently complained about the annoyance'. Brown's highlighting of the signifiers of respectable middle-class femininity acted as a direct foil to the police allegations. Appeal Judge Lord Ardwall stated that 'the sting of the charge . . . was that she was stamped as a prostitute', suggesting she had been 'branded unjustly for life'.[54] Legal cases such as this effectively reinforced the gendered framework of character assessment on which police judgements were based, maintaining as crucial the distinction between 'rough' and 'respectable' linked to sexual status. They reinforced, too, the stigmatisation and labelling of women routinely selling sex as 'common prostitutes'. In Edinburgh, Merrilees had no qualms about organising a 'sweep up' of 'the coffee stalls on the Mound' in the late 1920s, which involved the arrest and ultimately imprisonment of 'the inveterate prostitutes who were unhappily spreading venereal disease'. He admitted that this action led to a 'great outcry' in the local press, that '"poor and unfortunate girls"' had not 'been given a chance'.[55] In this case youth was correlated with innocence and victimhood. Once again the public 'outcry' was about wrongful arrest – of the wrong type of person – reinforcing the argument for an expeditious warning system to ensure that those who were genuinely young and vulnerable were sifted out.

As Settle has demonstrated, plainclothes officers were, nevertheless, able to exercise discretion within the warning system, by turning a 'blind eye' when it suited them. Although there was no need to prove 'annoyance', officers were encouraged to step up their activities in response to complaints from members of the public.[56] On other occasions, those involved in the sex industry were seen as useful informants concerning serious criminal activity. McNee's work in Glasgow's 'vice squad' covered the Charing Cross area in 1948:

> . . . there was a coffee stall which was a favourite place for prostitutes to gather. It was here that we too would spend part of the time – getting to know 'the girls' (indeed many of them were not much more than girls), listening to their gossip, exchanging pleasantries . . . Compassion and fairness on the part of the police were often rewarded by useful criminal information.[57]

Whilst McNee only served 12 months in this role (standard for the 1920s-40s), a report from 1958 suggests that by then officers remained in Glasgow's 'vice squad' for up to 4 years, enabling them to get to know the women who were working the streets and 'to quickly observe any young girls or women who were newly resorting to prostitution' and to whom assistance might be offered.[58] This local knowledge not only made it less likely that women would give incorrect names or addresses, but also meant that plainclothes officers knew where to find women if information was sought. As McNee observed, women who continued to sell sex 'knew the rules of the "game"'.[59] Thus, as recorded in 1958, they were able to 'loiter' in the vicinity of the coffee stalls and could only be legitimately arrested if they were 'seen to actually solicit', preferring instead to stand 'quietly in doorways', 'keeping much to themselves'.[60] Donald, who joined Glasgow City Police in the mid-1960s, explained that the plainclothes team who dealt with street soliciting were 'four older police officers' who 'knew the girls, they knew their backgrounds, they got information from them'.[61]

Yet this sense of continuity and local knowledge was already beginning to shift as the 1959 Street Offences Act encouraged the 'migration of prostitutes and their pimps from south of the border in search of a more lenient legal environment'.[62] As Donald reflected on this emerging transience: 'You were getting girls coming up from Liverpool and they did their circuit: Liverpool, Manchester, Glasgow, Dundee, Aberdeen, Liverpool, and they just kept moving, two or three weeks at a time. That way they never ever get done.'[63] The certainty that individual police officers were in command of accurate knowledge of a stable local population whose interests they represented had underpinned the effectiveness of the 'warning' system in previous decades.

If a welfarist approach shaped the plainclothes policing of street soliciting in Scottish cities, a more combative and retributive approach was adopted in the battle against the male 'bullies', 'ponces' and 'pimps' for which police officers reserved the lowest of opinions. In the first half of the twentieth century this was shaped by the disparate but intersecting rhetoric of moral purity, of hostility to 'foreigners' articulated through antisemitism and racism, and of feminist interventions to protect young women and children from sexual abuse.[64] Campaigns against what had come to be called 'the white slave trade' were networked across British cities, but in Glasgow the trajectory was also shaped by the strong Calvinist influence on civic life. As historian Ben Braber has shown, the wrongful and controversial conviction in 1909 of Oscar Slater for the murder of the wealthy 83-year-old Marion Gilchrist in Glasgow's West End (finally quashed in 1928) was driven by police and judicial bias that was shared across a wider popular constituency and grounded in 'xenophobia, anti-Jewish feelings and Slater's alleged involvement in prostitution' (as a suspected 'pimp').[65] Trial judge Lord Guthrie, also a temperance reformer and former legal adviser to the United Free Church of Scotland, directed the jury that Slater had benefited from 'the ruin of women, living for many years past in a way that many blackguards would scorn to live'.[66]

In the autumn of 1911 the campaign for the suppression of the 'white slave trade' in Glasgow came to a head when women's organisations, religious bodies and the poor law authority argued for more effective police regulation of 'brothel-keeping' and 'houses of ill-fame'.[67] Specific targets included unregulated Italian ice-cream shops in the city, which offended Sabbatarian sensitivities by opening on Sundays but were also seen as sites of sexual danger for their young clientele. A *Memorandum on the Social Evil in Glasgow*, written by Inspector of the Poor, James Motion, on behalf of both the Parish Council (the poor law authority) and the United Free Church, claimed that the police and magistrates were not performing their duties in relation to 'immorality' generally.[68] The situation rapidly deteriorated into a very public spat given extensive coverage in the Glasgow press. Chief Constable Stevenson admitted his surprise at the criticisms, given that prior to this 'charges have been levied at the police for being over-zealous and, indeed, harsh, in the execution of their public duty – especially in dealing with prostitutes' (a reference to the Jessie Brown case amongst others). 'Immorality in itself is not an offence against the law', he pointed out, and 'the police cannot prosecute for brothel-keeping the woman who personally takes men to or receives them in her own house'.[69] In fact, he argued, there was 'little police evidence of immoral conduct' in ice-cream shops and 'it would be considered an outrage if a policeman, without an information having been given by the girls or on their behalf, were to question the girls found there'. Rather, the portrayal of Glasgow in the *Memorandum*, which cited hyperbolic statistics for the number of 'women living an immoral life', was such as 'to malign the city' itself.[70] Thus Stevenson felt himself caught – as an intermediary – between the 'moral' lobby on the one hand and defence of the rule of law on the other.[71] He depicted the police, too, as assailed from all sides, with business proprietors allegedly threatening complaints or 'actions for damages' in the Court of Session as a vexatious tactic to escape police observations of their premises.[72] The dispute – which had many of the characteristics of a moral panic – was resolved through agreement amongst the institutions of the local state that the law needed to be strengthened to give the police more effective powers.[73]

Nevertheless, it demonstrates a concerted opprobrium against men who exploited women and children, which also resonated with working-class culture. Merrilees even states that in Edinburgh, as a plainclothes sergeant who encouraged 'older known prostitutes' to report on the men who were 'bullying' younger girls into prostitution, he and 'a number of specially chosen officers ... would go to the place indicated, get hold of the bully, take him discreetly to some quiet spot and there "Sing him a lullaby"'. This form of rough justice was seen as justified because of the continued difficulty of getting convictions (of men for living off the earnings of prostitution) under both the Immoral Traffic (Scotland) Act 1902 and the later Criminal Law Amendment Act 1912, given the Scottish requirement for corroboration and the fear that these men engendered in the women they sought to control. Merrilees's style of policing can also be viewed in terms of muscular Christianity, in which a 'heroic' commitment to protect the most vulnerable by waging war on the villainous was combined with his own staunch Calvinist morality. He welcomed the appointment of James Adair as PF for Midlothian (including Edinburgh) from 1932 to 1937, finding him to be an avid moral crusader whose values he shared, and depicts them as aligned in their desire to 'clear up vice in Edinburgh'.[74] As Settle has shown, this led to a concerted campaign against brothel-keeping, as well as the targeting of the prostitution ring associated with the Kosmo dance club, leading to the high-profile prosecution of its owner Asher Barnard in 1933 (which may also have had antisemitic undertones).[75]

Yet Davidson has demonstrated that a very different policing approach emerged in relation to the organised sex industry – including brothel-keeping – in Edinburgh in the years after the Second World War (compared to both the 1930s and to Glasgow). Indeed, the brothel in Danube Street, Stockbridge, run by Dora Noyce, was able to continue for 35 years (from 1943 until after her death in 1977) because of an implicit 'policy of relative tolerance'.[76] Although officers kept observations on the brothel and Noyce was brought to trial twice a year (paying either a substantial fine or serving a month in prison), there were no attempts to close it down because there were few complaints from neighbours or concerns about public health; indeed, Noyce ensured that the women who worked there received regular medical checks. Moreover, Davidson suggests that 'there appears to have been an informal agreement that, in return for information about the criminal underworld garnered in the course of servicing clients, raids on the brothel would be restricted'.[77] Rightly or wrongly, Noyce tended to be seen as benign by police officers, her sex and respectable demeanour differentiating her from the male 'pimps' hated by police. Unless there was considerable complaint about public annoyance in Edinburgh, the police took a permissive approach.

In Glasgow, however, Davidson charts 'vigorous application' of the law in the 1960s and early 1970s, particularly in relation to black and Asian men accused of brothel-keeping, leading to press reporting containing 'distinctly xenophobic, if not racist, overtones'.[78] Within a broader context of debates about immigration and race relations in this period, it is notable, too, that Dundee City Police were drawing attention to 'the number of Pakistanis who have settled in the city [who] . . . attract and harbour young girls' in the mid-1960s.[79] Black and Asian men were readily stereotyped 'as a sexually predatory "other"' within a broader white popular culture, deflecting attention away from white families and institutions.[80] This racist dynamic was nothing new. The 1911 *Memorandum* had referred explicitly to 'foreigners and Jews' (the former including Italians and Brazilians) as responsible for luring young women into prostitution.[81] Thus across the twentieth century the desire to protect vulnerable femininity ensured that a chivalric, paternalistic and even 'heroic' style of policing (sometimes implicitly rooted in a white Protestant identity) was adopted in relation to female 'prostitution'. The dynamics were very different when it came to the policing of homosexual offences.

Homosexuality

Until 1980, and thus for most of the twentieth century, sexual acts between males were illegal in Scotland, although prosecutions remained low.[82] A small number of individuals (consistently less than a dozen per year) were brought to trial in the High Court of Justiciary for the specific charge of sodomy or its attempt. The Criminal Law Amendment Act of 1885, which applied across the UK, had criminalised all acts of 'gross indecency', an offence that was tried in the lower courts in slightly larger numbers (an average of 85 per year for 1951–6).[83] Yet prosecutions for 'homosexual offences' that were 'private and consensual' and did not involve those under 21 remained extremely rare in Scotland (unlike in England and Wales) across the twentieth century.[84] Data prepared for the Wolfenden Committee (appointed to review the 'law and practice' relating to both homosexual offences and street prostitution) showed that only nine adult males were convicted of 'offences committed in private with consenting adult partners' in Scotland over the three-year period 1953–6, compared to 480 in England and Wales.[85] As Davidson has argued, this was not because of 'libertarian sentiments' but because of legal restrictions in 'a society reputed for its moral conservatism'.[86] Most significantly, the rule of corroboration made it extremely difficult to bring prosecutions relating to consenting behaviours that had taken place behind closed doors. Moreover, as the Wolfenden Committee reported in 1957, in Scotland cases were only brought by the PF when it was deemed to be in the 'public interest'.[87] Scotland was not included in the 1967 Sexual Offences Act, which officially decriminalised consensual sex in private, between males over 21 in England and Wales, largely because of the influence of the churches.[88] Thus the anomaly remained that private consensual sex between men was officially defined – through legal, religious and medical discourse in Scotland as 'illicit', 'immoral' and 'unnatural' – whilst, in effect, police and prosecutors were unlikely to act.[89] Indeed, in the early 1970s a succession of Lord Advocates publicly stated that they did not prosecute consensual activities in private involving those over 21.[90]

As historian Jeffrey Meek has shown, gay men in Scotland were unaware that 'private, consensual sex was unlikely to lead to prosecution'. Out of twenty-four self-identified gay or bisexual men whom he interviewed who had lived in Scotland between 1940 and 1980, 'only three recalled interactions with the police' and none had been arrested. Nevertheless, significant concern about risk and, in some cases, 'terror' of arrest was palpable.[91] Indeed, one of Meek's interviewees recalls threatening and insulting language that was used by two plainclothes officers who stopped him coming out of a public lavatory: '"They told me that they knew I was a poof and what I should do is go and jump over the Clyde Bridge, that I was no use to the world . . .".[92] These comments highlight the existence of high levels of prejudice against gay men and of the possibility of informal harassment by some plain clothes 'vice squad' officers.

If homosexual acts in private were not prosecuted by the CID, 'proactive' plainclothes policing specifically targeted public spaces in urban areas where men seeking sex with other men regularly met – open spaces (such as Edinburgh's Calton Hill and Glasgow Green), bars and commercial venues, and, especially, public lavatories – across the century. This was also, in part, about the targeting of male 'prostitution' (a further reason why the plainclothes 'vice squad' was drawn in). Senior police officers and magistrates in Glasgow and Edinburgh who gave evidence to the Wolfenden Committee clarified that most 'gross indecency' prosecutions were 'based on plain-clothes police observations on public lavatories' characterised as a 'vigorous campaign' against 'vice'.[93] In Edinburgh local 'cleansing' byelaws, which forbade 'loitering' for other purposes, were purportedly being used to deal with cottaging in public toilets as a more effective legal alternative to 'gross indecency' charges (which were harder to prove).[94] Gay men in Edinburgh learned tactics to avoid arrest: 'It was very easy if you went into one [public toilet] and got a nod from somebody and they wandered a few blocks down . . . That was a situation the police could not monitor.'[95] Nevertheless, from its foundation in 1969 to campaign for the rights and welfare of homosexual men, the Scottish Minorities Group (renamed the Scottish Homosexual Reform Group in 1978) argued that legislation was being used unfairly by police and public prosecutors.[96]

Within the culture of interwar policing, men who sought sex with men were stereotyped in terms of 'effeminacy and gender transgression'.[97] Meek's analysis of sodomy cases tried in the high court shows that in Glasgow during the 1920s groups of plainclothes officers undertook close observation of those reputed to be 'male prostitutes', aiming to witness men *in flagrante delicto*. Notably, cosmetics such as lipstick and powder were seen as important signifiers and were seized as supporting evidence.[98] This emphasis on effeminacy through the trappings of femininity contrasted with the hyper-masculinity of the police ideal. Published in 1966, Merrilees's memoirs looked back on the 'campaign against homosexuality' that he had launched in Edinburgh in the early 1930s with the robust endorsement of Adair as public prosecutor,[99] and which led to the closure of public urinals in the city and a raid on a club ('Maximes') that was seen as the centre of a male prostitution network.[100] Merrilees was keen to boast of his skills of disguise, dissimulation and mimicry (including of 'effeminacy'): 'I am afraid I almost left myself with a lisp, so authentic was my behaviour.'[101] Yet he was also careful to stress that his own masculine and heterosexual identity – as a policeman and husband – remained uncompromised. Describing undercover observations in the steam rooms at the municipal baths in Infirmary Street, his memoirs state: 'I . . . entered the steam compartment, and had only been there a few minutes before advances were made to me', whereupon 'I forgot myself . . . and I lashed out at two of these characters, flooring them'.[102] Aware of his diminutive height throughout his career (special permission was given to join Edinburgh City Police on the grounds of his skills at life-saving), Merrilees's memoirs emphasise his abilities as a pugilist and fighter and lay claim to a heroic masculinity.

Merrilees's memoirs shed further light on the criminological taxonomies and typologies, as well as perceptions of the relationship between urban space and 'deviant' sexualities, that shaped interwar urban policing. He referred to 'homosexuals' generically as 'unnatural' and as 'perverts', but also identified an 'effeminate sort' who used names 'of contemporary actresses or other well-known ladies' and 'were also referred to as bitches, poofs, pansies and whitehats etc.'.[103] He contrasted those who were 'really male prostitutes' with those who were 'effeminates', suggesting a distinction in terms of masculinities between those who, on the one hand, were not transgressive in gender terms but used sex for financial purposes and, on the other, those who were real 'homosexuals'. Furthermore, in an era in which the fear of homosexuality was elided with the fear of the pederast (given that all sex between males was illegal), he identified a further group of 'homosexuals' ('chicken chasers') whose preference was for 14 to 16-year-old boys.[104] The protection of children as well as concerns about blackmail and extortion certainly formed a crucial part of the agenda, but these were blurred with the stigmatisation of those who engaged in consensual homosexual practices. Moreover, this blurring of categories was formally inscribed into police training and practice, legitimising prejudice. The handbook *Scottish Criminal Law*, issued to officers across police forces in 1952, linked 'sodomy', 'gross indecency', 'indecent exposure' and 'lewd and libidinous practices' together in the same sentence as forms of 'moral degeneration' and as the actions of 'the pervert'.[105]

The use of stereotypes to identify, stigmatise and police those who are now described as the LGBTI community was remarkably persistent, as oral history interviews with former officers attest. Asked to reflect on the most significant changes that he had experienced across his 30 years of service, Charles, who joined Glasgow City Police around 1970, identified transformations in legal and cultural attitudes towards homosexuality as profound. Commenting on the initial training for new recruits at Tulliallan in the early 1970s, he said:

> Homosexuality . . . was one of the big training points. It was one of the training sessions that you got at the college. And then you're taught where to look and where to find people of that persuasion, that type of thing, and more or less to hunt them down. By the time I left it was totally different.[106]

Indeed, the 1980 edition of the Scottish police handbook controversially replicated some of the text of the version approved in 1952, instructing constables to give 'special attention to areas where moral degenerates may loiter' including 'public parks and lavatories – often frequented by perverted characters' to 'prevent crimes of indecency'. Whilst acknowledging that the law had recently changed to permit 'sexual acts between two consenting adult males in private', it reinforced the point that 'such conduct in public would be unlawful' through the use of stigmatising language.[107] In the words of campaigning lawyer Derek Ogg: 'The police are now being taught to treat a huge minority of Scottish citizens as alien, evil and morally inferior'.[108] On the cusp of decriminalisation in Scotland, the Scottish Homosexual Rights Group highlighted rumours of police entrapment and pressure on gay men to admit guilt; as a consequence, gay men were frightened to turn to the police when they were victims of burglary or assault. These rumours were emphatically denied by Scottish chief constables. They do, however, suggest low levels of trust in the police amongst the gay community (which had been, for many, configured as an underground sub-culture given their status before the law) into the 1980s.[109]

Indeed, the persistence of negative stereotypes – even after the Scottish decriminalisation of consensual private sex between men over 21 in 1980 – meant that it was extremely difficult for those who joined the police service in Scotland to feel able to identify openly as gay, whether male or female. Marc Burke, who began researching the experiences of gay police officers across the UK in 1990, found that at that point 'only a very negligible percentage . . . had come out at work'.[110] 'Homosexuality' was 'still synonymous with criminality in the minds of many police officers' and gay officers faced considerable 'role conflict'.[111] In the early 1990s prejudices within policing began to be openly and collectively challenged by gay officers themselves with the foundation, across the UK, of the Lesbian and Gay Police Association. In 2004 its Scottish members were given permission by ACPOS to attend the London Gay Pride March in uniform for the first time, providing symbolic affirmation of the importance of diversity in policing and of the need to work with and on behalf of lesbian and gay (and subsequently LGBTI) communities.[112] Analysis of the attitudes that shaped the policing of homosexuality in the first half of the twentieth century underlines how significant a journey this has been.

Thus in some areas of 'vice squad' activity (street betting and street soliciting) we see a sensitivity to the local economic needs of working-class women, children and families. Yet an intolerant attitude – shaped by religious belief and moral conservatism within wider Scottish society – meant that the use of public space by gay men was rigorously policed. In all three examples, however, the police agenda was driven by perceptions of 'public interest' rather than a simple law enforcement model. 'Public interest' was often discriminatory and far from inclusive. Moreover, police understandings of 'public interest' were shaped by the politics of gender, which constructed some groups as social threats and others as victims requiring protection.

CHILDREN AND YOUNG PEOPLE

In the second half of this chapter, we move on to provide an overview of the specialist policing strategies and tactics that were used in Scotland to deal with another distinct and often marginalised demographic group – children and young people – highlighting further the very significant use of 'quasi-judicial' process giving considerable latitude for police discretion. We also highlight the uneasy tension between interventions that were akin to social work and those that evoked controversy and complaint as 'heavy-handed'. Yet police responses also operated on a continuum. Despite increasingly politicised rhetoric that, by the 1960s, debated criminal justice policy in terms of 'soft' and 'hard', individual officers drew on a range of tactics on a day-to-day basis. The dynamics of age, generation, gender, religion and social class very explicitly shaped the tramlines of these interactions, but so too did 'situational variables' that included the type of offence alleged, the 'demands' of those reporting an incident, and the local 'reputations' of young people, families and neighbourhoods.[113] Public criticism emerged when police assessment of these factors was out of kilter with local opinion, leading to complaints within local communities that police action was unfair.

The warnings system and Juvenile Liaison Schemes

Given concerns about rising levels of 'juvenile delinquency' in Scotland at the beginning of both World Wars and again in the 1960s, considerable paid police time was occupied with children and young people.[114] From 1908 to 1968 children and young people were formally processed through the institution of the juvenile court which, in most towns and cities in Scotland, was held in the same building as the adult police court or sheriff court (although through separate hearings). However, from 1905 onwards in Glasgow, divisional superintendents also dispensed their own semi-formal justice to juveniles for minor first-time 'offences' through a police 'warnings' system (sifting them out of criminal justice as a deterrent measure).[115] Warnings were administered at the police station on a Saturday morning or after school. A total of 3,995 warnings were dispensed to Glasgow youth in 1936, dropping to 1,209 in 1946 and 1,291 in 1956, but rising again to 3,824 by 1964.[116] A similar system had been introduced in Kilmarnock in the 1920s, in Dundee in the mid-1930s, and in Aberdeen in 1937. The model varied from place to place (sometimes including the Lord Provost, head teacher or PF depute), but tended to involve a youth leader, church minister or a probation officer who attended at the station and ensured follow-up guidance or supervision. Working in Glasgow's Marine Division around 1932–3, Charles Macdonald recalled a 'plague' of 'children, mostly boys, smashing windows and streetlamps':

> It was our task to trace them and in this I found a friend in the local parish priest, Father McLoughlin. He was able to assist in identifying the culprits and on the condition that they would not be prosecuted he lent his support to a series of official reprimands to be conducted in the police station. This joint approach worked remarkably well, particularly in gaining the support of the parents.[117]

In Coatbridge, arrangements were made with parents that they should cover the cost of any damages but deduct the amount from their child's pocket money, resonant of models of restorative justice as well as those based on practical and ethical considerations ('khadi justice'). Indeed, Coatbridge Chief Constable Daniel McLauchlan was described by a Scottish Office civil servant in 1944 as 'an enthusiast in social welfare' who believed the juvenile court was 'too formal'.[118] The Scottish Office was surprised to discover the existence of 'an extra-legal police warnings system' when it began investigating wartime responses to delinquency but recommended it for general adoption across Scotland in 1945 (whilst stressing that formal records of decisions should be kept).[119] This endorsement contrasted with Home Office disapproval of the equivalent use of 'cautioning' south of the border (and zealous use of the juvenile court by the Metropolitan Police).[120]

As previous research has suggested, the approach in many parts of urban Scotland entailed police 'collaboration with youth leaders, head teachers and church ministers, as well as involving parents, in a regulatory complex that was community based rather than driven by national policy directives'.[121] Chief constables of Glasgow praised the preventive work of youth organisations in every annual report. Moreover, individual police officers used their leisure time off-shift to supervise boys' clubs in the city or work with the Boys' Brigade and scouting troops, maintaining a close connection between policing and voluntary social work which was forged through the ideals of paternalism, active citizenship, muscular Christianity and civic responsibility.[122] Judo and boxing formed an important staple of 'rational recreation' in boys clubs, with the aim of teaching young men to 'stand up' for themselves and to take fighting off the streets. Uniform, military drill and deportment remained a central focus of the Boys' Brigade, the Protestant youth movement that originated in Glasgow and had significant membership in the west of Scotland. This was a social welfare approach that was squarely located within a broader disciplinary paradigm concerned with character building.[123]

The idea of the Juvenile Liaison Scheme (JLS) was first introduced into Scotland in 1956 by David Gray, then Chief Constable of Greenock, as an initiative which he saw as 'really a natural development' of the Scottish police warnings system.[124] The crucial difference was that police officers undertook the direct supervision of youngsters themselves, rather than referring them on to others. This was not new in the UK; the first JLS was piloted in Liverpool in 1949, influenced by the model of the Juvenile Bureaux set up by police in several North American cities.[125] Any juvenile who admitted committing a minor offence and had not previously come to police notice would be 'warned' by the police and then placed under the supervision of a plainclothes Juvenile Liaison Officer (JLO). The JLO undertook home visits, befriended child and family, and liaised with schools, churches and youth clubs regarding further support. Those over the school leaving age of 15 were helped into suitable employment. The aim was entirely preventive – to keep children out of court – unlike the law enforcement focus of the CID. JLOs were often chosen because of their experience of youth work. Greenock's first JLO had previously run a swimming club for boys and reportedly described his approach as 'a mixture of authority, giving of advice and a sympathetic fatherly interest'.[126] In 1960 the staff was expanded to include a male sergeant and female officer, with girls now included in the scheme under her supervision (often for running away from home and placing themselves in 'moral danger' rather than for committing criminal offences). Metric indicators suggested that the scheme was successful compared to other modes of intervention. In Greenock 29 per cent of boys supervised through the JLS in 1956 were recorded as having reoffended within the next 5 years, compared to 40 per cent of those brought before the Glasgow Juvenile Court.[127]

The Greenock JLS initiative reflected Gray's broader approach to policing, which recognised the need to encourage and promote better relationships between police officers and local residents – working in conjunction with other social services and civil society organisations – as the central tenet of crime prevention. In this line of thinking, 'community' was a concept that had to be built, and the police, as one social service amongst others, had a crucial role to play in establishing its shared values. The focus was initially on the Weir

Street/Gibbshill area, an interwar housing scheme to the east of Greenock, which was officially badged as a 'Community Improvement Scheme' (CIS) in 1958. Gray argued that 'children broke the law not so much from badness but because they were conforming to the pattern of behaviour which existed in the area', embracing an ecological theory of crime causation. As a result of the CIS initiative 'fences [were] repaired, play areas created and tenants encouraged to cultivate their gardens'. Four uniformed officers were specifically 'instructed to get to know the people and give them encouragement in raising the standard of the area' with the aim to 'push the old-fashioned concept of the police as a heavy-handed law enforcement machine further and further into the background'.[128] A crime prevention campaign entailed the distribution of leaflets and stickers.[129]

Yet youth work lay at the heart of the project as long-term social investment. Gray voiced concern that Roman Catholic children were proportionately more likely to appear before Greenock's juvenile court and made concerted efforts to work with local priests when the JLS was first set up. A 'Youth Committee' of the Greenock Social Services Association was also initiated in 1956, chaired by Gray, its membership including the organiser of the Roman Catholic Boys' Guild (as vice-chair), as well as representatives of schools, churches and youth organisations, the probation service and the local authority children's department.[130] Cycle proficiency lessons (as well as a road safety exhibition involving white mice) were initiated for children during school holidays.[131] Thus the JLS was part of a broader package of initiatives involving police-community collaboration across the religious divide that was launched to break down a cycle of deprivation/depravation. Gray took the JLS idea with him when he was appointed Chief Constable of Stirling and Clackmannan in 1960, and the neighbouring Burgh of Coatbridge introduced its own scheme in the same year. Further schemes followed in Perthshire and Kinross (1961), Kilmarnock (1962), Argyll (1965) and Inverness (1965).

Nevertheless, the JLS model was not without controversy in Scotland. Some probation officers saw the JLOs as amateurs encroaching inadequately on their own brief. They had a point, given that the 1931 Probation of Offenders (Scotland) Act had formally prohibited the appointment of either serving or former police officers to these roles. Indeed, in Glasgow from 1905 until 1931 the police had overseen probation in the city, appointing serving policemen to take on the role of probation officers in the divisional courts.[132] Yet as Fergus McNeill has argued, this role did not entail the scientific casework to underpin rehabilitation that had emerged elsewhere by the 1930s.[133] In relation to the JLS, social work critics were concerned that once again what was on offer was an old-fashioned supervision rather than effective intervention to turn around lives.[134] From a civil rights perspective, too, there were concerns that young people were being bounced into admitting offences without diligent judicial process (including evidence of corroboration), and that the police were taking the place of prosecutor and judge. Finally, the majority of chief constables in Scotland – including Glasgow, Edinburgh, Dundee and Aberdeen – did not think that the JLO role was 'proper' police work, stating their opposition in a joint submission to the Committee on Children and Young Persons chaired by Lord Kilbrandon from 1961 to 1964.[135]

Yet when it was finally published, the Kilbrandon Report overwhelmingly endorsed the continuation and expansion of the JLS model as in the interest of 'good police–public relations'.[136] Lord Kilbrandon (a sheriff and Queen's Counsel) was himself a huge enthusiast. Also significant was the input of criminologist John Mack, who secured research funding from the Carnegie Trust to assess the scheme's success together with researcher Margaret Ritchie, and both became key proponents. A conference on the future of the JLS model, held at Tulliallan in 1965, led to their involvement in the design and delivery of residential training courses for new and serving JLOs to counteract the criticism of amateurism.[137] When non-judicial Children Hearings, grounded in a welfare model, were introduced in Scotland in 1968 to replace the juvenile courts (which were continued in England/Wales), the JLS model was retained and extended to all parts of Scotland as a 'bridge' between policing and social services.[138] Gray's role as policy entrepreneur, developing innovative approaches to the problems facing contemporary policing, was further enabled by his appointment as Chief HMICS in 1970, which he used as a springboard to promote the 'community policing' brand to other police districts (this time in the form of 'community involvement branches', which the Scottish Office circular of 1971 recommended should be set up in all forces).[139]

Yet those who took on the role of JLO in Greenock, Coatbridge and other burghs in the mid-1960s did not have an easy ride. They struggled with the reactionary views of police colleagues 'mainly ... older officers, many of senior rank, who thought this type of work was not police work'.[140] According to Mack, an uncompromising law-enforcement attitude predominated within Scottish urban police culture at mid-century which tended to view probation and the juvenile courts as soft.[141] Similarly, the equation with social work, children and families, and thus with femininity, meant that JLOs were likely to encounter the view that their work was 'going soft on offenders'.[142] Nevertheless, JLOs themselves recognised the necessity for the range of tactics that formed the broader police repertoire, sharing the view of uniformed colleagues that a tough approach was sometimes required. Sociologist Maureen Cain found, in a study of Lancashire JLOs, that work styles and orientations formed a spectrum from 'punitive' to 'welfarist', with a mid-point position most common.[143] Moreover, across their careers, individual officers moved between policing roles and drew on a range of styles and approaches that reflected their assessment of situational variables. As we will next demonstrate, at the same time that the JLS model was mainstreamed across Scotland as an example of best practice, complaints of heavy-handed tactics towards young people in Glasgow were leading to significant public outcry. If the 'community ethos' was increasingly accepted in relation to younger children playing street football or shoplifting, who could easily be absorbed into the category of harmless 'innocents', the 'hard man' style of policing was still very much in evidence when it came to the problem of teenage 'gangs'.

The 'Untouchables'

The resurgence of concerns about violence in the mid-1960s – based on a very apparent increase in murder rates linked to 'the use of fatally dangerous weapons' – was rapidly turned into a 'youth' problem in Glasgow. More specifically, it was mapped onto the phenomenon of territorial 'gangs' associated with the city's newest housing schemes, especially Easterhouse. The media, local politicians and the police can all be said to have played a part in the stigmatisation of young people in Easterhouse, which in turn led to a deterioration in their behaviour – or 'deviancy amplification' – as Gail Armstrong and Mary Wilson observed as a result of their ethnographic research at the time.[144] Angela Bartie has carefully delineated the creation of a moral panic (using Stanley Cohen's definition) at a very precise point in January 1966, when members of a tenants' association in Easterhouse were reported by the press to have given chase to a large group of youths who 'had been causing trouble in the area'.[145] This led to 'stylised' media depictions of the 'gang' problem, including in an episode of the current affairs programme *24 Hours* – for which the BBC later apologised as being 'distorted'.[146] A very public debate continued in a highly polarised and politicised manner, in which 'hard' and 'soft' 'solutions' were proposed in the context of pending local government elections (which led, in 1968, to Labour losing long-standing control of the council). Whilst Labour suggested 'treatment-oriented' or 'social welfare' approaches, councillors associated with the (non-socialist) Progressive Alliance called for the reintroduction of corporal punishment – including the 'birching' of young offenders (discontinued across the UK in 1948) and the capital sentence for murder (suspended in the UK in 1965) – as a deterrent to violent behaviour.[147] Chief Constable James Robertson used the events to call for increased police powers to stop-and-search for offensive weapons, a cause that was taken up by Conservative MPs in parliament. Yet this was declined by Secretary of State for Scotland Willie Ross (Labour) on the grounds that the police already had sufficient powers under the 1953 Prevention of Crime Act.[148]

The 'media fest' culminated in a 'weapons amnesty' in July 1968, organised by popular entertainer Frankie Vaughan (who was spurred to take action after seeing the BBC programme) and 'his promise' to 'gang members' 'to help them organise a youth centre of their own'.[149] Armstrong and Wilson have commented that this intervention was 'embarrassing' for the Progressives since it was based on a model of co-operation, reconciliation and recognition of young people's agency, but it was impossible to refuse the offer even though James Anderson, as Progressive Convenor of the police committee, was publicly critical.[150] The resultant Easterhouse Project, which brought together artists, social workers and criminal justice practitioners to work with young people, has been described by Bartie as 'an innovative attempt to tackle youth violence, run by and for gang members with the support of a Board of Trustees (including Chief Constable Robertson) chosen by the gang members themselves'.[151] Thus the Easterhouse Project is an important example of police involvement in a community-led project that prioritised social intervention. This model of a truly 'grassroots' voluntary initiative was, nevertheless, hard to sustain (particularly given continued press scrutiny and lack of financial security) and the Easterhouse Project was closed and re-launched as a police-led community involvement project at the end of 1970. The officer selected to take on this role has described his careful negotiation of the twin identities of police officer and youth worker in order to create a balance between requisite levels of trust and authority:

> I made contact with various elements of the gangs whilst we were getting the place cleared up and ready for use again, and I invited them to come down to the project. They all knew I was a police officer, and I made it quite clear from the start that anything happening inside the project, I would deal with as a community worker; what happened outside, I would deal with as a policeman. We made certain rules: no weapons, no alcohol; if they were drunk, they wouldn't get in . . . I also encouraged other groups in the community to use it. I did so by inviting people from the churches and from the community association, the housing association, to come onto a local committee to actually run it, again so that the people there would take an ownership of it and see a use for it, rather than it just being for the 'bad boys'.[152]

Thus all local residents – young and old – were encouraged to take responsibility. Like the earlier JLOs, however, he faced challenges from other officers who did not see it as 'proper' police work: 'I . . . think it was a bold move by the chief constable to involve one of his officers in it, and . . . a lot of my colleagues asked, "What are you doing? You're not being police officers."'[153]

Yet the resolution that was found in the Easterhouse Project was not the only police response. Whilst debates were playing out amongst councillors, Robertson was also recruiting and making use of newly formed mobile teams of young plainclothes officers (the generation who wore bomber jackets and grew their hair) as an anti-violence strategy. According to former officers themselves, a key trigger for this was the Easter weekend of 1968 when 'gang' members had descended on the city centre and there were '21 serious assaults on Sauchiehall Street in one afternoon . . . the level of violence in the city that weekend was so bad that everybody was pitchforked into the city centre.'[154] Their accounts emphasise high levels of physical danger given the use of lethal weapons, and the necessity of physical force to defend the 'law-abiding'. According to one former officer, who worked as part of the 'Echo 10' team (six constables and a sergeant) in Easterhouse (and named after 'the call-sign for the vehicle' which was part of 'E' Division), their approach was welcomed by older residents alarmed by gang fights near their homes: 'there was actual butcher's knives and stuff like that, it was real dangerous stuff'. He relates a particularly violent episode, in which the team 'were all dressed very roughly and . . . had gone in amongst a gang', when a man who was passing by was unintentionally struck with baton by an officer:

> I think it was he who had phoned for the police because it was all taking place outside the close where he lived and the sergeant picked him up and he said, 'We'll need to take you to the hospital, it looks as though your jaw's broken.' 'Oh no,' he says, 'it doesn't matter, I'm just glad that you got these bastards.' He said 'They've been here every night causing all kinds of bother and I phoned the polis, and the panda arrives and they just laugh at the panda. The panda drives away because he sees all these people fighting with swords and knives.'[155]

Nevertheless, in most cases the plainclothes team could only resort to crowd dispersal: 'You would get thirty or forty of them getting together and it was real battles . . . Unfortunately they recognised the van and as soon as they saw the van coming, they used to shout, "The polis!" and most of them would go away.' In these scenarios, the tactic (used widely in Glasgow policing) of noting 'the main characters' so that 'you could come back for them' was crucial.[156]

The group was rapidly nicknamed the 'Untouchables' – after the popular American series shown on British TV in the 1960s that depicted Eliot Ness's law enforcement team battling against Al Capone and his mob in prohibition Chicago. Rapidly, too, it acquired a reputation not just for toughness, but for its controversial targeting of young people, using BoP to arrest those 'appearing in public groups of three or more'.[157] Where the police saw this as 'come-back' for violent incidents, young people articulated it as harassment. Armstrong and Wilson argued, on the basis of their interviews with Easterhouse teenagers, that this led to an escalation of conflict between the police and youngsters, and a deterioration in the behaviour of those charged with minor offences: 'I got done for breach of the peace for nothing, well next time it'll be something . . . Might as well get the jail for something.'[158] Thus 'what began as a myth ended in a *real* social problem'.[159]

The problems also seem likely to have stemmed from the failure to develop an effective policing strategy for Easterhouse in earlier years: there was a significant vacuum that the 'Untouchables' of Echo 10 were left to fill. Whilst shops, a youth centre and other amenities were late to arrive, so too was a local police station. Back in 1957 HMICS Sidney Kinnear had been taken on a tour of some of the 'new housing areas' surrounding the city which he described as 'only lightly policed' by officers on Vespa motor cycles.[160] Temporary police 'huts' had been constructed at Drumchapel and Castlemilk in 1956, with a new permanent police station for Drumchapel opening in 1957. In marked contrast, there was no temporary police 'hut' at Easterhouse until June 1969, and a permanent police station or 'sub-divisional office' did not open until April 1973.[161] It was also in 1969 that Easterhouse was first given its own Unit Beat area teams, each consisting of two uniformed constables in a Panda car, and based at the temporary office. Indeed, until 1969 Easterhouse was policed 'by [a] Landrover and mini-van' sent out from divisional headquarters, with the result that 'policemen had little local knowledge'.[162] These worked in parallel with Echo 10. Thus Easterhouse was never covered by the traditional 'beat man' system and, even after 1969, the lack of shops and other basic amenities meant that officers stationed there (in uniform as well as plainclothes) rarely interacted with residents: 'there was nowhere for police to have a kit-kat and get to know anybody personally'.[163] In this context and without a history of preventive police work embedded within the social relationships of area, the 'Untouchables' not only attracted opprobrium from parents and teenagers but also, according to Armstrong and Wilson, had a detrimental effect on young people's interactions with uniformed officers. They cite the following examples from their interviews: 'the Touchies made us turn against the beat police, soon as we see *any* kinda polis we start smashing their van up now'.[164]

Yet this was not simply a product of the lack of investment in Easterhouse. The tensions between plainclothes police and young people were felt in other parts of Glasgow, culminating in the high-profile public campaign of 1973 against alleged misuse of police powers – which was mostly focused on the 'Untouchables' – led by Bill Hatton, Labour Councillor for the Whiteinch ward in the north-west of the city. In June 1973, Hatton, who had been collecting cases reported to him by parents – of harassment, wrongful arrest and the bringing of false charges – began to publicise them through the local press. Deputy Chief Constable James Kelso reportedly told journalists that 'he had no knowledge of the allegations' and that he was 'astonished at this generalised attack on the police'.[165] The *Evening Citizen* reported that, prior to his election as councillor, Hatton's own son had been 'stopped and forcibly searched by the "Untouchables" squad as they made their way home one night' for no apparent reason (Hatton had complained but this was not upheld following investigation).[166] In August 1973 Hatton distributed copies of a 24-page dossier of allegations (in anonymised form) to members of the city council, much to the disapproval of Labour Convenor of the police committee, Agnes (Nancy) Ballantyne, who accused him of 'unethical action' in not submitting the dossier to her or to Chief Constable David McNee.[167] Hatton's justification was that 'young people are afraid to make complaints against the police', that 'certain sections of the police are fighting crime by scaring the wits out of lots of decent young people who are anything but wrong-doers' and that some young people in the city were 'accumulating records of convictions without having broken the law'.[168]

Letters extracted in the dossier (thirty in total) capture the viewpoints and emotions of both parents and young people, as these two examples demonstrate:

> Parent: 'My son, who is 16 years of age and still at school, and two of his friends, were sitting on a wall in the square in front of my window. I had warned him not to play football, so I kept a close watch on him. After keeping check for roughly twenty minutes and seeing that they were just sitting and talking I went for a walk with my dog. I was away at the most for five minutes in which time they had been 'booked' for disorderly behaviour. They had seen two plain clothes detectives entering the square they knew they were police but not having done anything they just sat and watched. On being approached one of the boys said "Are we not allowed to sit in our own square?" The reply was "when you see us, run" or words to that effect.'[169]
>
> Young male: 'This boy and girl asked me for a light for their cigarette, which I gave them, when the plain clothed policeman came to me in a van and and lifted the boy, girl and myself and we were taken to [the police station] charged with attempted housebreaking and I do honestly admit I have had previous convictions but believe me I am definitely innocent this time as I can't pass a police [sic] but they lift me . . . my mother wanted me to write to my MP because the police went to my work and I lost my job.'[170]

Parents were extremely anxious and concerned about their sons, reporting detrimental effects on mental health, economic prospects, and family life: 'this is upsetting me writing this as I am reliving the whole thing again'; 'my son is afraid to go out, his dad has to meet him and take him home by car when he goes to his youth club'.[171] They defended young people from misrepresentation – 'most people are so down on the youth of today and its [sic] such a pity' – and upheld their children's right to use the streets, meet friends and engage in leisure.[172] Some felt their own value system was being challenged:

> I . . . brought my family . . . up to respect the police and walk the streets in a decent manner. I always tell them if you ever see trouble turn away from it, trust the police to help you but I was wrong.[173]

A number saw themselves and their children as responsible, 'decent' and law-abiding, with wrongful arrests resulting from officers failing to distinguish between actual offenders and teenagers who were simply in the wrong place at the wrong time. One parent described her son as 'not a wild boy . . . [but] a prefect at school . . . well thought of by the teachers'.[174] Despite this experience this parent nevertheless stated: 'I am not anti-police. Have since tried to help them in their fight against crime regards house-breaking, and will continue to do so as long as I can.'

Perhaps most revealingly, the dossier included an anonymous letter sent to Hatton by a serving police officer after reading the summer press coverage:

> Most of the trouble stems from the formation of the plain clothes squads, know [sic] as the Untouchables, and reading between the lines this would appear to be your main reason for complaint. I can assure you they are detested as much within the Force as by the public.[175]

The dossier offers a rare moment in which young people and their families describe in their own words their perceptions of a very particular style of urban policing – and exposes even police concerns that legitimacy was damaged. It is not our intention to make judgements about veracity and culpability from research materials that are inevitably partial. Rather, it is the gap between these two counter-narratives that interests us as significant. On the one hand the police justified 'come-back' (arrest after the event for a lesser charge of BoP) as a necessary tactic within a broader general context of endemic serious violence. On the other hand young people described their treatment on particular occasions as unfair, even when they admitted they had offended at other times. Thus the rules of 'come-back' do not appear to have been understood and accepted in the same ways by both parties. Perhaps even more significantly, many of the correspondents were less concerned about the principle of provocative police tactics, but rather that they were used indiscriminately (as a result of inaccurate local knowledge) on those whom they felt should have been seen as 'law-abiding' and 'decent'. The methods used by the 'Untouchables' undermined police legitimacy – because they were not seen as fair or just in accordance with the broader moral value system of residents.

Indeed, Hatton's dossier and the attendant publicity was one of the factors that led to the recognition by McNee, encouraged by Gray, that fresh initiatives were needed to rebuild police relationships with the public through 'community involvement', youth work, and a new public relations department. The Glasgow police annual inspection papers for 1973–4 glossed over the whole saga and did not comment on the phasing out of the 'Untouchables', but they did, tellingly, report on the creation of a 'new' mobile 'Support Group' (to replace them) which would 'try to avoid giving cause for public complaint'.[176] When Gray visited the city for his routine inspection in 1975 (the last one before Glasgow City Police was folded into the new regional Strathclyde police force) he met with the police authority, now chaired by Labour's Bashir Maan:

> At the conclusion of the meeting one of the Labour members mentioned that at one time he had been a great critic of the police for the rough handling of some of his constituents. Mr McNee, he said, had changed all this and now received few complaints.[177]

These comments chime with the observation made by Ritchie and Mack in 1974 of the aspiration to replace the '"hard man" police image' with a 'community ethos'.[178]

Nevertheless, the 'law enforcement' ethos remained apparent amongst older Glasgow officers prior to regionalisation. Sceptical of Children's Hearings, some viewed them pejoratively as an even lighter touch than the juvenile court: 'They were just getting a wee pat on the back and that was it. And some of them were right bloody wee neds who needed a good kick up the . . . but you couldnae do these things.'[179] Charles was aware that 'cops tended to disregard what kids did, because there was an awful lot of paperwork' and 'it was not worth all the work'.[180] Yet for Donald, whose formal police role was to liaise with the reporter to the children's panel in the early 1970s, gradual change was discernible: 'Older police officers . . . saw their jobs very much as an enforcement agency' but 'I think we were moving from police force to police service, where you saw yourself . . . as looking at ways in which you could use the law for the betterment of people.'[181] Given the previous 'strong opposition' to the JLS model in Glasgow from 'senior officers', McNee avoided this label but developed an adapted form that made use of uniform beat officers to supervise offenders (praised by Gray as a welcome expansion of their responsibilities). Piloted in one of Glasgow's Divisions in 1974, it was rolled out as a 'Youth Advisory Service Scheme' following the creation of the new Strathclyde Police in 1976. From 1971 onwards, the Easterhouse project was brought within the new 'Community Involvement' division, which focused on youth work (including an initiative in Blackhill).[182] Thus the clashes of the late 1960s and early 1970s began a re-thinking of the central principles and values that underpinned occupational identity.

Conclusions

This chapter has shown that there was a diversity and complexity to specialist plainclothes roles within urban police forces, each generating different effects in terms of police legitimacy, public confidence and the responses of distinct demographic groups. Nevertheless, common themes and trends are apparent across the examples we have analysed. Working in plainclothes had greater potential to build trust, to break down social barriers and to tap into broader information circuits than the uniform enabled. Yet it also provoked anxieties that were sometimes well-founded – often amongst marginalised groups who lacked legal status – regarding espionage and entrapment, harassment, and unfairness. These groups were overwhelmingly male – whether working-class teenagers or gay men – and thus the more ebullient forms of plainclothes work (used by the 'Touchies' and the 'Vice Squad') entailed the playing out of competing masculinities. The lexicon of 'hunting out' and 'going in' depicted a debacle, in which the police waged a battle of wits or brawn against those viewed as anti-social or dangerous. Until the 1980s plainclothes officers were encouraged, through training and formal instruction, to target homosexual men who used public spaces for 'cruising' by constructing them as an 'immoral' other, outside the boundaries of the 'law-abiding' community, alongside child abusers, and 'pimps' or male brothel-keepers. In so doing, a model of police masculinity as heterosexual as well as chivalric in its defence of those who were young, female, and innocent was reinforced (which was sometimes also racialised).

Yet plainclothes officers had the capacity to use discretion, which they often exercised with a sensitivity to working-class values, interests and needs in urban areas. This was most apparent in relation to street gambling; where arrests were made, they often resulted from complaints from wives and families. In relation to prostitution-related offences, although there was no formal requirement to prove 'annoyance', arrests were often stimulated by public concern, young women soliciting were viewed with considerable sympathy as victims of circumstance, and links between the police and local social workers were used to prioritise welfare rather than penal intervention. Indeed, a changing configuration of the relationship between 'law enforcement' and 'social work' is apparent across time. A significant number of police officers undertook voluntary social work in their spare time, out of a broader sense of social responsibility, but in relation to a demarcation of work and leisure. Nevertheless, their identity and status as police officers was carried with them into their voluntary work, and the two fields were seen as complementary.

Yet amidst the cultural change of the 1960s, 'social work' and 'law enforcement' were increasingly presented – within press coverage of public debate but also within rank-and-file police culture – as diametrically opposed and politicised 'soft' and 'hard' responses to social problems. Moreover, social fears as well as social expectations tended to converge on young people and their futures. For older rank-and-file police officers what was at stake was a value system that encouraged deference, conformity, duty and the performance of 'gendered respectability'. This was increasingly challenged by an alternative model that preferred self-actualisation, self-fulfilment, democratic participation and inclusivity.[183] Experiments with the JLS, the police-led incarnation of the Easterhouse Project, and other Community Involvement initiatives, sought to broker what was in fact a new intermediary path (partway between 'police' and 'social service') that aimed to engage young people by encouraging them to 'take responsibility'.

Finally, this chapter has demonstrated that the evidential requirement for corroboration in Scotland significantly shaped the tactics used by plainclothes officers as well as the decisions of prosecutors. This was most apparent in relation to street soliciting and homosexual offences, for which very distinct patterns were apparent in the twentieth century in comparison to England and Wales. Although homosexual acts in private were illegal until 1980, prosecutions were minimal, and police attention was overwhelmingly focused on cruising and cottaging, where zealous and (probably disproportionate) surveillance was used at key points. With regard to street soliciting, an elaborate system of cautioning emerged, through which the police were overseeing their own 'quasi-judicial' process, which was also directly mirrored in the methods that emerged to process youth offending across a similar period. When it came to minor offences, urban police forces sifted significant numbers out of the formal criminal justice process by dealing with them internally at the station. Assessment of 'public interest' rather than fetishisation of law enforcement remained the key determinant of police decision-making.

This book has dealt, so far, with policing styles and approaches in distinctly urban environments by focusing on Glasgow and industrialised areas of west-central Scotland. We have seen how differing (and sometimes countervailing) effects were created for multiple communities through the proliferating range of specialist roles that developed in urban and suburban areas as the role of the beat man became increasingly restricted. In marked contrast, however, in rural areas, police officers – often working on their own rather than in teams – remained generalists for most of the twentieth century, investigating offences as well as performing administrative and preventive functions. As we demonstrate next, the high degree of autonomy and discretion that this entailed was a very significant factor in shaping the distinct contours of rural policing.

Notes

1. Barrie, 'Britain's oldest police?', 126; Goldsmith, 'City of Glasgow Police', 83 and 101.
2. PP, *HMICS AR*, 1946, Cmd. 7247.
3. *McNee's Law*, 39.
4. PP, *HMICS AR*, 1930, Cmd. 3912.
5. Glasgow Police Museum and GCA, GCA, SR22/40, City of Glasgow Police, CC ARs for 1932 and 1946.
6. PP, *HMICS AR*, 1946, Cmd. 7247.
7. NRS, HH55/1727, Glasgow, inspection report, David Gray, August 1974. In other cities (notably Aberdeen) beat men were routinely used as crime enquiry officers for minor offences; McNee began to implement this in Glasgow in 1974 (PP, *HMICS AR*, 1974, Cmnd. 6065, 19).
8. Banton, *Policeman*, 7.
9. Brogden, *Mersey Beat*.
10. Emsley, *English Police*, 72.
11. Interview with Brian.
12. Interview with Donald.
13. Interview with Brian.
14. Davidson, *Illicit and Unnatural*, 91.
15. Colquhoun, *Life Begins*, 26.
16. Mack, 'Full-time miscreants', 43; interview with Brian.
17. Banton, *Policeman*; Evans, *Inside Job*.
18. For example, Colquhoun, *Life Begins*; Merrilees, *Short Arm*.
19. Mack, 'Full-time miscreants'. The article refers to 'Worktown', but Scottish Office files clarify the research centred on Greenock: NRS, HH60/883.
20. Mack, 'Full-time miscreants', 39.
21. See Hobbs, *Doing the Business*.
22. Mack, 'Full-time miscreants', 39.
23. The Manuel case has been extensively covered through 'true crime' writing, including Muncie, *Crime Pond*. For a semi-fictionalised account see Mina, *Long Drop*.
24. Mack, 'Full-time miscreants', 49.
25. See especially Muncie, *Crime Pond*.
26. Interview with Donald. See also Evans, *Inside Job*.
27. Interview with Donald.
28. GCA, CC AR, Glasgow, 1956.
29. Ralston, *Real Taggarts*, 165, 114 and 3.
30. Knox, *Court of Murder*, 72.
31. Colquhoun, *Life Begins*, 'Acknowledgement'.
32. Lawrence, '"Scoundrels and scallywags"'; Stallion, *Life of Crime*.
33. TNA, HO 335/5, SPF, 12 April 1950, Q.6269.
34. Ibid., Q. 6309 and Q. 6308.
35. PP, *Criminal Statistics for Scotland*, 1960, Cmnd. 1343; figures are not simply for street betting but include prosecutions for illicit gambling in clubs and other locations.

36. McNee, *McNee's Law*, 40.
37. Muncie, *Crime Pond*, 18.
38. *Scotsman*, 17 December 1936; Merrilees, *Short Arm*, 75. The first documented use of cine film to secure conviction for street betting in Great Britain was in Chesterfield in May 1935: Williams et al., 'Police filming'.
39. Settle, *Sex for Sale*, 24, citing CC ARs, Glasgow 1904 and 1922.
40. Settle, *Sex for Sale*, 24.
41. Burgh Police (Scotland) Act 1892, s. 391, ss. 22. The 1892 Act was adopted in all royal burghs except Greenock and the four cities of Glasgow, Dundee, Edinburgh and Aberdeen. However, Glasgow, Greenock and Dundee incorporated the solicitation clauses word-for-word into local byelaws; Aberdeen remained the exception until 1938. See NRS, HH60/263 and PP, *Report of the Committee on Homosexual Offences and Prostitution* (1957), Cmnd. 247, 84.
42. PP, Cmnd. 247, 84.
43. Aberdeen was the exception. 'Annoyance' had been included in the 1862 General Police & Improvements (Scotland) Act, which was very similar to the English legislation. The Lord Advocate's office claimed that the removal of the word 'annoyance' in the drafting of the 1892 Burgh Police Act (which replaced the 1862 Act) had been unintentional and its implications had not been realised at the time: NRS, HH60/263.
44. See Goldsmith, 'City of Glasgow Police', 355–72 on the clampdown on street soliciting in Glasgow (as in Edinburgh) from around 1870 which he sees as driven by the Corporation.
45. PP, Cmnd. 247., Appendix 2, Tables XII and XVI.
46. Settle, *Sex for Sale*.
47. On Glasgow in 1907 see PP, *Royal Commission, Minutes of Evidence*, vol. III (1908), Cd. 4260, James V. Stevenson, Q. 39804–40247, esp. Q. 39931 and Q. 3933. For Edinburgh and Glasgow in later decades see TNA, MEPO 2/10287 and PP, Cmnd. 247.
48. *Scotsman*, 28 January 1928.
49. Merrilees, *Short Arm*, 65. NRS, HH60/263, suggests warnings were in use in Edinburgh by 1925.
50. Merrilees, *Short Arm*, 77; MEPO 2/10287, 11.
51. Settle, *Sex for Sale*.
52. NRS, JC31/1909/41, Jessie Brown v. George Neilsen (Burgh Prosecutor, Glasgow). Reference has been found to only one other Glasgow complaint or appeal (see *Scotsman*, 28 January 1928), in which a woman who was wrongfully arrested was awarded damages of £300 by a jury (the arresting constable was also dismissed by the chief constable).
53. PP. *Hansard* [HC], 15 June 1909, col. 823.
54. *Scotsman*, 15 December 1909; *GH*, 15 December 1909. He was referring to the very wording of the charge: 'being a common prostitute, you did . . .'.
55. Merrilees, *Short Arm*, 76.
56. Settle, *Sex for Sale*, 32.
57. *McNee's Law*, 40.

58. TNA, MEPO 2/10287.
59. *McNee's Law*, 40.
60. TNA, MEPO 2/10287, 8.
61. Interview with Donald.
62. Davidson and Davis, *Sexual State*, 32.
63. Interview with Donald. As he also points out, the problem of drugs became a very significant factor by the 1980s.
64. Bland, *Banishing the Beast*.
65. Braber, 'Trial of Oscar Slater', 270.
66. Quoted in Ibid., 267.
67. *GH*, 4 February 1911.
68. GCA, T.PR 1.16, *Memorandum on the Social Evil in Glasgow*; *GH*, 4 October 1911.
69. *GH*, 1 December 1911.
70. Ibid.
71. *GH*, 14 December 1911.
72. Ibid.
73. *GH*, 23 December 1911. The Burgh Police (Amendment) Act 1911 allowed local authorities to control the opening hours of refreshment houses and to require registration of those permitted to open on Sundays or in the evening.
74. Merrilees, *Short Arm*, 74.
75. Settle, *Sex for Sale*, 39–45, 157, 174–5.
76. Davidson, *Illicit and Unnatural*, 120.
77. Ibid., 121. Davidson and Davis, *Sexual* State, 17 also suggest Leith 'was being treated virtually as a "tolerance zone"' by the 1950s.
78. Davidson, *Illicit and Unnatural*, 122.
79. NRS, HH55/734 HMICS inspection, Dundee, report of Janet Gray, 26 October 1964.
80. Jackson with Bartie, *Policing Youth*, 126.
81. Settle, *Sex for Sale*, 157.
82. Davidson and Davis, *Sexual State*, 41–96; Meek, *Queer Voices*.
83. PP, Cmnd. 247, Appendix 1, Table X. Note that gross indecency was rolled into a generic statistic for offences under the Criminal Law Amendment Act, making it impossible to be certain about the precise trend across time.
84. PP, Cmnd. 247, 50; Meek, *Queer Voices*, 40.
85. PP, Cmnd. 247, 21.
86. Davidson, *Illicit and Unnatural*, 207.
87. Meek, *Queer Voices*, 42.
88. Davidson and Davis, *Sexual State*, 41–91.
89. Davidson, *Illicit and Unnatural*.
90. Meek, *Queer Voices*, 50.
91. Ibid., 41.
92. Quoted in Meek, *Queer Voices*, 41.
93. Davidson and Davis, *Sexual State*, 45, citing TNA, HO 345/16.
94. Ibid.

95. Alan Alexander (b. 1937) in Cant, *Footsteps & Witnesses*, 43.
96. On the SMG/SHRG see Dempsey, *Thon Wey*; Davidson and Davis, *Sexual State*; Meek, *Queer Voices*.
97. Meek, *Queer Voices*, 27.
98. Ibid., 25–7; see also Houlbrook, 'Man with the powder puff', for England.
99. Adair later sat on the Wolfenden Committee, famously opposing the recommendations made for decriminalisation in the majority report.
100. Merrilees, *Short Arm*. Merrilees, who became Chief Constable of Lothian and Peebles Constabulary in 1950 following a high-profile career in Edinburgh City Police, was a local and national celebrity whose success story (from 'poor bairn' to OBE) was told on the popular ITV show *This is Your Life* in 1959.
101. Merrilees, *Short Arm*, 121.
102. Ibid., 119.
103. Ibid., 116.
104. Ibid., 118.
105. Anon., *Scottish Criminal Law* (1950), Section 2, 7–8.
106. Interview with Charles.
107. Anon., *Scottish Criminal Law* (1980), Section 2, 8.
108. *Scotsman*, 20 September 1980, quoting Derek Ogg, SHRG solicitor.
109. NRS, GD467/1/2/8.
110. Burke, *Coming Out*, 211. His interviews were mostly with officers who served in English forces.
111. Burke, 'Homosexuality'; Burke, *Coming Out*, 38.
112. Scottish LGBTI Police Association, 'Our Story', https://www.lgbtipolice.scot/history (last accessed 1 January 2020).
113. Wolcott, *Cops and Kids*. Our discussion throughout this section also draws on Bartie and Jackson, 'Youth crime', and Jackson with Bartie, *Policing Youth*.
114. Smith, 'Official responses' and 'Juvenile delinquency'.
115. PP, Cmd. 874, Q. 73333 Superintendent William Miller Douglas.
116. NRS, HH60/434; GCA, SR22/40, City of Glasgow Police, *CC AR* for 1946, 1956 and 1964. In comparison 6,648 children or young persons were dealt with by the juvenile courts in Glasgow in 1956 and 8,144 in 1964.
117. Van Slingelandt and Macdonald, *Long Way*, 65.
118. NRS, HH60/434.
119. Ibid.; Bartie and Jackson, 'Youth crime'.
120. Jackson with Bartie, *Policing Youth*, 27.
121. Bartie and Jackson, 'Youth crime', 87.
122. Colquhoun was a judo instructor at a Gorbals youth club in the late 1940s: Colquhoun, *Life Begins*, 51. McNee was an active member of the Boys' Brigade until he reached the age of 18, and was appointed as its vice-president in 1980: McNee, *McNee's Law*, 28.
123. White and Hunt, 'Citizenship'; Jackson with Bartie, *Policing Youth*, 168.
124. NRS, ED39/134, D. Gray to A. J. Betts, Scottish Office, 12 June 1956.
125. Mays, *Growing Up*, 139.

126. NRS, ED39/134, 'The Greenock Police Juvenile Liaison Officer Scheme', typed notes of A. J. Betts.
127. NRS, ED39/134, Report, the Juvenile Liaison Scheme in Greenock, 1956–61.
128. NRS, ED39/134, Report of a conference on the work of juvenile liaison officers, 22–24 June 1965, address by Chief Inspector Robert Campbell, on Greenock and Ravenscraig (also the focus of a CIS).
129. *Greenock Telegraph*, 16 July 1965.
130. NRS, ED39/134, D. Gray to A. J. Betts, 12 June 1956.
131. *Greenock Telegraph*, 25 May 1956.
132. PP, Cmd. 874, Q. 73333, Superintendent William Miller Douglas.
133. McNeill, 'Remembering probation'.
134. NRS, ED39/134, miscellaneous correspondence, 1960.
135. Jackson with Bartie, *Policing Youth*, 36.
136. PP, *Report of the Committee on Children and Young Persons, Scotland* (1964), Cmnd. 2306, 60. For the contrasting approach in England and Wales see Bartie and Jackson, 'Youth crime'.
137. Mack, 'Police Juvenile Liaison Schemes', 369; NRS, HH60/883, Greenock JLS; Mack, *Police Juvenile Liaison*.
138. Schaffer, *Community Policing*, 48.
139. Ibid., 47.
140. NRS, ED39/134, Conference report, 22–24 June 1965.
141. NRS, GD281/66/4.
142. Cain, 'Role conflict', 378.
143. Ibid.
144. Armstrong and Wilson, 'Delinquency'; Armstrong and Wilson, 'City politics'.
145. Bartie, 'Moral panics', 388, citing *GH* 10 January 1966; Cohen, *Folk Devils*.
146. Bartie, 'Moral panics', 390.
147. Armstrong and Wilson, 'City politics', 73.
148. Bartie, 'Moral panics', 394–5. Murray, 'Proactive turn'.
149. Bartie, 'Moral panics', 385.
150. Armstrong and Wilson, 'City politics', 75.
151. Bartie, 'Moral panics', 399. See also Bartie and Fraser, 'Easterhouse Project'.
152. Interview with George.
153. Ibid.
154. Interview with Donald.
155. Interview with Brian.
156. Interview with Brian.
157. Bartie and Fraser, '"It wasnae just Easterhouse"', 220.
158. Armstrong and Wilson, 'City politics', 80.
159. Ibid., 81.
160. NRS, HH55/1237, Glasgow, inspection report, 1957.
161. NRS, HH55/1727, Glasgow, inspection papers, 1973.
162. NRS, HH55/1727, inspection report, 1969; Armstrong and Wilson, 'City politics', 68.

163. Armstrong and Wilson, 'City politics', 71.
164. Ibid., 81.
165. *Evening Citizen*, 13 June 1973.
166. *Evening Citizen*, 14 June 1973.
167. *GH*, 3 August 1973.
168. *Evening Citizen*, 14 June 1973; B. Hatton, 'Complaints against the Police' (Glasgow: privately published/printed pamphlet, 1973–4), 24 pages, here 1–2.
169. Hatton, 'Complaints', letter 1.
170. Ibid., letter 7.
171. Ibid., letter 4; letter 2.
172. Ibid., letter 5.
173. Ibid., letter 18.
174. Ibid., letter 4.
175. Ibid., letter 8.
176. NRS, HH55/1727, Inspection papers and report, David Gray, August 1974.
177. NRS, Inspection report, David Gray, July 1975.
178. Ritchie and Mack, *Police Warnings*, 45.
179. Interview with Ronald.
180. Interview with Charles.
181. Interview with Donald.
182. PP, *HMICS AR*, 1976, Cmnd. 6891, 24; NRS, HH55/1727, Inspection report, David Gray, August 1974.
183. Jackson with Bartie, *Policing Youth*, 168.

5

POLICING THE RURAL

Rural policing in Scotland can be characterised in terms of deep continuities across the twentieth century and a temporality that was cyclical, shaped by the rhythm of the seasons and the iterative patterns of everyday routine. This chapter examines the styles of policing that were generated in the most sparsely populated parts not only of Scotland but of the UK, highlighting the ways in which officers negotiated their police identity whilst living and working within small communities.[1] It focuses in particular on the Highlands and Islands region, which in 1900 (and until the amalgamations of the 1960s) was covered by the northern county constabularies of Inverness, Ross and Cromarty, Caithness and Sutherland (as well as by separate police forces for Orkney and Shetland).[2] The area covered by Inverness County Police[3] was vast and by far and away the largest in Britain – some 2.75 million acres – stretching from the Moray Firth on the east coast to the western isles of Skye, Harris, North Uist, South Uist and Barra (although not Lewis, which was in Ross-shire). With an authorised strength of around 65 across the first half of the twentieth century, this equated to an average of 41,900 acres per officer. Sutherland County Police, in the far north and north-west, ostensibly policed 1.2 million acres on an authorised strength of just 18, an average of 67,000 acres per officer.[4] In practice, given that large swathes were uninhabited and road links limited, police work was concentrated around settlements, with villages acting as important hubs or nodes. Yet geographical distance and area nevertheless created particular challenges in terms of transport, communications, and support networks for isolated officers.

Across the twentieth century crime rates in the Highlands and Islands were consistently the lowest in Scotland and the majority of police time was spent on administrative functions. According to police data for 1946 only 182 crimes or offences (or one every two days) were recorded across the entirety of Sutherland, whilst officers had overseen the dipping of 309,267 sheep.[5] Later, amidst the perceived national 'crime wave' of the early 1960s, criminologists calculated a crime rate of only 9 offences per 1,000 population in Sutherland and 8.5 in Shetland, in contrast to 72 per 1,000 in Glasgow.[6] This chapter suggests that very low crime rates in northern counties (in comparison to the dense urban and industrial central belt) were in part because the policing function was shared with other 'traditional' entities and authority figures who predated the apparatus of the modern state: the Church (elders and ministers), family (heads of household), and landowners (through factors and gamekeepers). The police officer was most likely to be called upon when the legitimacy associated with these other structures broke down. It also argues that low crime rates were themselves a function of the style of policing that was used in relation to settled rural communities: as preventive, diffusive and explicitly grounded in the concept of policing by consent. This style was developed and learned across the twentieth century through practice and word of mouth – rather than being taught in training school or police manuals – and in response to local cultures. Yet it was also a very pragmatic response to the challenges of policing such large areas in a way that might be deemed efficient with limited resources: a small and dispersed group of officers and, until the last quarter of the twentieth century, little in the way of technology or equipment. Thus the policing style that came to be associated with the 'highland bobby' or 'village constable' (terms used at the time and by former officers themselves) was a product of the political economy of policing rural areas.

Whilst highlighting the importance of specific local context in shaping the dynamics of police-community relationships, the chapter shows that it is possible to determine a model or type – that can be traced through and across archival documents and oral history interviews – which is a distillation of the characteristics and experiences of rural Scottish policing. It was a model that had emerged by the early twentieth century and remained in place until at least 1975. The chapter will begin by analysing the spatial, social and temporal contours of policing amongst the settled rural communities of the Highlands and Islands, in which officers were embedded and for whom the 'gentle' or diffusive style was forged. Yet in many parts of the Highlands and Islands there was a clear divide between the settled population and groups of itinerant 'outsiders' – vagrants, Travelling people, and transient 'navvies' or male labourers – who were often viewed as an external threat to property and security and as 'trouble'. Thus the second half of the chapter examines the cultivation of other policing styles and repertoires to deal with these groups;

significantly, these incorporated more robust tactics and the use of physical force, but for some officers they also involved a more conciliatory form of mediation between settled and transient populations. Arguably, the arrival of migrant construction workers – as the harbingers of technological and social change – ruptured the deep continuities of rural policing even more than did wartime in many areas. The chapter finishes by commenting briefly on the transformations of the late twentieth century, and their implications for the experience of rural policing and police-community relationships.

THE VILLAGE CONSTABLE AND POLICE LIFE

Personnel records that survive for recruits to the county constabularies of Inverness (1901–68), Caithness (1900–67), Orkney (1920–67) and Shetland/Zetland (1929–64) reveal a distinctive demographic pattern: police officers in the Highlands and Islands were consistently 'local' across time (in contrast to Glasgow City Police, 70 per cent of whose recruits were migrants in the early years of the twentieth century).[7] Of recruits to Inverness County Police, 77 per cent were born either in Inverness-shire or in a neighbouring county (see Appendix 1, Table A.7). As this chapter will show, officers in Inverness-shire were, as a matter of principle, rarely stationed in their native settlements and a policy of rotation was preferred (a model used in most counties). Some officers and their families stayed in a village for significant amounts of time in the first half of the twentieth century when police recruitment was static and recruits remained in the job for life. Ardersier had the same village constable for a period of 18 years (1919–37), Cannich for two periods of 17 years (1895–1912 and 1920–37), and Daviot for 19 years (1921–47). Nevertheless, most officers experienced moves across huge distances from east to west coast within their careers, given the size of the police district. After the Second World War, postings tended to be shorter (around 5 years), officers were deliberately moved across divisions and those who were married were expected to undertake island duties for a period of at least 2–3 years. For example, an officer might move from the island of Barra (as the only officer on the island), to Lochboisdale on South Uist, to Beauly on the east coast, to Portree on Skye and then on to the large Divisional station at Fort William across his service. Nevertheless, there was invariably a degree of cultural affinity, including an understanding of rural life and, in some cases, language. Unsurprisingly, in comparison to the City of Glasgow (which predominantly attracted industrial workers), recruits to Inverness County Police were more likely to have worked in agriculture or forestry before joining – 18% in the period 1956–68 – although nearly a quarter had been engaged in clerical work, suggesting that excellent record-keeping skills were seen as necessary in rural policing (see Appendix 1, Table A.8). Given wartime and military service, a high proportion of those who joined in the 1940s and 1950s – here as elsewhere – came from services backgrounds.

In Caithness, Shetland and Orkney, recruits were even more 'local', with the vast majority born within the district itself – 64 per cent, 73 per cent and 82 per cent respectively – creating a very distinctive dynamic of local policing delivered by native officers, which persisted until regionalisation in 1975.[8] Thirty-eight per cent of Caithness recruits had worked in agriculture, fishing or (in several cases) game-keeping in the county before joining, whilst 26 per cent had worked in manual trades including work as joiners, carpenters, and masons. Of the twenty Shetland recruits for whom personnel records are held in the Highland Archives, a fifth had previously worked at sea (the most predominant occupation), while two had served as officers in other Scottish police forces before returning home to join Zetland Police.

Finally, in terms of demographic trends, police officers in the Highlands and Islands, like their Glasgow counterparts, were overwhelmingly Protestant (and within this, Presbyterian) (see Appendix 1, Table A.10).[9] Only 3.6 per cent of Inverness County recruits self-identified as Roman Catholic across the years in which religion was recorded (1936–68), despite the prevalence of Catholicism on the western isles of Barra and South Uist.[10] Former officers who were interviewed suggested religion was rarely an issue in the Highlands and Islands (in contrast to Clydeside's reputation for 'sectarian' tension). Nevertheless, a strong tradition of Sabbatarianism on Skye led to high-profile disputes related to the erosion of Sunday observance. In 1965 Free Church minister Reverend Angus Smith (and thirteen others) was arrested and charged with breach of the peace for obstructing the slipway at Kyleakin in a peaceful 'sit-down' against the first Sunday ferry service, leading to press coverage of the protest across the UK and globally.[11]

Rural officers were geographically embedded within settlements, living on their 'patch' rather than outside of it (as in urban areas). Moreover, the workplace was also home and the material fabric and lay-out of police buildings shaped the experience of family life. In Inverness-shire, Caithness and Sutherland, as in other counties, 'larger' village police stations consisted of accommodation for a married village constable and his family as well as a small police office and two cells (for detention or imprisonment of up to 14 days); smaller stations were often simply houses and were rented by the police authority rather than owned by them. The inferior standard of accommodation received repeated comment from HMICS, the SPF and officers themselves. In 1900 HMICS recorded that in some 'old county stations' there was no separate police office so that business had to be transacted in the family living room, which was 'often very inconvenient, when the family is large, or when there is sickness in the house'.[12] At Tongue police station, Sutherland, the parlour had itself been converted into a police office with two cells by the 1930s, so that living accommodation was restricted to a kitchen, scullery, two attic bedrooms and a box-room. Thus police business was part of domestic space, often literally intruding into it. One constable wrote to his Chief Constable to request a bell for the office door, as well as a sign for the front, because the office entrance was at the rear of the property: 'very often strangers walk into the kitchen or sitting room looking for the office and on occasions they have walked upstairs'.[13]

Attempts to modernise accommodation were gradual and piecemeal until after the Second World War and were rarely considered a priority. Police authorities were reluctant to commit limited resources or to raise rates, and these economies were further affected by interwar cuts to police budgets. Other problems included the difficulties of negotiating with landowners where housing stock was rented, as well as the slow arrival of amenities such as electricity, mains water and telephone to remote areas. Electrification did not reach parts of the northern counties until the 1940s. Sutherland County Police had no telephone link even at its headquarters until 1926, and Bettyhill station was one of the last to get a telephone in 1943, pushed on by the exigencies of war.[14] The condition of some stations led to individual protest. In 1935 the police constable at Melvich, Sutherland, complained to his police authority that the damp penetrating the sitting room and bedroom was so severe that he would make arrangements for his wife and children to live elsewhere.[15] Remedial repairs were made but plans to rebuild were put on ice when war broke out in 1939, as indeed they were elsewhere. The police constable based at Beauly's Victorian police station, which suffered from persistent problems with blocked gutters and drains, reported in August 1945 that:

> the rain is splashing in through the roof of the Police Office here. There is a continuous drip above a window and I cannot work in it as it is. If it is not attended to the papers in this office will be ruined.[16]

Considerable resilience was required to maintain pride in record keeping in such adverse circumstances.

Difficulties with the standard of accommodation were not restricted to rural areas – nor to Scotland – and plans for the provision of appropriate police housing were built into directives for post-war reconstruction. In 1945 the Scottish Police Council unanimously agreed that houses of a suitable standard should be provided for all police officers, and police authorities and housing authorities were instructed to work together in 1946 to ensure that police houses were included in all new housing areas.[17] The building of a new police station at Castle Bay, Barra, which had been delayed by war, was finally completed in 1952 as part of a wider programme of building projects planned by Inverness County Police in the Western Isles.[18] Yet the patching of Victorian stock continued in some cases (Beauly and Ardersier) until they were vacated as beyond repair and replaced with new-build in the early 1970s.[19] Police families together faced the disruption (including to children's schooling) of moving their home when village constables were rotated to new posts. They arrived at their new destination to find that wallpaper and skirting was indelibly faded, indicating the shape of the previous occupants' furniture. The condition of kitchen and scullery was often poor, requiring DIY expertise and considerable adaptation to render them serviceable. Permission had to be sought to carry out repairs or decoration, with police authorities unwilling to sanction other than the most necessary expense.

Accommodation and fuel were provided 'free', on the assumption that a rural officer's wife would play an important support role. In the first decades of the century she might be paid an additional annuity (around £10 in 1914) to act as matron for the police cells and to escort and search female prisoners.[20] Across the century, the village constable's wife was crucial to the effective running of the station, not simply because of her assumed domestic service role, but in taking and relaying messages, and acting as a first port of call when her husband was out. For example, in December 1940, when an airplane crashed down into a field near Dalcross aerodrome, police headquarters at Inverness telephoned Ardersier village police station, receiving important details of the incident from the wife of the constable (since he was already at the scene). She cared for an injured pilot at the police station until a car arrived from Inverness to take him away.[21] These details reveal how the hidden work of police wives (often missing from other record keeping) underpinned the smooth running of the station. As Weinberger has demonstrated for England, police wives acted as 'unpaid assistants' and even, as a 'proxy policeman'.[22] As one officer who served on Skye in the 1960s explained:

> My wife was as much a policeman as I was . . . She was expected to clean the office and buy the materials out of her own wage. When I was out she had to take calls and record them in [the] duty books . . . handwritten, Stephens blue/black ink and red ink, pens with nibs. If I was out, my wife could get six, seven, eight, nine, ten calls a day some days and she had to write all that in the book . . . When we did eventually have a baby, she'd be standing there with the baby in one arm and the phone up here and trying to write.[23]

It was partly because of gendered assumptions about the support role of the police wife that county constabularies were so slow to appoint women as paid officers.

The structures, rhythms and encounters of everyday policing were meticulously recorded in the station occurrence book, which was established in the

1860s as a key part of the bureaucratic apparatus through which the police organisation monitored the activities of rural officers, who worked on their own for long periods of time. As one former officer recollects of the mid-twentieth century: 'In the rural you see, you were an individual, you acted as an individual, you made decisions as an individual and you used discretion as an individual.'[24] The occurrence book (and its successors the 'journal', 'log book' and 'duty book') was part of an inspection and audit trail, since it was countersigned by a supervisory officer when he visited the station. As Paul recalled, 'My sergeant was in Beauly [half an hour away] and he would come and visit me once a month. He came up, looked at the book, initialled it, a cup of tea, biscuits, a blether'.[25] Slightly different models were used in different constabularies, although that used in Inverness-shire and which we describe here was fairly typical. A daily entry was required in the occurrence book, detailing hours of duty, the nature of those duties, distance travelled, places and people visited (in black ink), as well as information about the incidents and cases that constituted 'occurrences' (recorded in red). Sample entries were provided in the frontispiece, enabling imitation as well as consistency, although the variation in approach and interpretation is striking. Some officers (or perhaps even their wives) recorded a minimum of information, whilst others were more prolific diarists. An entry from the occurrence book that we presume was completed by the police constable stationed at Dunvegan, Skye, in November 1944, not only exemplifies the formula used but shows how, in time of war, the rituals of everyday life persisted undisturbed in some parts of the country:

> 11 November Saturday
> At 10am engaged about station till 11am and patrolled by way of Lonmore and then attended sheep dipping at Kilmuir and returned to station 1pm. Resumed 2.30pm and patrolled by way of Dunvegan pier and castle, and district returning at 5.30pm. On duty 6½ hrs, travelled 7 miles.
> Night duties, resumed 7.30pm and patrolled in village generally and visited Young Men's Club, then returned to station at 10.30pm. On duty 3 hrs, travelled 3 miles.[26]

For the historian the occurrence book is a rich dataset providing insight into the temporal, geographical and social contours of the village constable's day or, at very least (since we cannot certify its accuracy) of what was possible, probable and expected. Thus it can be seen as a narrative of typicality, if not to be taken entirely at face value. The occurrence book was a response to a certain set of requirements for record keeping and can only be understood in light of the purpose for which it was written. It is not a personal diary. It rarely contains personal reflection or insight. Its focus is on factual events.

Yet, it is suggestive of the performance of the police role and identity, and of the importance of the routine. By analysing the formulaic and the iterative, moments that are discordant or do not fit with the previous narrative can be more clearly identified and interpreted. Deconstructing and contextualising the social categories that are referenced and not explained but simply assumed can help shed light on the power dynamics at play. Finally and crucially, the station occurrence book can be read alongside other accounts including more personalised memoirs (early twentieth century) and oral history interviews (for the period within living memory).

Policing the Settled Community

Routine and the everyday

An initial comparison of occurrence book, journal and log-book entries for stations across Inverness-shire from around 1900 to 1970 demonstrates striking continuities in the roles of officers and the duties in which they were engaged. Given the centrality of livestock farming to the rural economy, the 'worrying' of sheep (and sometimes cattle) by stray or out-of-control dogs was a serious problem that generated persistent concern and diligent investigation across time.[27] Those relating to the theft of livestock (particularly poultry but also sheep and cattle), and the poaching of game (deer and pheasants) as well as river-poaching of salmon also persisted, and in some cases the police carried out night watches in attempts to identify culprits.[28] Across the century and into the 1980s, too, police constables were involved in the annual cycles of renewing firearms certificates and, as inspectors for diseases of animals, for attending or overseeing sheep dippings, for ensuring that appropriate licences were in place for the movement of livestock, and for checking that diseased animals were appropriately logged and disposed of.[29] These patterns were common across rural counties.

Whilst officers clearly performed a role as the regulatory arm of the state, the visits to local farms that these occasions necessitated built the bonds of social familiarity. As a former officer who joined Sutherland County Police in the 1960s explained:

> One of the best ways of getting to know the community was, oddly enough, the sheep dipping papers. They were brilliant, because you didn't post them out. You had to go to every farmer, every crofter, every person that owned sheep, you had to have a dipping paper for them, which was returned . . . The other thing that was great was firearms certificates, because in the Highlands there is a huge abundance of licence holders, for firearms and shotguns, of necessity, and you would get dished out firearms certificates to deal with every month. You kept the registers in

the stations in those days and you just took the pages from the register and called all the people and renewed their firearms certificates and had a word with them and a cup of tea. So very quickly you got to know most of the people living in the parish. Within a year you got to know almost everybody.[30]

The legitimacy of policing was underpinned by the recognition that officers ensured the smooth running of the events and business transactions associated with the farming year. Until at least the 1940s, officers were required to be in attendance at farm auctions or 'displenishing sales', which usually took place in May, attracting large crowds who lingered on in public houses into the evening. This was to ensure good order but also the legitimate exchange of property at the sale.[31] Village constables also acted as inspectors of weights and measures in the first half of the twentieth century, which again required an annual inspection over several days.[32]

It is notable that the village officer continued to provide an important communication and support service across time. Station log books for 1969 and 1970 show that it was still very common for officers to be asked to deliver messages about relatives who were ill or in hospital, given that many private households did not yet have telephones. In 1970, too, as in earlier decades, local residents were still notifying the police station when they were due to be away or on holiday, with the (realistic) expectation that the constable would check all vacant property daily while they were away.[33] Moreover, the receiving and return of lost property was a standard component of their work in the 1960s just as it had been in the early 1900s. The security and protection of the property and livestock of the settled population was thus a crucial focal point of the work.

Considerable time was spent patrolling the breadth of the local beat which might cover a radius of around 15 miles either on foot or by bicycle (usually their own, for which they received an allowance), cementing affinity with people and place.[34] In the years before the installation of telephones village constables were required to meet with neighbouring officers of adjoining stations around once a week at various fixed 'conference points' to exchange information. It was one of the ways in which the duties of individual village constables was checked, co-ordinated and (where a superior officer was involved in the conference) supervised. But it also had a further function, since they undertook a round journey and called in to talk to landowners, estate managers and gamekeepers, farmers, store owners, schoolteachers, clergy and their wives *en route*. Norman Morrison wrote of the friendly reception provided by farmers during his time as village constable in Port Charlotte, Islay, in Argyllshire 1897–1900: 'when calling at their houses on my daily rounds I would be lavishly and hospitably welcomed to their table'.[35] A Sutherland police officer recollected of his 1950s childhood on the far north-west coast:

> The policeman was at [the village] frequently, not for any reason other than to have a look at all the people and have a patrol along the road and see that things were going fine, and called in to get bits of news and local gossip or whatever.[36]

This routine presence and visibility also ensured further acquisition of 'knowledge' and the building of relationships of trust with key individuals within the settled community. To take another example, in 1904 the police constable stationed in the tiny hamlet of Tomnacross, a sub-station within Beauly district, covered an average of 8 miles per day during his dayshift, heading out at around 10am each morning, making a series of calls at local farms, estates or the Manse, attending a conference point, and arriving back around 3pm. Each evening from 6pm to 11pm (with the exception of Sunday) he patrolled in the vicinity of the Megston Inn, the only licensed premises on his patch, covering a further 4 miles.[37] Village constables in the villages of Beauly and Ardersier recorded that they worked even longer days of 13 or 14 hours in the 1920s and 1930s. Attending church – whether the Church of Scotland or the Free Church – was an integral part of any Sunday duty but in many villages night patrol was still undertaken in the evening despite closure of licensed premises. It was not until the 1950s that a 'day of rest' (expanding to two by the 1960s) was formally indicated in many station journals; although it had been legislated for since 1914 it was abandoned everywhere during the war. Nevertheless, as Frederick recalls: 'The public expected you to be available 24 hours a day ... Even at night somebody might come to your house door.'[38]

Evening patrol of larger villages was concerned with the enforcement of licensing laws, the prevention of disorder and, crucially again, the protection of property. Licensed premises such as pubs and hotels were usually visited between 10pm and 11pm most days of the week, whilst licensed dances – which were held in village halls occasionally in the 1920s and regularly on Saturdays by the 1950s – might not finish until after midnight. Indeed, by the 1950s and 1960s, village hall dances were attended by large crowds (bussed in from the nearest towns) and could be a rough affair leading to breach of the peace and even assault charges, as the accounts of officers stationed at Beauly and Cannich testify.[39] It was in relation to dances in village halls that rural officers were most likely to be assaulted or sustain injury in the 1950s, through incidents associated with them.[40] The constable's job was to ensure all was in order as crowds dispersed. Finally, he 'inspected property' as the Beauly police constable put it in 1953 – checking all premises were secure – before retiring to the station around 1am.[41] In both wars, the routine of the village constable was simply expanded to take in a greater range of duties, including patrol of 'vulnerable points' (if not already covered), liaison with special constables (who undertook much of the 'watching'), and warning local people regarding contravention of the lighting regulations.

However, this routine, whilst important to the semblance of order, might be disrupted and immediately abandoned in cases of obvious emergency (the most frequent in occurrence books being serious or fatal accidents on railway or road, reported suicides, missing children and, particularly on Skye and in Lochaber and Cairngorm, mountain rescue). Unlike their counterparts in city police forces, who passed information over to specialist departments for further investigation – most obviously the CID – the village constable was a generalist who invariably saw matters through from start to finish, taking statements as well as fingerprints and photographs at scenes of crime, leading and carrying out investigations, referring the matter to the Procurator Fiscal (PF), and making arrests. In emergency situations (and where back-up and corroboration was needed) constables often worked together with their 'neighbour'. Thus in 1918 the Beauly police constable cycled out late one May evening to meet his counterpart at Kirkhill station following the discovery of the body of a local man in a wood, a suspected suicide (indeed, Beauly and Kirkhill constables across the century acted as back-up for each other). A doctor had been called to examine the body, and the two constables attended the scene, studied the gun and the note found on the body, and carried out investigations and interviews. They summoned and briefed the PF who took the formal precognitions and confirmed the case as suicide.[42] Indeed, it was only in the years after the Second World War that CIDs were formalised in county constabularies. By the 1950s, following the initial enquiry of a case, a village constable would inform the CID based at the divisional headquarters. Nevertheless, as occurrence books show, the local officer would continue to investigate and take statements, or to work closely with a detective constable sent out from HQ. On island locations in particular, the onus remained on the local officer, as Frederick recalls:

> You were left to your own devices as it were. When we had some serious crime you had to . . . solve it yourself because it was about 24 hours before you got any mainland assistance . . . There was a series of crimes which the CID couldn't solve and – after the CID had left the island – I made the right contacts and cleared up the crime.[43]

Stationed in Sutherland in the 1970s, another officer described an incident in which he was called out to an oil platform over a mile offshore in the early morning hours to deal with a fatal accident: 'The next day I notified health and safety . . . and they flew up in the helicopter. They were absolutely amazed when they were asking "Where's your inspector?" and I said, "I'm everybody. I'm the only guy here".'[44]

Whilst a small proportion of incidents led to prosecution, informal resolutions were just as likely to be found, with the village constable acting as a mediator in disputes between neighbours, tradespeople and creditors, and sometimes family members, including husband and wife. Examples from the occurrence books that were kept during the interwar period by the Ardersier constable reveal the role of the village constable in resolving conflict. In March 1923 an Inverness shopkeeper complained that a young domestic servant living on the officer's beat had fraudulently obtained clothing. When the constable visited the servant to investigate further, she claimed she had been unwell and gave him the money to take to Inverness, which was duly returned to the shopkeeper.[45] In 1933 he assisted a woman who had been away from home to work as a housekeeper but upon her return, 'found the door locked against her and could not get in although she knew her husband & family were inside'. The constable recorded that her husband had told him 'that his wife had left without saying where she was going, that he had managed without her while she was away, but that he was prepared to take her in'.[46] Over-boisterous street play by children and the proximity of village life sometimes led to further friction between adults. One father lodged a complaint at Ardersier police station that a woman in the village had called his 8-year-old son 'a low class filthy boy . . . of low class parents'. The woman denied the defamation and complained that the children had been creating a disturbance outside her home. The constable mounted watch outside her house that evening but no further incidents materialised and the friction seems to have abated.[47] Finally, disputes sometimes spilled over into threatening behaviour, with neighbours turning to the police constable for assistance without invoking the formal letter of the law. In September 1933 a male labourer alleged that another local man had 'threatened him with a spade' but that he 'would not lodge a complaint for prosecution but wanted [the man] warned'. The constable called on the man, warning him that if there was 'any further trouble he would be reported'.[48] These specific incidents are indicative of the trust that might be placed in a particular officer by ordinary villagers – labourers and domestic servants – to advise, assist and defuse conflictual situations.

Oral history interviews provide access to the kinds of informal intervention that are unlikely to have made it into the occurrence books at all:

> I had a situation one night where a guy threatened to shoot the whole family . . . I was on my own, it was an off-shore Island, accessible at low tide. I got there and the family was hiding behind a rock. And eventually the guy, who was rolling drunk, fell asleep and the lady said 'oh we'll have to get rid of that shot gun', the shot gun was lying beside him, I got rid of the shotgun and unloaded it and she said 'I wish I could destroy that shotgun' and I bent the barrel of the shotgun round the house, threw it in the sea and she went back home . . . That was using your discretion,

because I knew, fine, if I locked the guy up, the family weren't going to speak against him. I had no corroboration. I was the odd man out. So the best thing to do was to get rid of the shotgun. And I did.[49]

Whilst officers on the mainland could call on their 'neighbour' for assistance in serious cases where corroboration might be needed, the island constable had to draw on his own resources and make his own judgements. Informal solutions were crucial given there was little back-up, but their long-term effectiveness was grounded in the trust and respect that officers built up locally over time. The fine balancing that was required in the exercise of discretion in order to maintain police authority and legitimacy will be examined next. Trust had to be earned and could not be assumed.

Legitimacy and discretion

The popular memory of nineteenth-century policing was one of physical conflict rather than moral force in some areas of the Highlands and Islands. This was the legacy of police involvement in the forced eviction of tenants during the clearances and, subsequently, the Crofters' Wars of the 1880s when heavy-handed police involvement had reinforced assumptions that they were 'agents of the proprietorial class'.[50] To deal with the land disturbances in Skye, Inverness County Police had rapidly doubled in size between 1880 and 1883: from 40 to 94 officers (authorised strength).[51] As crofters continued to protest against landowners' actions in the Glendale area in 1883–4, permission was sought from the War Office to arm police officers with revolvers.[52] In 1884–5 and again in 1886, Sheriff Ivory led two military expeditions to Skye, involving gunboats of marines whose presence on or near the island was supposed to intimidate crofters (a tactic that was also used in relation to the land raid at the Park Deer Forest on Lewis in November 1887).[53] As crofters received some recognition and protection in the years after the Napier Commission, they shifted their energies into political campaigning, including the winning of parliamentary seats in 1886, and away from physical resistance; fears of unrest dissipated.[54]

Nevertheless, tensions over land and crofters' rights lingered on in the form of land raids in the Western Isles in the years after the First World War and, in 1948, on the Knoydart peninsula.[55] Settlements on Barra, South Uist, Skye and parts of Lewis were known by the police to be 'anti-police', 'anti-landlord' or 'anti-authority' across the twentieth century and stories were told of police officers in Barra 'being thrown over the pier for over-policing' in the 1960s.[56] Officers who served on Skye in the 1950s to 1970s were aware of the popular memory of conflict:

> There was always this Highland clearances . . . there's a wee bit of suspicion of authority. They sort of held back a bit until they really got to

> know you. You had to gain their confidence. But there was always this cloud.[57]
>
> There's always been an anti-authority in the island. I put it down to the fact, going back to the Highland clearances, the police and the Army were persecuting people. They were standing up for the landlords and not for the local people. I can understand, down through the generations that has continued.[58]

Contestation over land use and ownership was also apparent in attitudes towards poaching. Rural officers certainly cultivated contacts with estate factors and gamekeepers and their co-operation was viewed as an important resource. Large estates employed teams of river-watchers to prevent salmon poaching, but requested police back-up if events became confrontational or violent.[59] Yet officers in Sutherland and the Western Isles were aware that salmon poaching was not seen as a 'proper' crime in some settlements:

> It was an age-old tradition that they were poorer people and they saw the fish going past in their nets in the sea or in the lochs or in the rivers. They thought, and they'd [been] brought up by their forefathers before them, that they were entitled to the fish. Because who did they belong to?[60]

Some officers had considerable sympathy for this view: 'if someone complained that someone was working a monofilament net for catching cold iron – salmon – you'd have to do something. But it's not a thing you would chase after'.[61] Whilst gamekeepers expected police support, officers in the Western Isles were reluctant to be drawn in and keen to avoid situations in which they were viewed as unfair or partial:

> There was still this feeling that if the estate saw anything at all, they expected the police to drop everything and come out and deal with it. In the end we got the message through loud and clear to a couple of them, but it was up to them to catch the poachers and get the evidence and then hand it over to us . . . We had to show them that we were not going to be taking sides.[62]

Highland officers were employed to uphold the protection of property. Yet, by the mid-twentieth century, they understood (and sympathised with) the values of the community they policed (having grown up for the most part in the Highlands and Islands themselves):

> I see a lot wrong with putting a net across a river or a loch that somebody pays for, I don't agree with that. If you put a net out in the sea and you catch a couple of fish in the summer and take it home and feed your family,

> I see nothing wrong with that. I would never be chasing people in the sea for stuff like that.[63]

As one former officer who served in Caithness explained: 'it depends on the kind of poaching'.[64] Large-scale commercial poaching was undoubtedly viewed as a serious illegality. By the late 1950s the theft of red deer by highly organised groups of poachers using lorries and armed with sten guns was identified as a very significant problem in Ross and Cromarty. This was far removed from the romanticised figure of 'John MacNab' (the fictional character in John Buchan's novel) who 'shot and removed stags under the noses of stalkers'.[65] Thus organised poaching was clearly distinguished from the opportunist occasion in which a local individual took fish for personal use.

For similar reasons – relating to ideas of moral economy and customary right – it has been suggested that police officers (unlike customs officials) had been slow to intervene when islanders salvaged whisky from the wrecked *SS Politician* that ran aground off the coast of South Uist in 1941 (the series of events that inspired Compton Mackenzie's 1947 novel *Whisky Galore*). Writer Arthur Swinson, who interviewed local people in 1962, commented of one account relayed to him:

> the constable in this story was waiting to see if the whisky was found . . . if it was then he would have to bring a charge. But if it was not, even though the old lady had given herself away, he had no wish to take action.[66]

Clearly a local resident had admitted possession, but without corroboration there was no charge – and the officer was not inclined to search it out himself.

Ultimately, respect for the police could not be assumed but had to be won in rural areas and was contingent on the approach and behaviour of individual officers. On Skye newly posted officers and their families were expected to follow Sunday observance and were requested by neighbours not to hang out washing on the Sabbath (although it could be difficult to comply with this request in relation to police work). In the Western Isles generally knowledge of Gaelic acted as a form of cultural capital, assisting officers to break down initial suspicion when they were first posted. One officer, who had grown up on Harris and served on other islands, saw himself as 'fortunate' to be a 'fluent Gaelic speaker': 'they accepted you more . . . and helped you more . . . It's funny how that language . . . binds people'.[67] Another former officer argued that Gaelic was his 'main weapon'. When he first arrived at a new posting he made sure he visited a 'notorious pub', to warn them to abide by 10pm closing times:

> As I was going out the door I met one of the guys at the door and he said, 'Have you nothing better to do?' I said to him in Gaelic, 'I'm away now,

> you can go back in', because I knew that's what they were doing ... Of course they were absolutely flabbergasted because they'd been talking about me in Gaelic. All of a sudden I was the best guy. The next Friday I went down, the place closed well on time. They probably came back in again but they were very, very friendly. That cracked the ice because I'd always discovered that Gaelic was a brilliant thing to have in the island, even on the mainland.[68]

Social capital was important, too. Oral history interviews all show that police embeddedness within the settled community was facilitated by civil society connections, such as church attendance and membership of local societies, fishing and shooting associations, sports teams (including shinty) or through youth club volunteering.

Given that individual constables were often isolated from each other (particularly on the islands) with high levels of autonomy, it was the relationship that was forged though everyday encounters that was more important than formal structures of governance in building trust. One officer with wide experience of working in a one-man station commented:

> I found it very, very useful to get out into the street at busy times and stop and speak to folk and it was amazing what you would find out. They trusted you. You were one of them, they treated you as one of them ... I had very widespread beats, some were 20 odd miles one way or the other, eventually you got around there and you made contacts throughout the area. They would give you a phone number and that was it. I think the important thing was that first of all they trusted you – you had to get their trust first – and secondly you had to know who you could trust.[69]

Relationships with settled communities in the highland counties were interpersonal and individualised rather than professionalised – 'a lot to do with your personality' as one officer put it – but involved very high levels of discretion and responsibility.[70]

The exercise of 'discretion' was emphasised by many former officers interviewed as crucial in establishing this trust in rural areas. It had a particular meaning for them within a broader policing ethos and was a key component of their identity as 'a highland bobby'.[71] Bruce explained the approach that had been cultivated in Orkney, which he learnt from older officers and which contrasted with the 'city-based' style encountered at training school:

> One of the things ... [one of the] older officers always said was, 'Occasionally, when things go wrong, you have to caution and charge somebody with a crime' ... He said [that] when you went to the house to do that, 'If

you don't get offered a cup of tea afterwards and a scone or some baking, you haven't done your job properly.' He said, 'You can be a police officer but still manage to do it in such a manner that it doesn't cause offence, fear or dislike. If you do it properly, you can achieve both.'[72]

Former officers viewed the style of the 'highland bobby' as entailing persuasion and prevention – achieved through 'discretion and diplomacy' – rather than the 'firefighting' they associated with their city counterparts.[73] As one man who joined Sutherland County Police in the 1960s explained of his whole career:

> If you live in that kind of area, if you've got your book out all the time, booking people for everything, you get less and less information from the public . . . If you were over-zealous in your application of the law, then you would never get on right with the community, never. If you use common sense when you are dealing with the law – I'm not saying you let people off with crime [but] it's far better to give people a warning.[74]

He identified a careful balancing act ('common sense') that might involve acknowledging a likely problem but coming up with a preventive solution that was (at least in the interim) informal and enabled a negotiation around shared values. As Lawrence argued in relation to the example of drink driving: 'it's not about enforcing the law . . . it's also about keeping the peace . . . When do you take the [car] keys off somebody rather than [say] "Well it's an offence, I've got to charge him" . . .?'[75] These insights strongly suggest that the style of policing used within settled communities in rural areas was an important factor in the maintenance of low rates of reported crime.

Ultimately the diffusive and preventive style of policing that resulted from the exercise of discretion by individual officers created potential for significant strength in terms of the building of trust and legitimacy, but there was also potential for major weakness. Officers who were interviewed tended to reflect on their own best practice, often in comparison with a predecessor whom they had replaced. One interviewee recalled being posted to a one-man island station:

> The Chief Constable, I remember, personally asked me if I would consider going . . . he said 'two or three of the officers before you have, perhaps, become too integrated in the community'. He said 'I want you to go and put some respect back into the police uniform'.[76]

Another recalled that 'the guy who was there long before me was bone idle, he never did anything'; he found that the local hotel flagrantly ignored closing hours, which he had to reinstate upon arrival in order to rebuild 'respect' for the police in the area.[77] Drink (resort to alcohol) was a common problem underpinning this decline in effectiveness, acknowledged in relation to colleagues in several interviews.[78] One officer was promoted to an inspector's role in order to remedy previous deficiencies: 'The Chief Constable took me in and said . . . "I'm getting complaints from there regarding drink and not attending to duties that they should be attending to . . . I want you to go there and do a job for me."'[79] Lawrence described the problem of 'crossing that line' as follows:

> You had to go in so far but not too far in to maintain your place in the society . . . if you went into the local pubs in a heavy drinking area then you couldn't do your work . . . you couldn't hold your place in society and you'd be reported.[80]

Indeed, he hinted at the pressure on officers to behave in an exemplary manner given the scrutiny and constant surveillance of the 'community': 'you're always in the spotlight – it's as if you're under the microscope all the time in some of these smaller areas'.[81] Similarly a former officer in Caithness in the early 1950s commented on the 'tightrope' that he felt he walked:

> In a country station, everything you do is held up to scrutiny. You've got to be 100 per cent right all the time. You've got to be diplomatic; be careful what you say . . . Or you would lose face, you'd lose reputation.[82]

The policeman's authority amongst the settled community was derived from moral force, which had to be continually maintained. Within a relatively large geographical area trust in the police might rise and fall in line with the behaviour of one officer: 'If you start playing games and favouring one more than the other, it would spread like wildfire.'[83] Officers were expected to get to know the settled community, but not too well; a careful balancing of insider/outsider status was required for optimal efficiency as far as the police organisation was concerned. In Inverness-shire the necessity for an appropriate social distance was maintained through the principle of rotation to new stations every 4 to 6 years to prevent officers 'going native'.[84] As one officer put it, 'It took you a year to get to know the place and you were useful for the period, but at the end of the 5 years you probably weren't doing your job because you knew them too well.'[85]

In Shetland, Orkney and Caithness smaller distances were involved and officers were policing communities in which they had themselves grown up, or were a few miles down the road and in which they had relatives. From the perspective of the inspectorate of constabulary, based in Edinburgh, this was undesirable. In 1946 HMICS Sydney Kinnear had argued that Zetland

Constabulary should amalgamate with other forces to create a larger policing district precisely because 'The local members of the force are related through marriage etc to so many people that they cannot carry out their duties in an unbiased manner.'[86] Yet it was resisted at the local level. What highly localised policing meant from the perspective of the police officer was explained by Albert, who served in Caithness: 'We're a tribal society. We're all related or we all know each other. Among ourselves we speak quite a strong dialect. It was quite difficult for a southern officer to understand really.'[87] Being local, for him, acted as a further check on behaviour: 'if you arrested somebody, it wasn't the police that arrested them; it was that particular policeman who arrested them'. Although he had grown up inside the community, joining the police inevitably set him apart to some degree: 'If you're a policeman in the county . . . it's something like the minister. People treat you like there's something wrong with you . . . You join company [at social events] and there's silence, and then another subject is talked about'.[88]

'Discretion' was used as a vital tool in the rural context to enable an officer to both assert his authority and provide a conciliatory solution that necessitated future co-operation (elements in the creation of 'respect'). The use of informal resolution – advice, persuasion, warning, and occasionally turning a blind eye – was central to the 'gentle' policing style in small settlements. Nevertheless, interviews with former officers suggest that this approach, which aligned the values of the settled community (seen as law-abiding for the most part) with those of the state, was most compromised by the introduction of the drink driving limit and the roadside breathalyser in 1967. Given concerns about serious accidents and fatalities caused by drink driving, police forces adopted a zero tolerance policy. As one officer commented: 'Starting to breathalyse drunk-drivers: that was extremely unpopular, I suspect. It was never, that sort of information was never fed back to you [by local people], but you got inkling'.[89] This was a major shift from earlier approaches: 'At one time nobody ever reported a drunk-driver. In my early days it was just rife . . . but if you did somebody in the early days for it, you were a sod of a cop'.[90] The introduction of the breathalyser was described as dividing local opinion – between those who saw it as important for public safety and those who saw it as state interference – and testing the equivocal relationship between officers and settled population further at this point.

Given that village constables in 'one-man' stations were isolated and self-dependent, local people who served as special constables were well-regarded as an important resource: 'the eyes and ears' of policing who 'knew everybody' and 'knew all the relationships'.[91] This was in contrast to urban Glasgow where they were viewed negatively because they were 'not proper police'. Whilst there is little extant information about the occupations of special constables, it is significant that for Ross and Cromarty a third were recorded as gamekeepers during the First World War, since knowledge of local terrain was also important given fear of a 'hostile landing'.[92] Across the century, special constables in rural areas could be drawn upon to accompany a regular officer if corroboration was needed and to help in the event of serious accidents. At elections they performed regulatory duties at polling booths. On occasion, too, they might be used informally by community members as an intermediary, to pass on information to the police without doing so officially. Nevertheless, special constables and police officers alike had to be reticent and discrete about the role:

> We were . . . very aware not to land them in it too much with their neighbours and fellow islanders because that would have spoiled them as special constables . . . We were careful not to put them in difficult positions but still use their local knowledge and expertise.[93]

Regular officers were aware of local sentiment that viewed them as 'a spy in the camp' or as 'the other side' whilst respecting them highly as 'good solid upright people whose first priority was to ensure law and order and that things were done properly'.[94] Thus careful use of special constables was part of the balancing act between 'insider' and 'outsider' status that county officers negotiated on a daily basis.

Policing Migrant Communities

This chapter has demonstrated that trust and legitimacy had to be (constantly) won. Nevertheless, policing in the Highlands and Islands in the twentieth century can also be characterised – for the most part – as taking place on behalf of and in the interests of the settled population amongst whom a style of policing as diffusive, rooted in diplomacy, persuasion and moral force was cultivated. 'Trouble' tended to be associated with the arrival of itinerant 'outsiders', and in particular with different transient populations passing through or moving into an area. The settled population demonstrated prejudices, across the century, against nomadic groups including those labelled or 'othered' as 'tramps', 'hawkers', or 'tinkers'. The arrival of migrant male construction workers heralded the building of roads, aluminium smelters and hydro-electric schemes in the highlands in the first half of the twentieth century; these were followed by the influx of male labour to Dounreay Nuclear Power Development Establishment in Caithness (from 1954) and to the north sea oil industry (from 1964). Examining police responses to each of these groups in turn, the final part of this chapter will identify differing police styles and tactics to those used in relation to the settled population.

Vagrants

The establishment of county police forces in nineteenth-century Scotland was in large part a response to fears of vagrancy amongst a settled population reluctant to sustain the expense of accommodating the homeless poor, who had been displaced from the industrialising cities.[95] As Smale has argued in his study of Alfred List, the architect of policing in the Scottish Borders, the association of the vagrant with criminality was linked to weakness of character rather than poverty *per se* and it was used to expand the surveillance of this 'dangerous' group. Thus 'the border forces were formed with the single objective of providing surveillance of the vagrant, that great figure of fear and blame, with police stations positioned on the major vagrancy routes in and out of the counties'.[96] Hostile attitudes lingered on into the twentieth century across rural areas and were part of living memory in the northern counties as in the Borders. In the 1950s a church minister in Ardersier recorded that 'A hundred years ago "outsiders" or "incomers" were not welcome. Inhabitants not long since dead, could recall tramps being stoned out of the village.'[97]

Police officers across Scotland were required to conduct a bi-annual 'vagrancy census' from 1888 (when first introduced) up until the Second World War. This was a head count of all 'vagrants, beggars and migratory poor' (the official terminology) after full search of the local area had been made each June and December. Indeed, occurrence books demonstrate this was part of the cycle of duties of the village constable. In the summer months the homeless moved through the countryside (whilst wintering in towns in lodging houses) and it was in June that they were more populous. In Inverness-shire in June 1909, for example, 492 'vagrants' were recorded in public places compared to 273 in December.[98] Vagrancy and criminality continued to be closely linked through public discourse in the years before the Second World War (and the creation of the welfare state). In his annual report of 1909 (quoted at length in *The Scotsman* newspaper) HMICS Lieutenant-Colonel Ferguson complained of the 'number of tramps, vagrants, and professional beggars in Scotland . . . who beg and commit petty thefts and cause considerable damage by fires when they lie out about stack-yards and out-houses at night'. Airing his views on social policy, he expressed support for proposals (put forward in 1906 but never realised) to send all 'vagrants' to labour colonies. A high proportion of those listed as 'vagrant' were children – 36% of those passing through in Inverness-shire in 1909 – and he supported calls for them to be sent to residential industrial schools.[99]

In towns and cities, powers to prosecute for begging had long been in force (as a result of the 1862 Police Act as well as earlier local initiatives); the 1889 Local Government (Scotland) Act enabled county councils to introduce similar byelaws if they wished, whilst the similarly titled Act of 1908 made it compulsory.[100] In theory this intensified the criminalisation of 'vagrants' in the Edwardian Scottish countryside, although in practice officers tended to warn and move people on. Those who had been issued with a pedlar's certificate, which licensed them to trade goods as travelling sellers, were immune from prosecution (and classification or harassment as a 'vagrant') if they were genuinely selling wares. Nevertheless, there was a tendency to elide 'hawkers' with 'tramps' as suspicious and predatory, and to scapegoat them as thieves and arsonists within a broader popular culture. This is demonstrated through examination of police station occurrence books from the first half of the twentieth century. For example, after a haystack was destroyed by fire near Ardersier in March 1923 it was recorded that there was no trace of 'tramps or suspicious persons having been about'; when clothes were stolen from a washing line in November suspicion fell on 'a man of the hawker stamp' who had been asking if he could borrow old clothes for his wife.[101] The police constable stationed at Rhiconich in Sutherland received a call from a merchant in a neighbouring village in July 1936 'about two tramps who were causing an annoyance to his son'. Characteristically, whilst no official complaint was lodged or charge pressed they were warned and told to leave the district the next morning.[102]

The language of social identity used in police records drew directly from the wider social classification systems used by the state and from specific local cultures and fears of 'the outsider'. Whilst individuals were conventionally described in terms of occupation and place of residence or origin, occurrence books also referred to 'two young men tinkers [who were] . . . married tinsmiths . . . presently of no fixed abode' (1903); 'a tramp labourer of no fixed residence' (1913); 'a man of the hawker stamp' (1923); 'a man of the tinker class' (1939); and 'persons of the tramp class' (1963).[103] The label of 'tinker' or 'hawker' – like that of 'tramp' – was not simply an occupational category; it was used as a broader ethnographic and criminological signifier that was concerned with social and moral status.

Scottish Gypsy/Travellers

In the twenty-first century Gypsy/Travellers have been accorded legal protection by the Scottish Government as an ethnic group under equalities legislation.[104] The term 'tinker' (now pejorative) was used very widely in the first half of the twentieth-century to refer to Scottish Travellers: those who were often Gaelic speakers, made a living as tinsmiths and traders in metal goods, and who shared 'a strong sense of kinship based on close family ties', regarding themselves as 'distinct from gypsies or other itinerant groups'.[105] Some autobiographical accounts affirm that they were treated with respect by the settled population, with whom they shared similar values: 'I've taken a peat or two, I've even taken a salmon or two, for the pot, but the Travelling people here in

Scotland were always very law-abiding, very religious, very strict, they go on well with the local people.'[106] As in other accounts, poaching (like taking turfs) was presented not as 'proper crime' but as customary right; shared moral values with settled highlanders are emphasised. Some Travellers saw themselves as well-regarded for performing an important economic role bringing goods into an area: 'Most people liked us – they liked us coming round – we were useful, we were company, we were honest'.[107]

Nevertheless, a 1918 Departmental Committee, set up to investigate the conditions in which they were living in Scotland and to recommend how their plight might be improved, stated that 'tinkers' were 'very much a class apart'. In the words of an Argyllshire poorhouse official, 'the community seems to look upon the tinker as something beneath it'.[108] In contrast, police officers were described as playing a supportive role, despite dealing with 'the tinker class' frequently because of reports of drunkenness: 'the police, we are told, are looked upon by them as their best friends, and when in any difficulty they apply to the policeman for help, which is always given and appears to be appreciated'.[109] The law made it an offence to camp without permission, although Travelling people claimed 'customary rights' to camp on common ground. In the years after the First World War a harder approach emerged on the part of landlords and settled communities.[110] For John Stewart, who was born in 1910, 'the real tinker traveller . . . [would] shift to any place where he could put his camp up and no have a dose o keepers, policemen, farmers and gentlemen comin down shoutin at him [sic]'.[111] Police occurrence books, read alongside other documentary evidence, suggest that those labelled 'tinkers', like Gypsy/Travellers elsewhere, were increasingly accorded 'little legitimacy in rural space' and treated as of 'pariah status'.[112] There are hints, too, that police officers sometimes acted as mediators, balancing the expectations of the settled that 'tinkers' should be moved on immediately against the wellbeing of Travelling people, although their actions were limited. On Skye in 1923 the Dunvegan police constable received reports from a crofter that 'tinkers' were camped on common grazing and 'that as he had a quantity of peat in the vicinity of said camps, he wished the tinkers removed by the police'. The group (nine adults and ten children) were warned by the officer and they agreed to move on when the stormy weather had cleared, suggesting that a compromise solution was reached.[113]

A 1936 report on the problem of 'vagrancy' in Scotland commented that the 'tinker' population faced 'an increasing disinclination on the part of landlords and factors to afford permission to camp on their ground . . . the consequence is that tinkers are being driven from place to place, even from county to county.' A crucial difficulty was that (under the 1908 Children Act) the state required all school-age children to be in attendance for a minimum of 200 days per year otherwise parents would be prosecuted and families separated.

In order to meet this requirement, stability was needed in the form of accommodation or a place to camp. The 1936 report continued:

> We learn that police officers, inspectors or poor, and others are repeatedly appealed to by distressed tinker parents, almost at their wits' end, unable, on the one hand to get houses or permission to camp, and on the other, dreading the consequence of failing to send their children to school as laid down by the Act.[114]

To counteract these acute fears, the Church of Scotland's Mission Committee experimented with a scheme of 'permit camps' in Perthshire, which enabled them to settle in one place for 6 months, allowing children (and parents) to fulfil the school attendance requirement.[115] Thus interwar police officers were in an ambivalent position, mediating between the needs and very real fears of Travelling people seeking to comply with school attendance law and the demands of the settled, who claimed property rights.

In the post-war years, the Scottish Travelling People were presented as a fading group, although the work of the folklorist Hamish Henderson in collecting story and song accorded them very significant cultural recognition. Evidence suggests that Travellers were increasingly stigmatised as they struggled to adapt economically – in an era associated with a welfare state (assumed to alleviate poverty) and growing consumerism (which meant their goods were no longer wanted). Whilst Caithness County Council aimed to accommodate them in social housing in the late 1950s, the local press highlighted the 'prejudice' of their neighbours and the 'problem of integration'.[116] One Inverness-shire church minister wrote in 1965 of social attitudes in his parish: 'The owners of "basket" caravans and dealers in floorcloth were frequent summer visitors . . . [but] the few tinkers who remain have degenerated into beggars, with a decreasing number of housewives having compassion upon them'.[117] Duncan Williamson's memoirs recall encounters with the 'polis' in which he and others were told to move on because of complaints made at the station about 'begging'.[118] Similarly, Sheila Stewart's memoirs highlight the bullying and prejudice she experienced as a child in Perthshire in the late 1940s. She recalls the song 'It's a hard life being a traveller', sung by her mother Belle Stewart, which described Travellers setting up camp to earn money from fruit-picking: 'but it was very hard to keep them there / When the policemen said to go'.[119] Occurrence books for some areas of Inverness-shire in the 1950s show that 'tinkers' who were known to be scrap-metal dealers were routinely visited and targeted by police in the search for stolen goods as notions of a 'traditional' way of life were further eroded.

Police officers undoubtedly acted to reinforce prejudices (and persecution through school attendance laws), but there are also hints from a range of post-war sources that some constables continued to mediate between the distrust of the settled population and Travelling people, recognising the poverty and adversity of the latter. Sheila Stewart recounts a story in which a 'policeman' intervened in a dispute in a public house to assist a Traveller who had only a piece of leather to pay for his beer: '"Now," said the policeman, "I will give you one of my half crowns and I'll keep this one, and that's the argument finished".'[120] One former police officer who served in Caithness in the 1950s spoke with pride of learning 'tinkers' cant', and befriending and assisting Travellers – 'we'd fill in forms for them and help them that way' – and of giving a framed photograph of a deceased son to a grieving mother after a fatal car accident.[121] Another spoke of lending small amounts of money (always paid back) to a 'wife' who was part of 'a large tinker community'.[122] Travellers' 'cant' referred to the police as 'the hornies', and there was recognition (on both sides) that they were likely to be warned if not arrested for drinking or fighting.[123] Another former officer, who joined Caithness police in the late 1940s having served in the marines during the war, distinguished between the majority of Travelling people whom he viewed as 'kind-hearted as could be' and whom were treated with respect – 'If I was passing in the car I would stop, and go and sit in their tent with them and have a yarn, you see' – and the few individuals whose bad behaviour through drink was seen as a nuisance. Yet he went on to describe the use of rough justice and physical intimidation in relation to one particular man who was persistently arrested and imprisoned for being drunk and disorderly across a period of many years:

> I would take a stick to him, and I would kick his backside and put him down on the pavement and make him pray, that kind of thing, with my feet on his fingers; oh, I had no mercy with him. But, by gee, he respected it, you see, and of course it was unknown to anybody; he never told people that.[124]

This account – and the silent complicity it suggests – is shocking in the context of twenty-first century policing, but its frankness reveals the circumstances under which aggressive policing tactics might be used in more rural areas in the years after the Second World War.

Construction work and migrant labour

The industrial development of the highlands in the twentieth century brought another transient population: migrant male labourers. During the building of the railways in the Scottish Borders in the 1840s tensions between police and gangs of navvies (a large proportion of whom were from Ireland) had erupted into violence and disturbance, leading to increasingly 'robust' policing tactics, and the stigmatisation of 'navvies' as a group (and Irish navvies in particular).[125] Into the twentieth century manual labourers were associated with 'trouble' by many within the settled community. First published in 1913, Patrick MacGill's semi-autobiographical novel *Children of the Dead End* described the outcast status of the Irish 'navvy' in rural Scotland: 'The children hide behind their mother's petticoats when they see us coming, frightened to death of the awful navvy man who carries away naughty children'.[126] Part of the prejudice was a result of his need to resort to begging between jobs, eliding him with the 'tramp': 'A few gave me some food, some cursed me from their doors, and a great number mocked me as I passed . . . Others would say "Get out o' our sight, we we'll take tell the policeman about you . . ."'[127]. MacGill's protagonist 'Dermod' undertakes periods of casual work digging potatoes on the farms of Argyllshire, in the building of the railways around Glasgow, and then in the construction of the vast aluminium smelting plant and hydro-electric dam at Kinlochleven (1905–9), which has been described as the 'last construction project built by the hard labour of itinerant Irish navvies unassisted by machinery'.[128] Construction workers slept in sub-standard dormitory-style huts, in which beds were shared between day- and night-shift workers (and thus constantly occupied). Spare money was spent on alcohol and gambling come pay-day, which was a moment of release from the toil and sheer danger of construction, leading to flare-ups amongst a hard-drinking minority who acquired a local reputation for violence.[129] The policing of Kinlochleven itself was split between Inverness-shire and Argyllshire constabularies, with the former responsible for the Kinlochmore area (to the north of the river Leven) and the latter for Kinlochbeg (south of the river), thus drawing in both constabularies.

In the years 1924–43 the British Aluminium Company was engaged in further industrial construction – namely the 'Lochaber Project' slightly further north at Fort William – bringing 3,000 working men into the area at its height.[130] At the same time there was a new surge of road-building projects, associated with the rise of motor traffic, including the reconstruction of the Inverness-Perth road and the Glasgow-Fort William road, drawing in further migrant labour, whilst the population of Kinlochleven continued to grow. A small increase (of five) in the number of officers employed by Inverness County Police was approved by the Secretary of State, and district beats within the Fort William Division that had been amalgamated in the early 1920s were reinstated. The Chief Constable argued that 'such public works . . . attract . . . a large number of people . . . amongst them many of the tramp and criminal classes' (camp followers who sought to benefit indirectly from the earnings of construction workers) as well as genuine labourers looking for work.[131] Tensions between community expectations and policing priorities – as well as the fear of the 'outsider' and 'new' populations – are highlighted in a controversy surrounding the reassignment of a village police constable in 1927. Sixty residents of Onich and North

Ballachulish (including hoteliers, clergy, storeholders and the school mistress) signed a petition to the Scottish Secretary complaining that they were 'not being afforded the police protection we are entitled to'.[132] They argued that 'the fact that there is no resident police constable soon becomes known amongst the tramp fraternity', that there had been 'a considerable increase in the number of vagrants etc passing through this district', and that, as a result, a large house had been broken into in the absence of its owners.[133] The Chief Constable of Inverness-shire told the Scottish Secretary that the beat itself had not changed and Onich was still visited three times a week; the officer had been moved to Kinlochmore precisely because of an influx of population there, and the 'trivial' cases referred to by petitioners were just as likely to have happened if he had been resident. The residents' campaign highlights expectations that the village constable should be at the centre of the settled community, to guarantee security of property and home from external threat.[134]

Interviews with former officers who served in the northern counties in the 1950s to 1970s make it clear that conditions in the labour camps of this era (with the further expansion of hydro-electric schemes and, subsequently, the development of the nuclear and oil industries) had not changed much since MacGill's day. A very different style of policing was reserved for the male workforce – across a range of construction projects – in comparison to the settled population:

> We were hit out of the blue by hundreds and hundreds of workers who didn't necessarily behave themselves at night . . . there were lock-ups, nine or ten people locked up every night . . . it was just a huge shock in everybody's system when the industry [aluminium] came.[135]

> I remember the first crowd of Irish labourers who arrived at the railway station to start work there [Dounreay], the very first. We went up and looked at them. My word, what a tough-looking crowd they were. Very nice blokes but mercy, they were tough. They were taken out there and I remember their first pay-day. A whole mob of them in the town in their working clothes, and they in with money and they were . . . well, the cells were full.[136]

> They'd fight over anything; fight in the billets or fight, even in the bar . . . it was quite rough, yes at times . . . It was the only time I ever drew my baton in thirty years . . .[137]

> So I had two types of policing. I had these very tough men, who lived a very sparse and very hard existence building these things on the one hand. I had a local, domestic population, who were quite couthy and quite gentle on the other hand. So I found very quickly that I really had to vary how I did my job with each.[138]

The interviews clarify that a 'gentle' and diffusive approach was used with the settled population and that differing tactics involving 'toughness' were needed with the male labour force.

Physical force and the 'firefighting' style of policing was inevitably called upon to deal with some of the situations in the camps (hence the comments 'I drew my baton' and 'the cells were full'). Indeed, while Sutherland was noted for its very low crime rates, it was anomalous amongst Scottish police districts in combining this trend with the highest rate for violence against the person across the whole of Scotland in 1954–5. Criminologists Shields and Duncan found this rate was almost entirely a result of assaults on police officers 'due to the presence of migratory workers engaged in hydro-electric schemes in this area'.[139] Bruce, who served on Orkney, felt that 'the Orkney public really liked their police and were very proud of them and very supportive'. This contrasted with the workers who were brought in to construct the oil terminal on Flotta in the mid-1970s whom he sensed had 'a common bond against everything':

> Sometimes when I was on the island doing enquiries, it would be lunchtime, so the security man would take me to the canteen . . . You would go in, 1,000 people all eating. You would come in the door and it was like the piano player stopped playing at the saloon. The place just went silent. Then some wag would start singing the *Z Cars* tune . . . It was extremely intimidating especially for a young fellow. It taught me very early on how to handle in my own mind that amount of resentment. It's like a wall coming towards you; you can almost touch it, it's so solid.[140]

The intensive and crowded all-male environments in which workers, removed from home and family, found themselves, created very different challenges for officers to those associated with the settled population. 'Toughness' of character was needed to counter the hyper-masculine culture, and this had to be grounded in physical presence: 'It was them against us; it was a real division. Because I was on my own, the uniform I put on became a uniform of armour.'[141]

Nevertheless, officers were very aware that non-confrontational tactics were still very likely to be necessary:

> At worst it would be a slight scuffle but that was the worst it ever got. That wasn't luck; that was good judgement. That was a lot of thought on my part, and a quick learning curve of diplomacy and that the tongue is far mightier than anything else. The last thing that I could afford to do would be to encourage any sort of physical backlash because I had no back-up.[142]

These comments resonate with Norman Morrison's much earlier observations of his work amongst the navvies at Kinlochleven in the years 1913–16:

> I had often to go single-handed in the small hours of the morning to their shacks in order to quell fights and disturbances when, literally, skin and hair were flying. The disturbances often looked ugly and threatening and would have, if not carefully and delicately handled, led to riot and bloodshed . . . On the spur of the moment I had to size up my man and decide whether I should approach him with a humorous and nonchalant remark, or whether at once I should take up a firm, stern attitude.[143]

Thus police narratives demonstrate strong continuities across the twentieth century in highlighting the judgements, tactics and styles of policing that were used to deal with migrant workers; whilst these might be broadly characterised as 'tough' in contrast with the 'gentle' tactics used for the settled population, both might entail high levels of diplomacy in situations where individual rural officers were acting on their own.

Morrison – who had himself read *Children of the Dead End* – was a strong believer in social progress, education and the potential for reform, and his memoirs depict his orientation in policing as one of social service.[144] For him the navvies were 'humane, honourable, conscientious and kind-hearted' despite being 'troublesome when under the influence of liquor'.[145] Indeed, MacGill's novel recorded occasional assistance from police officers – 'the man put his hand in his pocket and took out a sixpence which he handed to me' (in this case in an urban area) – that were more tolerant than that of the general population.[146] This chimes, too, with accounts of the practical help that police officers in northern rural areas provided for Indian pedlars travelling from Glasgow in the 1930s. Testimonies collected by Bashir Maan suggest that, when the prejudices of 'local people' who were "scared of us dark strangers"' made it difficult to find lodgings, they would go to 'the local police station' where the police 'were always very helpful and obliged' by 'finding them lodgings or accommodating them in the "cells"' (if no other option).[147]

Military populations and wartime

Finally, the conditions of wartime created not only increased movement of populations but also an intensification of its regulation and surveillance into which the police were drawn under the Defence of the Realm Acts. Indeed, in the Second World War the area north-west of the Great Glen became a 'protected area' to which unauthorised access was prohibited.[148] A large number of military personnel were stationed in the Highlands, most significantly on Orkney where the British naval fleet was based during both wars. Whilst those in the armed forces came under the jurisdiction of military police, civilian officers undertook inquiries relating to those absent without leave or evading conscription altogether. Police work entailed the monitoring of any 'suspicious' persons (who might be spies, fifth columnists, prisoners of war, draft dodgers or deserters), as occurrence books attest. In the First World War, for example, those on the 'tramp' as 'vagrants' were 'met and challenged' regarding their identity; in some cases they were searched and, if of military service age, required to produce certificates to show they were unfit.[149] Wealthy visitors to the area's large country houses (as well as their servants) were kept under observation if assumed to be 'enemy aliens'.[150]

Yet the presence of servicemen – as well as visiting seafaring populations (merchant navy and trawlermen from Scandinavia in Kirkwall and Lerwick) – was also a matter of significant continuity across the century given permanent military bases. Wartime can thus be seen as an accentuation rather than a disruption to police routine. Whilst not viewed pejoratively as lower status (given the widespread experience of military service and the status of the Scottish regiments) soldiers were, nevertheless, more likely than the settled population to be associated with minor offending. The example of Ardersier is a useful one to explore here, given its two-mile proximity to Fort George barracks, which formed part of the village constable's beat and which, until 1960, acted as the Highland Brigade Depot, where all recruits to Highland regiments received their preliminary training (and were, thus, constantly passing through).[151] The sampling of occurrence books for 1923 and 1933 (as for 1943) shows that most reports of criminal offences – in the main, incidents of theft and dangerous driving – were linked with depot soldiers. Thefts were either reported to have taken place at the barracks itself – for example, when a set of field-glasses went missing from the musketry store (May 1923), a diary and money were taken from a lieutenant's dressing chest (March 1933), and a gold watch disappeared from the officers' mess (November 1933) – or in the village of Ardersier, particularly the theft of bicycles.[152] When it came to the disciplining of soldiers for drunkenness or disorderly behaviour, the local constable worked with the military police. Ardersier police cells were rarely used in 1923 other than for soldiers when, across a number of weekends in June, men 'of the Gordon Highlanders were confined in the cells here for drunkenness by the military police'. In September the Ardersier constable was obliged to phone the 'garrison police' for assistance because soldiers were creating a disturbance in the village, and he was required to give evidence at Fort George when the case was heard by the military authorities.[153] There is nothing to suggest that the relationship between the village constable and military police was other than amicable, and the occurrence books record the close communication between these parties and frequent visits to Fort George as part of the village constable's daily duties.

As studies by Marika Sherwood and David Smale have shown, prejudice against male migrant labour in rural Scotland more generally was enhanced in wartime in relation to black and minority ethnic populations.[154] This was starkly evident in relation to the British Honduran Forestry Unit camped near Duns in the Scottish Borders. Coverage of the men's arrival in the pages of *The Scotsman* in September 1941 used racist tropes to present them as an exotic 'other'.[155] A moral panic quickly developed locally regarding criminality, immorality and miscegenation (relationships between white women and men of colour), leading to police raids on the camp, increased hostility between the police and the men of the unit, and their return home in 1943. As one official put it, there was 'no real evidence' that the unit behaved 'in a worse way' than other wartime lumberjack crews (such as the Newfoundland Overseas Forestry Unit, based in Inverness-shire), but the fact that they were men of colour meant 'their immoralities' got 'more publicity', were viewed as 'more shocking', and the police felt pressurised by local opinion to act.[156] In this incident racism added a further dynamic to the labelling of the migrant male labour force as 'outsiders'.

Conclusions

This chapter has identified deep continuities across much of the twentieth century – and up until at least the 1960s – in the tempo and spatial configuration of rural policing in the Highlands and Islands, which had concomitant effects on policing styles. Officers were embedded within village communities and policing tended to take place on behalf of the settled population whose values they often (but not always) shared. They were involved in a careful balancing of their own insider/outsider status, and the drawing of this line affected whose interests were represented. In rural counties just as in complex urban environments, 'communities' were multiple and heterogeneous. Some officers attempted to dilute the demands of the settled majority with regards to Travellers, whilst others refused to take sides in disputes between landowners and crofters. Police legitimacy could not be assumed (and there were legacies of conflict in some areas) but was grounded in the ability of individual officers to command and retain respect. High levels of autonomy – associated with their position as generalists – meant that relationships with the settled population were personalised and styles of policing were based on moral force, diplomacy and gentle persuasion. When it came to the policing of the transient male labour force, the performance of physical 'toughness' became an important strategy, although diplomatic skills were also a requisite given lack of back-up.

It is a truism that the practice of effective policing is always context specific, since it is a response to a particular confluence of demographic, political, social and cultural factors. Nevertheless, this chapter also suggests that the delivery of policing in rural areas – in Scotland and, inevitably, other parts of Great Britain – was profoundly shaped by a set of commonalities related to its political economy and organisation. Island policing was in many regards simply an accentuation of patterns common elsewhere. Technologies were harnessed to improve communications across the twentieth century, but their introduction was slow and their effects even more gradual for small island constabularies than in other rural areas. In 1960 the entire motor fleet owned by Zetland police authority consisted of just one car; Orkney had two police vans, a scooter and motorbike; neither constabulary was using police wireless communication as yet.[157] A specifically Scottish dimension can be identified in the legal requirement for corroboration, which was one of the factors that led to a reliance on informal resolution in the case of single-man stations (although working with 'partners' and special constables was one way round the issue).

Significant technological and social change – combined with wider structural change within policing itself – led to shifts in the geography of policing and reconfiguration of the police-community relationship in the last third of the twentieth century. The older focus on settlements (as nodes of communication through which individual officers were embedded within networks and localities) was partially replaced with a focus on the policing of highways as vectors for movement of traffic (and indeed criminality). The opening up of tourism from the 1960s and attempts to encourage resettlement led to a more fluid population becoming a new norm in the Highlands and Islands (rather than the divide between settled and transient communities which has been highlighted here). Aspects of this transformation were shared with other parts of the UK. Malcolm Young's ethnographic work on a more rural force (West Mercia) in England has similarly charted the replacement of 'local' policing by 'local' officers with reactive 'firefighting' policing delivered from great distances, as well as the central imposition of 'community' initiatives in place of the informal ties and use of discretion that formerly characterised the work of the village constable.[158] Yet any nostalgia for a former era of policing needs to be offset by a recognition of aspects of low morale amongst officers in the first half of the twentieth century on account of low pay and sub-standard accommodation. Moreover, there were few opportunities for promotion in the counties (relative to city forces) given the small number of personnel employed, and little in the way of reward for long service other than the police pension. Furthermore, whilst high levels of autonomy and discretion could be productive, leading to the creation of deep qualitative relationships, these were highly dependent on the individual and could lead to ineffective policing (from the perspectives of both the police authority and the local community) given the remoteness of many rural police stations.

The consolidation of the county constabularies of the Highlands and Islands into the far larger (regional) police district of Northern Constabulary in 1975 not only made greater specialisation and professionalisation possible but, concomitantly, created career development opportunities that made policing a more attractive occupation. At the same time, within the new Northern Constabulary, the role of the 'village constable' continued much as previously into the late twentieth century, particularly in some of the remote island settlements. 'Local' police officers continued to be generalists (often covering large distances) but were now more supported by a range of specialist units to provide technical back-up. Interviews with former police officers who served in the Highland and Island areas that became Northern Constabulary presented its creation as optimising the benefits of both discretionary policing and professionalisation (in combining both together).[159] These high levels of satisfaction were a result of improved resources (and working conditions) that in part resulted from economies of scale that made policing more resilient. In contrast, rural officers (in Ayrshire, Lanarkshire and Argyllshire) who became part of the new Strathclyde Police after 1975, spoke instead of a negative experience in which the bureaucratic model that had been crafted in Glasgow City was effectively rolled out everywhere.

The idea of village policing proved to be remarkably long-lived in the Highlands and Islands. Interviews conducted by researchers in 2010–12 with current Northern Constabulary officers (on the cusp of the creation of Police Scotland) demonstrated the continuation of many of the key features we have described here: the importance of negotiating consent with communities; of finding informal resolutions and a 'long-lasting fix' rather than delivering '"by the book" policing'; of acting as a mediator rather than law enforcer; of shouldering high levels of responsibility in which they 'routinely take on the work of higher ranks and specialist units'; and of the experience of being constantly on call.[160] Whilst some of the village police stations that are referred to in this chapter – including Ardersier, Beauly and Bettyhill – were closed in 2011, over 40 per cent of the police stations in the Highlands and Islands were still staffed by a single officer in 2013.

Notes

1. The Highlands and Islands were defined as 'remote rural' by the Scottish Household Survey: 6-fold urban rural classification (2003) because they were constituted of settlements of less than 3,000 people, with a drive time of over 30 minutes to a settlement of 10,000 or more (with the exception of areas around Fort William and Inverness).
2. These areas came under Northern Constabulary from 1975 until 2013 (which also incorporated parts of Argyllshire) and now constitute the Highland and Islands Division of Police Scotland. Thus the terms 'northern counties' and 'Highlands and Islands' are used here to denote an administrative region. Caithness amalgamated with Orkney and Zetland constabularies in 1969 to form the first (or 'old') Northern Constabulary, to which others were added in 1975.

3. Inverness County Police was more commonly referred to as Inverness-shire Constabulary in the nineteenth and earlier twentieth centuries. We use the term County Police in this volume to enable ease of comparison throughout between city, burgh and county constabularies or forces. This applies, similarly, to Caithness Constabulary (here Caithness County Police) and Sutherland Constabulary (here Sutherland County Police).
4. PP, *HMICS AR*, 1900, Cd. 548. These figures were static until 1950 (whilst population of the Highlands and Islands was in decline). By 1960 the authorised establishment of Inverness-shire was 91 (including four women) and for Sutherland was 27 (one woman): *HMICS AR*, 1960, Cmnd. 1390.
5. HAS, R91/B/6/2 Sutherland Police Committee, minutes, 14 October 1947.
6. Shields and Duncan, *State of Crime*, 45.
7. Personnel records exist for all officers recruited to Inverness (N=233) and Caithness (N=92) county constabularies (HAS, R91/D8 and HAS, R91/E/8). For Shetland/Zetland (N=20) and Orkney (N=23), records (also in HAS, R91/E/8) are sparse before 1938 when they came within the Police Act. The authorised strength of Zetland was 11 in 1945, and 16 in 1957; for Orkney it was 12 in 1945, and 20 in 1960; for Caithness it was 24 in 1945, and 39 in 1960. PP, *HMICS AR*s: 1945, Cmd. 6936 and 1960, Cmnd. 1390.
8. HAS, Caithness, R91/E/8, Personnel files. Nevertheless, officers who had joined prior to amalgamation could not be forced to move outside of their original district under the terms of the 1967 Police (Scotland) Act.
9. Information about religion is not systematically recorded in personnel records for Caithness, Orkney and Shetland, but in all cases where given was Protestant.
10. Whilst a number of recruits came from Harris and Lewis across the period there were none from Barra or Benbecula and only one (who was also Catholic) from South Uist, reinforcing perceptions of these areas as 'anti-police' (although a small number joined Glasgow City Police at the end of the Second World War).
11. *GH*, 7 June 1965; *The Guardian*, 7 June 1965; *New York Times*, 7 June 1965.
12. PP, *HMICS AR*, 1900, Cd. 548, vii.
13. HAS, R91/D/9/10/6 letter, Beauly constable to CC, 2 July 1947.
14. PP, *HMICS AR*, 1926, Cmd. 2901; HAS, R91/B/6/1.
15. HAS, R91/B/6/1.
16. HAS, R91/D/9/10/6.
17. PP, *HMICS AR*, 1946, Cmd. 7247. On the poor standard of police houses in England see Weinberger, *Best Police*, 106.
18. NRS, HH55/1819.
19. HAS, R91/D/9/10/6, and R91/D/9/10/2.
20. PP, *HMICS AR*, 1914, CD. 7849.
21. HAS, R91/D/9/19/A/9.
22. Weinberger, *Best Police*, 110–11.
23. Interview with Jack (pseudonym) conducted by Davidson.
24. Interview with Frederick (pseudonym), conducted by Davidson.
25. Interview with Paul (pseudonym), conducted by Davidson.
26. HAS, R91/D/D/5/3/9.

27. For example, HAS, R91/D/B/5/1/4, Ardersier, 25 October 1923; R91/D/D/5/3/11, Dunvegan, 12 May and 14 May 1953; R91/D/B/5/2/28 Beauly, 19 February 1969.
28. HAS, R91/D/B/5/1/9, Ardersier, 22, 14, 31 August and 1 September 1933; R91/D/D/5/3/11, Dunvegan 10, 11 and 12 August 1953.
29. HAS, R91/D/D/5/3/6 and R91/D/D/5/3/15.
30. Interview with Graeme (pseudonym), conducted by Davidson.
31. HAS, R91/D/B/5/2/4a, Beauly (Tomnacross) station, 1904.
32. HAS, R91/D/B/5/1/4, Ardersier 30 and 31 April 1923.
33. HAS, R91/D/B/5/2/28, Beauly, 1969; HAS, R91/D/B/5/1/37, Ardersier, 1970.
34. In 1928 the mode average 'district' beat in Inverness-shire was 14 miles, the longest 28 miles and the shortest 9 miles, See NRS, HH55/313, Inverness-shire, inspection report, 1928.
35. Morrison, *My Story*, 38.
36. Interview with Graeme.
37. HAS, R91/D/B/5/2/4a.
38. Interview with Frederick (pseudonym), conducted by Davidson.
39. Interview with Terence (pseudonym), conducted by Davidson; interview with Paul.
40. Interview with Bernard (pseudonym), conducted by Davidson.
41. HAS, R91/D/B/5/2/15.
42. HAS, R91/D/B/5/2/5.
43. Interview with Frederick (pseudonym), conducted by Davidson
44. Interview with Gavin (pseudonym), conducted by Davidson.
45. HAS, R91/D/B/5/1/4.
46. HAS, R91/D/B/5/1/9, 12 April 1933.
47. Ibid., 30 May and 1 June 1933.
48. Ibid., 7 September 1933.
49. Interview with Frederick (pseudonym), conducted by Davidson.
50. Cameron, 'Internal policing', 439; Carson, 'Policing the periphery', Part II.
51. PP, *HMICS AR*, 1883, 154. In 1890 authorised strength was reduced to 65.
52. *Scotsman*, 10 December 1884.
53. Cameron, 'Internal policing', 450.
54. Cameron, *Land for the People*.
55. Cameron, 'Seven men'.
56. Interview with Roy (pseudonym), conducted by Davidson; interview with Lawrence (pseudonym), conducted by Davidson.
57. Interview with Jack.
58. Interview with Gavin.
59. Interview with Terence.
60. Interview with Lawrence.
61. Interview with Albert (pseudonym), conducted by Davidson.
62. Interview with Gavin.
63. Ibid.
64. Interview with Albert.
65. PP, *Hansard* [HL], 18 August 1958, col. 581, Lord Mansfield.
66. Swinson, *Scotch*, 115.

67. Interview with Lawrence.
68. Interview with Gavin.
69. Interview with Frederick (pseudonym), conducted by Davidson.
70. Interview with Paul.
71. Interview with Graeme.
72. Interview with Bruce (pseudonym), conducted by Davidson.
73. Ibid.
74. Interview with Graeme.
75. Interview with Lawrence.
76. Interview with Bruce.
77. Interview with Paul.
78. Ibid., and interview with Terence.
79. Interview with Jack.
80. Interview with Lawrence.
81. Ibid.
82. Interview with Albert.
83. Interview with Terence.
84. Interview with Stanley (pseudonym), conducted by Davidson.
85. Interview with Frederick.
86. NRS, HH55/940, Zetland, inspection report, 14 November 1946.
87. Interview with Albert.
88. Ibid.
89. Interview with Bruce.
90. Interview with Graeme.
91. Interviews with Bruce and Bernard.
92. HAS, R91/A/8/2, refers to 345 police 'Guides and Special Constables' in Ross and Cromarty.
93. Interview with Bruce.
94. Interview with Paul.
95. Carson and Idzikowska, 'Social production', 286–8.
96. Smale, 'Alfred John List', 53–4.
97. Barron, *County of Inverness*, 3–4.
98. PP, *HMICS AR*, 1909, Cd. 5085.
99. Ibid., 5; *Scotsman*, 19 April 1910.
100. PP, *Report of the Departmental Committee on Vagrancy in Scotland*, 1936, Cmd. 5194, 55–6.
101. HAS, R91/D/B/5/1/4, 3 March and 28 November 1923.
102. HAS, R91/b/5/15/2, 1 July 1936.
103. HAS, R91/D/C/5/3/51, Fort William, 8 November 1903; R91/D/C/5/3/63, Fort William, 11 February 1913; R91/D/B/5/1/4, Ardersier, 28 November 1923; R91/D/B/5/1/13, Ardersier, 30 September 1939; R91/D/B/5/1/32, Ardersier, 25 August 1963.
104. Clark, 'Sites, welfare', 148.
105. Leitch, *Sandy Stewart*, 'Introduction'.
106. E. Davies, 'The pearl fisher's son', in Neat, *Summer Walkers*, 36.

107. A. J. Williamson, 'Singer of the flying cloud', in Neat, *Summer Walkers*, 53.
108. NRS, HH55/237, *Report of the Departmental Committee on Tinkers in Scotland* (Edinburgh, 1918), s. 63, evidence of Mr D. McCallum, chairman of the Lorn[e] Combination Poorhouse Committee, Argyll and Bute.
109. Ibid.
110. Leitch, *Sandy Stewart*, xxiv.
111. Quoted in Ibid.
112. Halfacree, 'Still "Out of place"', 129; Leitch, *Sandy Stewart*, xxi.
113. HAS, R91/D/D/5/3/2, 3 November 1923.
114. PP, *Report of the Departmental Committee on Vagrancy in Scotland* (1936) Cmd. 519. s. 90.
115. Leitch, *Sandy Stewart*, 44.
116. *Caithness Courier*, 9 July 1958; 11 November 1959.
117. Barron, *County of Inverness*, 211.
118. Williamson, *Horsieman*.
119. Stewart, *Traveller's Life*, 69–70.
120. Ibid., 25.
121. Interview with Albert.
122. Interview with Terence.
123. See for example, Tobar an dualshais, http://www.tobarandualchais.co.uk/en/fullrecord/38045/1 (last accessed 1 January 2020), Jeannie Robertson, 'Bing avree, barrie gadgie, here's the hornies bingin tae the glimmer', recorded 1954. Interview with Terence: 'we [the police] were always dealing with them because their men when they got drink were like the Indians'.
124. Interview with Denis.
125. Smale, 'Alfred John List', 72.
126. MacGill, *Children*, 166.
127. Ibid., 104.
128. Miller, *Dam Builders*, 11.
129. Ibid.; Wood, *Hydro Boys*, 111.
130. Ibid.; Perchard, *Aluminiumville*.
131. NRS, HH55/311, CC's report to Standing Joint Committee, Inverness County, January. 1925.
132. Ibid., petition, 27 December 1927.
133. Ibid., Letter from residents' committee to Scottish Secretary.
134. Ibid., CC to Scottish Secretary, May 1928.
135. Interview with Graeme.
136. Interview with Albert.
137. Interview with Terence.
138. Interview with Bruce.
139. Shields and Duncan, *State of Crime*, 51.
140. Interview with Bruce.
141. Ibid.
142. Ibid.
143. Morrison, *My Story*, 56.

144. Ibid., 63.
145. Ibid., 57.
146. MacGill, *Children*, 104.
147. Maan, *New Scots*, 142.
148. Crang, 'Second World War', 563.
149. HAS, R91/D/B/5/12/7, Laggan, 15 November 1916.
150. Ibid., 12 October 1915, 11 and 14 August 1914.
151. Barron, *County of Inverness*, 3–4.
152. HAS, R91/D/B/5/1/4 and R91/D/B/5/1/9.
153. HAS, R91/D/B/5/1/4.
154. Sherwood, *British Honduran Forestry Unit*; Smale, 'Policing in the Scottish Borders'.
155. *Scotsman*, 12 September 1941.
156. *Scotsman*, 1 February 1940; *Evening Telegraph and Post*, 4 April 1941.
157. PP, *HMICS AR*, 1960, Cmnd. 1390.
158. Young, *In the Sticks*.
159. Rosenbaum, *Community Policing*, and Fielding, 'Theorising'.
160. T. Fenwick, R. Dockrell, B. Slade and I. Roberts, 'Rural policing: understanding police knowledge and practice in rural communities', SIPR Research Summary No. 10 (2011), http://www.sipr.ac.uk/Plugin/Publications/assets/files/Research_Summary_10.pdf (last accessed 1 January 2020); Fenwick, 'Learning policing'.

6

WOMEN IN SCOTTISH POLICING

In September 1915 Emily Miller was appointed as a plainclothes investigation officer attached to the CID of Glasgow City Police, the first woman to be employed in a policing capacity in a Scottish force. Her duties were very specific: to take statements from women and children who were witnesses in cases of assault and sexual violence and to support them in court. By 1939 there were still only 37 female officers in the whole of Scotland (within an overall police strength of 7,387). The pace of appointment increased incrementally in the aftermath of the Second World War: to 139 women in 1950, 271 in 1960 and 382 in 1970, but even then they constituted only 3.7 per cent of all serving officers.[1] This chapter demonstrates that, despite their small numbers, an analysis of women's 'specialist' role sheds significant light on the dynamics of gender in shaping police identities and relationships with communities. Indeed, the campaign for women's appointment was led from outside policing in the first half of the twentieth century. Women's groups from across the political spectrum claimed citizenship and recognition as part of the 'public' whom the police were required to serve; they argued that female police officers had a 'special sphere' of usefulness in responding to the needs of female and child 'victims' of crime. This chapter highlights striking continuities in ideas and rhetoric across the twentieth century. Women's policing work was presented as intersecting with social work, as being preventive and community oriented in its focus, and as requiring interpersonal skills and what would now be seen as emotional literacy. Yet their contribution was also viewed as niche – as necessary but specialist, contained and, crucially, restricted to a minority. Small numbers of female officers were employed precisely because they were seen as a complementary corollary of the dominant model of mainstream policing, which was grounded in physical force and equated with masculinity and the male body.

Campaigning for Female Officers: the First World War and its Aftermath

Whilst Miller was heralded as the 'first official appointment in Scotland', women had long been involved in voluntary, unpaid and support roles.[2] By 1900 it was established in rural areas that police wives would undertake essential work, cleaning and maintaining police premises and looking after female prisoners; this free labour, based on assumptions about the male breadwinner and feminine domestic responsibility, continued across the twentieth century. In larger towns and cities working-class women (often wives or widows of serving officers) were sometimes employed in small numbers as female turnkeys or matrons to work with female prisoners. Very unusually in 1875 Rachel Hamilton (née Johnston) had been sworn in as a Special Constable during the riots at Partick Cross, Glasgow, when supporters of Irish Home Rule clashed with the Orange Order. She had worked as a shipyard labourer and foreman navvy, her height and physical strength receiving comment.[3] However her role and profile were exceptional in the UK, contrasting markedly – in terms of social class and ideas about gender roles – with that of the women who became involved in policing duties during and after the First World War, whose contribution was delineated in terms of middle-class femininity.

The outbreak of war in 1914 led to the development of two very significant initiatives for women's police work across the UK led by largely middle-class women involved previously in social work or (in some cases) the campaigns for female suffrage. Firstly, a private organisation that explicitly styled itself as the Women Police Service (WPS), led by former rescue worker Margaret Damer Dawson and former suffragette Mary Allen, trained women and sought to place them in paid posts. Its most significant activity in Scotland took place at HM Gretna Munitions Factory, the largest cordite factory in Britain, when, in October 1916, the WPS was contracted by the Ministry of Munitions to provide 'policewomen' to supervise the 11,000 female munitions workers who arrived from all over England, Scotland and Wales. As a result, 150 uniformed members of the WPS were employed at Gretna. They escorted female munitions workers from barracks onto trains to the workplace each morning, checked passes and searched the women, ensured compliance with regulations, and supervised behaviour during breaks. During the evening they patrolled the new townships of Gretna and Eastriggs (specially built to support the work of the super-factory).[4] They were never an official part of the police service, which sought to distance itself from the WPS, in part because of its connections with suffrage militancy which had led to direct conflict with the police. Nevertheless, the work of the WPS had symbolic importance and, by winning the Ministry of Munitions contract, it demonstrated women's capacity for security and regulatory roles.

At the same time, the National Union of Women Workers (NUWW), an umbrella organisation for women involved in voluntary, philanthropic and social work, inaugurated a nationwide 'patrol' movement that received police recognition. Women patrols were designed to deal with the effects of 'khaki fever', a phenomenon which can be interpreted as a 'moral panic' about the many young women (including those in their teens) who reportedly flocked to towns where soldiers were garrisoned, attracted by the thrill of men in uniform.[5] Concerns were voiced in terms of the protection of both feminine virtue and vulnerable youth, intertwining strategies of care and control. Women patrols were to give up a few hours each week to walk in pairs through streets, squares, parks, railways stations and other public places to act as a deterrent and offer assistance to young women and children. From its early days in 1914 the 'patrol' idea was promoted across Scotland by the Scottish Branch of the NUWW (also referred to as the Scottish Unions of Women Workers or SUWW).[6] In an era in which women had not yet won the vote, the SUWW was an influential lobby group, led by some of the most prominent women in public life, mostly but not exclusively aligned with the Conservative/Unionist and Liberal parties. In the years 1914–18 the list of its Standing Committee members included the Countess of Aberdeen (convenor), leading constitutional suffragist Lady Frances Balfour, feminist lawyer and peace campaigner Chrystal Macmillan, eminent Aberdeen-based geologist and women's rights campaigner May Ogilvie Gordon (later to become a Liberal candidate for parliament), pioneering Dundee-based woman doctor Emily Thomson, Edinburgh-based Girton graduate and Classics teacher Jane Ewing Hannay, as well as 'Mrs Thomas Johnston' (Margaret Freeland Johnston, née Cochrane), wife of the socialist politician.[7] Without referring to ideas about equal rights, they found common ground in arguing for women's contribution to public life and duty as citizens.

As a result of their successful lobbying, the Scottish Secretary provided an official endorsement for the patrols, permitting them to wear an armband and a badge (there was no uniform as such) and to carry a card signed by the local Chief Constable. On 5 December 1914 the Scottish Office sent a circular to all chief constables requesting that 'the police under your control will do all that is in their power to assist the efforts of these women workers'. It was made clear, nevertheless, that the work was 'mainly preventive', that it involved 'girls and women who would not ordinarily come under the notice of the police', and that it 'is not designed to relieve the police of their duties with respect to disorderly or illegal conduct on the part of prostitutes or others'.[8] Thus it was not to be seen as police work as such, but as subsidiary work generated by the exigencies of war. The Scottish Office view, although not formally stated, was that 'this kind of thing ought to be run by private organisation . . . to discourage suggestions which were made to us that the patrols should be appointed and run by the police'.[9]

By 1915 the SUWW claimed it had recruited 482 women patrols, who were working as volunteers in 23 different towns or cities across the length and breadth of Scotland.[10] They operated in the largest numbers in Dundee, Glasgow and Edinburgh. Their prominence in smaller towns can be explained by the presence nearby of military bases, such as Stobs camp in the case of Hawick in the Scottish Borders. The SUWW highlighted the need for 'sympathy, patience and tact', referring to 'the excitement amongst young women and girls . . . which . . . though natural and in itself innocent, requires to be kindly and firmly dealt with and kept within bounds'.[11] Their approach emphasised a benevolent befriending – 'to act as a steadying influence on girls and young women and in general to look after their interests' – and was aligned more with social work than policing.[12] Indeed, the movement specifically aimed to recruit volunteers who had experience in educational or social work with girls.[13] For example, Lady Katherine Scott, who became the Patrol Convenor for Hawick, was a former Sunday School teacher inspired by evangelical convictions who had also undertaken voluntary work for the Young Women's Christian Association in London.[14] As the initial 'excitement' of war evaporated, the problem of 'khaki fever' dissipated in the smaller towns and the patrol movement focused on the running of girls' clubs to divert adolescents into rational and 'healthy' recreation as an alternative to the streets. In the cities, particularly Glasgow and Edinburgh, the business of street patrolling persisted across the war years 'safeguarding the young in crowded centres'. In Edinburgh the patrols took on the duties and powers of park keepers in 1917, according them further official recognition.[15]

The particular trajectory that women's entry into policing took in Scotland was profoundly influenced by the work of the National Vigilance Association (NVA). Indeed, the SUWW Patrols Committee worked closely with local branches of the NVA and there was significant overlap in membership (for example, Lady Frances Balfour was prominent in both). The NVA had been set up in London in 1885 as a 'social purity' organisation to campaign against obscenity and immorality as well as the organisation of prostitution and the sexual exploitation of women and girls (the 'white slave trade'), the latter being an area of concern that was also highlighted by Edwardian feminist and suffrage groups (as part of the argument for why votes for women were needed).[16] Vigilance Association branches were founded in Glasgow in 1910 and in Edinburgh in 1911 in response to localised concerns about the prevalence of child sexual abuse.[17] In addition to lobbying to change the law, they had developed a portfolio of specialist social work ('moral welfare' and 'rescue') to protect and assist vulnerable young women in the years immediately before the First World War. As Viviene Cree has argued, they established a 'co-operative' relationship with the police, which involved some sharing of information and cross-referral.[18] In Glasgow, concerns about 'immorality' in the city had led to an unsuccessful proposal to the city's magistrates in 1911 – promoted by the Vigilance Association and endorsed initially by Chief Constable Stevenson – that 'female detectives' might be employed to take statements from female witnesses in cases relating to the Criminal Law Amendment Act (which defined offences relating to age of consent and criminalised brothels).[19] Indeed, Miller's appointment as a paid statement-taker in 1915 was the direct result of further approaches made by Glasgow Vigilance Association to magistrates, the Chief Constable and the police authority. Miller herself had undertaken paid investigative work and court duties for the Glasgow Vigilance Association since its inception in 1910 (as well as having worked as a psychiatric nurse), and thus had 'extensive experience' already.[20] Moreover, in Edinburgh the NVA (Eastern Branch) was involved in the establishment of voluntary patrols in the city and went on to fund the appointment of two paid women patrols from February 1919.[21]

Thus two models were advanced: one relating to plainclothes statement-taking in the CID, the other to street patrol (and, potentially, uniform). Both had emerged during a period of rapid social change in which women were permitted to try their hand at a wide variety of occupations previously reserved for men, given emergency conditions. It was a time in which new 'modern' occupations including social work and probation were still under construction and gaining professional definition. It was also a period in which middle-class women were negotiating new work roles and identities. Finally, it was a time in which women were actively asserting their citizenship, firstly in terms of the contribution they might make (their national 'duty' during wartime) but, secondly, in terms of the needs of women and children (rights and protections); the latter was to dominate at war-end. These broad trends were international (as well as national) but the precise contours that they took on the ground were shaped by local conditions (including resource distribution, geographies and regulatory frameworks) and the agency and networks of campaigners and supporters. In 1914 the SUWW had rested its case for official recognition on the argument that patrol work was for the war's duration and did not replicate police work. In Scotland (unlike England) the patrols were run purely as a separate voluntary organisation and they were not part of the police establishment or funded by police budgets. By 1917, however, the SUWW was thinking ahead and embarking on an orchestrated campaign for the employment of women by and within police forces – as both patrols and police officers – on a permanent and paid basis.

There were, however, legal and financial impediments – as well as cultural and political ones. The first attested and uniformed female police officer in the UK, Edith Smith, had been sworn in by Grantham Borough Police in December 1915. Yet, shortly afterwards, the Home Office advised that this was technically impossible since women, by virtue of their sex, were not 'proper persons' in the eyes of the law: it had long been established that they could not vote, or serve as MPs or on juries for similar reasons.[22] This legal interpretation – that even if women were appointed they could not be given equal status or powers of arrest to male constables – was accepted by the Scottish Office and chief constables as applying to Scotland. However, a financial impediment had also surfaced in Scotland specifically. The police grant from the Scottish Office was 'stereotyped' in such a way that funds could only be spent on designated areas that purportedly did not allow the allocation of resources to women (unlike in England and Wales where this had been allowed since 1916). Coupled with this, the Scottish Office grant was only a third of the police budget (until 1919), thus placing a greater burden generally on ratepayers who were reluctant to accept additional financial responsibilities. These financial restraints explain, to some degree, why the patrol movement remained separate from the police in Scotland whilst it was estimated that around 200 women were on police payrolls south of the border.[23]

Nevertheless, the legal and financial protocols acted more as a convenient smokescreen for those reluctant to commit real resources. In Glasgow a way had been found to employ Miller. In Aberdeen, Dorothy Maitland was placed on the police payroll as a 'police sister' from 1913 to undertake tasks that were coming to be defined as probation work; a similar arrangement was made in Ayr.[24] In Dundee, where the patrol movement had been particularly active, the SUWW approached the Town Council in 1918 with a proposal that Jean Thomson (née Forsyth Wright) – a minister's daughter who had been assisting the city police for the last 9 years in work relating to women and children – should be appointed as a paid 'policewoman'. Chief Constable John Carmichael agreed to her part-time employment for 4 hours a day, again as a 'police sister'. In fact, by her own account, Jean Thomson undertook a full day's work for half pay, reporting for duty at 9am and working into the evening as she patrolled dancehalls, cinemas and ice-cream parlours in full uniform for which she received only a half allowance.[25] Except for these four cases, chief constables waited for the Scottish Office to take the lead.

The tactics needed to be stepped up. To promote women's appointment to formal roles, the SUWW set up the Scottish Training School for Women Police (there were already NUWW training schools in Bristol and Liverpool to which it was affiliated) at 13 Newton Place, Glasgow, in 1918. The initiative was supported in kind by Glasgow Corporation (who granted access to the courts for training purposes), although funding came from a Carnegie Trust grant and from private subscriptions. The school's patroness was the high-profile Conservative and Unionist the Duchess of Atholl, but its committee also included 'Mrs Thomas Johnston'.[26] The school's 'Director', Edith Tancred (appointed in June 1918), had been a House Mistress at Cheltenham Ladies' College and had worked in boys' and girls' clubs in London before undertaking training with women patrols in Bristol and with the Metropolitan Police. Although never herself employed in a policing role in Scotland, she was an indefatigable campaigner for the cause who made it her life's work to persuade chief constables, local authorities and the Scottish Office that women were an asset to policing and to achieve fair pay, status and conditions. The Scottish Training School began by developing a training programme for women keen to take up police appointments and was responsible for the training of two of the women recruited as paid NVA patrols in Edinburgh.

Yet it became obvious that there was little point in training women if there were no jobs for them to go into. In January 1919 Tancred and the SUWW put the school's training work on ice, in order 'to educate public opinion in the need for policewomen'.[27] They mobilised social and political networks at grassroots level as well as contacts in the highest echelons of government, addressed public meetings (including ward meetings of town councils) and further developed a coalition of support amongst the panoply of women's organisations across Scotland. With votes won for some women in 1918, suffrage societies reconstituted themselves as Women's Citizens' Associations and they were drawn into the campaign for female police officers.[28] So, too, were local branches of the Scottish Co-operative Women's Guild who had over 17,000 members, whilst in Dundee the women's section of the Labour Party also joined the local campaign in the early 1920s.[29] By July 1919 seven of the largest towns in Scotland had 'resolved' to support the appointment of 'policewomen' – Edinburgh, Glasgow, Dundee, Aberdeen, Ayr, Dunfermline and Rothesay – and continued pressure was exerted on the Scottish Secretary to remove the impediments to their employment.

In August 1919 the Scottish Office finally released a circular to chief constables stating that the costs of appointing policewomen might be charged to police funds, ending the problem of the 'stereotyping' of police budgets. Whilst it recognised that 'the assistance of properly trained women would be of considerable value in certain spheres of police duty', it also stated that women could not be properly sworn in as constables with powers of arrest or regarded as regular members of a police force but instead should be regarded as 'auxiliary' in status.[30] The circular at least enabled Glasgow to press ahead. In October, plans to recruit ten female (auxiliary) constables were approved by the Scottish Secretary, and the first of these 'policewomen' – Georgina W. McLeod – took up her post as an employee of Glasgow City Police on 15 December 1919 (on an 'experimental' basis in the first instance and on half the pay of a new male recruit).

On 23 December 1919 the Sex Disqualification (Removal) Act came into being, specifying that 'a person' might no longer be disqualified from 'any public function' or 'civil or judicial office or post' on the grounds of their sex. It was this piece of legislation that paved the way for the appointment of the first women jurors and magistrates, and enabled women to practise as lawyers. Yet its interpretation in regard to policing remained contentious, and the Scottish Secretary decided to await the recommendations of the Departmental Committee on the Employment of Women on Police Duties, which had recently been announced by the Home Secretary and which (following further concerted lobbies by Tancred and the Scottish Training School) was to cover Scotland as well as England and Wales. Chaired by Major John Baird MP, the Committee reported in July 1920, clarifying that the Sex Disqualification (Removal) Act did, indeed, apply to policing and that women could 'be employed with advantage to the community' on a recommended set of gender-related duties including patrolling and statement-taking. It clarified, too, that women could be employed as 'an integral part of the police' with 'the legal powers and status of a constable' and that they should be 'specially qualified, highly trained and well paid'.[31] Nevertheless, it was not until 1924 that Glasgow's 'policewomen' were confirmed as full members of the force with pensions and powers of arrest.

Thus the First World War and its aftermath was a crucial period in which the established answer to the question 'who should police and on whose behalf?' was challenged on grounds of gender. The prominent campaigns of women's organisations are an early example of the call for more diverse policing styles, skills sets and police personnel. But how did these campaigns influence women's work as practitioners once in post? It is to this question that this chapter will now turn. Up until the Second World War, female police officers in Scotland were overwhelmingly employed in plainclothes in CIDs to take statements from female and child witnesses in sexual assault cases, reflecting the origins of their duties in moral welfare work. The one female officer who had worn uniform – Jean Thomson – resigned in August 1922 (a few months after her chief had decided against the employment of full-time 'policewomen' in the city); it was not until 1935 that a woman was again employed in Dundee when Annie Ross was appointed to the CID in plainclothes.[32]

The 'Special Sphere' of Usefulness: 1920–40

Throughout her campaigns, Tancred argued that there was a 'special sphere of usefulness' for female officers: 'in preventing girls from getting into trouble in the streets and in detecting and bringing to justice the vile and cowardly class of criminal who prey on girls and women'.[33] Women's policing work was presented as complementary (rather than overlapping) with that of policemen, and as entailing emotional labour and highly developed social skills. Whilst women claimed recognition of equal citizenship, they did so in such a way as to emphasise different needs, grounded in gendered experiences of motherhood and sexual violence. 'Equality' and 'difference' were not polar opposites but went hand in hand; nevertheless, the emphasis on 'difference' meant that women's police work was shaped by ideas about what has been labelled 'social maternalism' (the idea that women's role as carers and nurturers extended to the public sphere).[34]

Moreover, the Home Office issued a set of Police (Women) Regulations for England and Wales in 1931 (adopted in Scotland in 1934) which listed the duties that might be assigned to policewomen, highlighting work 'with women and children', thus giving official sanction to the idea of a 'separate sphere of usefulness'.[35] Although this early group of women officers were small in number, their personal and professional experiences are glimpsed in the minutes of evidence of a series of parliamentary committees – the Baird Committee of 1920 and the Departmental Committee on Sexual Offences against Children and Young People in Scotland (Child Assault Committee) of 1924–6 – enabling further analysis of the dynamics of gender and class that shaped their work as practitioners.[36] There was obviously a political agenda behind the act of giving evidence (the promotion of particular messages about the significance of policewomen's work) and clearly these minutes of evidence are not necessarily frank descriptions of the everyday to be taken at face value. Nevertheless, they reveal something of the attitudes and work orientations of this early group of female officers, of their perceptions of interactions with others, and of their possible effects.

Speaking in 1920, Jean Thomson stressed that 'a great deal of the whole importance of the work depends on your own personality and how you get on with people'.[37] Thomson spent time visiting Dundee's lodging houses (where the poorest women found a temporary bed for the night), through which she felt she built up trust:

> You get to know where the girls are living and what they are doing in that way. You gain the confidence of the girls. Many times they come to you in little difficulties. Perhaps it is not actual police work, but they find they are on the downward path.

Whilst Thomson performed a law enforcement function she also described a concomitant social welfare role that was preventive and rehabilitative (overlapping considerably with probation work):

> Girls who have been in trouble very frequently come to me. They want to get some work perhaps. They have not very much chance of getting it

unless they can get someone who takes an interest in them. I have case after case of girls coming out of prison who, even though they know I was instrumental in getting them into prison, seem to feel they can come and ask for help.[38]

Within social work rhetoric, 'befriending' did not assume a relationship of equals but was grounded in an ideal of an older trusted confidant who would provide inscrutable support and encouragement to those less fortunate. The relationship was grounded in distinctions of class and age as well as gender. Arguably, too, Thomson was uniquely placed to gain the trust of at least some of the women and children whom she was seeking to help, given that she too had experienced very significant adversity, which she alluded to in telling the Baird Committee that she was no longer supported by a husband and had three children who were cared for by her widowed mother.[39]

In 1920 Thomson, Miller and Tancred made powerful arguments that women and children found it easier to disclose abuse to a female officer whose availability was vital in enabling prosecutions to be brought. Tancred, who had shadowed Miller's work in Glasgow, explained that half of all sexual assault cases reported did not come to court because women withdrew their evidence when they realised how proceedings would be conducted. In Scotland (as in England) it was customary for the courtroom to be cleared of all women (other than the witness) in cases that were considered too 'indelicate' for them to hear:

A girl had been assaulted on a tram, and Miss Miller had taken her evidence and had got sufficient evidence for the Procurator Fiscal to prosecute. When the girl came into court and she found that the court was cleared, and there was no-one there but the men officials, she turned to Miss Miller and said: 'I am not going to give that evidence before all these men.' Miss Miller said: 'I hope you will, because you have got a good case and the man will get adequate punishment if you go through with it.' She thought a little and said 'Will you be in the court with me?' Miss Miller said 'Yes, I will be in the court, and this lady [Tancred] has the leave of the magistrate to remain.' She said 'Very well then, I will do it'. And she gave her evidence quite properly and clearly and the man was sentenced.[40]

Similarly, Phoebe Duncan, who was appointed as a Glasgow 'policewoman' in 1921, told the Child Assault Committee in 1925 that: 'Many mothers say to us that they are glad to see a woman come, and I think we get a full statement.'[41] Miller, who went on to train the new intake of Glasgow policewomen, discussed the emotional stress of conducting such work, which required considerable empathy and tact:

> On New Year's Eve I went to one aged two years and nine months. I was 25 minutes with that little girl before she would speak to me, and before I could mention the case at all I had to 'make friends' with her. I got her on her granny's knee and asked her about who had hurt her. That is where the strain comes in all the time – to get at the child's point of view.[42]

The 1920s saw what might now be labelled the 'discovery' of child sexual abuse in Scotland, as a result of the campaigns of the women's movement of this period. This paralleled concerns in England, although a specific aspect of the Scottish debates concerned the environmental problems associated with overcrowded tenement living – in Glasgow in particular – which was seen as an exacerbating factor. Children shared common spaces including poorly lit stairwells and lavatories with those of all ages and generations, to whose attentions they were vulnerable. In England and Wales, the 1925 Committee on Sexual Offences against Children was to recommend a very radical overhaul of court procedures (including some proposals that were not implemented until the 1980s).[43] In contrast, the most significant recommendations that were made by the Scottish Committee related to environment (that shared lavatories should be abolished and cinemas better lit), parental responsibility (for ensuring supervision, protection and education of their children), and finally – in common with suggestions south of the border – that 'woman police should take precongitions when available and suitable for the purpose'.[44] Indeed, this recommendation was reinforced by the Scottish Office which, in 1925, issued a circular that urged chief constables to appoint women to take precongitions (although it drew short of making it compulsory).[45]

In their evidence to the Child Assault Committee, Glasgow's 'policewomen' explained that although their work was not limited to sexual assault – they took statements from girls accused of theft, collected evidence in cases of fortune-telling by posing as clients, carried out observations on bonded warehouses, and escorted women and children in court – it nevertheless took up the vast majority of their time.[46] They were painfully aware of the deficiencies of the law. Helen Blair, also appointed in 1921, spoke of the difficulties of getting a conviction in cases involving very young children and suggested that such cases should be tried before a panel of expert judges instead of a jury, given their complexity. Her belief in children's testimony and her frustration at the legal system came through in a particular case that she described: 'The child could only tell you in very small language what had happened, and you really believed her story, but who is to convict a man on the evidence of a child of 2½?'[47] Phoebe Duncan drew attention to the isolation and vulnerability of some boarded-out children: 'in the case of one child . . . in which we secured a conviction . . . I said "[c]ould you not get anybody to tell what had happened to you", and she said to me no, that they were a mile from anywhere.'[48]

Indeed, as a result of comments such as this, the Committee also went on to recommend closer co-operation between the police, education and welfare authorities 'for the purpose of safeguarding the welfare of victims'.[49]

Yet whilst they were attuned to the existence of child sexual abuse and some of the difficulties confronting witnesses, women officers exhibited prejudices that were widely shared by other professional groups who gave evidence to the Child Assault Committee. Emily Miller equated the city's ice-cream parlours and fish and chip shops with sexual danger because '[m]ost of them are kept by Italians and these foreigners have a different standard of morals from our men', a racialised assumption about criminality that had long been circulating amongst police and vigilance workers in the city.[50] Miller also stereotyped child abusers as mainly 'degenerate weedy looking men': as a biological 'other' whose behaviour was shaped by physical and psychiatric flaws.[51] Helen Blair was unable to accept that intra-familial abuse straddled social classes although she acknowledged this was simply because she had only encountered it in what she saw as the 'slum' areas of the city: 'other people say it is prevalent in different classes where there is no overcrowding, but we do not hear of it'.[52] Arguably, her evidence can be read against the grain to suggest that the close proximity of tenement life meant that neighbours were more likely to be aware of such cases and found ways to report them to the police even if reluctant to do so directly; one case was said to have come to light because of 'an anonymous postcard sent in by a neighbour'.[53] If the work of female officers in this period was one of moral regulation and remained shaped by class prejudices (and included elements of mutual mistrust), it nevertheless chimed sufficiently with the concerns, ethical codes and values of working-class women.

Early women officers were circumspect in public about their treatment by male colleagues. Helen Blair was reported to have stated in 1926 that 'there was still a great deal of prejudice in the force' although the women in Glasgow 'had really gained the men's confidence'.[54] There were undoubtedly tensions. Emily Miller had submitted written evidence to the Child Assault Committee in May 1925 in which she stated: 'There seems to be a decided prejudice against the Women Police amongst the higher official, whereas it has been my experience that the lower ranks – the men who actually do the work – welcome their help.'[55] The first ten Glasgow women had been sent out in pairs to five of the largest Divisions to work in plainclothes with the CID under the line management of the male superintendent rather than a senior female colleague, and Miller was aware that they were not being used effectively. Whilst she was keen to stress that rank-and-file policemen welcomed women because they were reluctant to take these kinds of statements themselves, she was disdainful of the class background of male constables: 'the men generally are drawn from a section of the community whose standard of moral rectitude is liable to be blunted, because of circumstances beyond their control'.[56] Her background in evangelical 'social purity' work may be apparent here, alongside an equation of moral superiority with education and middle-class respectability. Her aloofness, which may offer an explanation for her departure from policing shortly before she gave evidence to the Child Assault Committee, is also illustrated in her disappointment in the 'type' of woman that Glasgow had recruited. She had hoped for a cohort that was 'educated, highly intelligent and tactful' and, ideally, 'experts engaged in various branches of social work'.[57] Yet the pay, conditions, and police culture generated by male colleagues meant that the work was 'not at all attractive to the type of persons most suited'. She stated pejoratively in her oral evidence that the new intake of Glasgow women was there (with one exception) 'because of, well, a job . . . as a living'.[58] By inference, this contrasted with her personal sense of policing as a vocation and duty.

If policing as a new occupation for women in the interwar period failed to acquire equivalent professional status to teaching and social work, the recruitment profile nevertheless differed from that of male officers with regards to previous occupational background, class and social status. Personnel records exist for twenty-one women (out of a total of thirty-three) who joined Glasgow City Police between 1920 and 1940.[59] Recruits included a domestic science teacher, a nurse and a 'mission worker' (evangelical social work), the kind of expertise that Miller had hoped for. The vast majority, however, were drawn from previous occupations in white-collar work (including a third from clerical work and a quarter in the service industries including sales), contrasting with the dominance of industrial manual labour amongst male recruits. The Police (Women) Regulations of 1931 and 1934 specified that recruits must be between the ages of 22 and 55, unmarried or widowed and, indeed, would be required to resign upon marriage.[60] Of the interwar Glasgow recruits, it is notable that four joined as widows (the remainder were single), whilst the mean average age on joining was 28, somewhat older than male recruits. In terms of religion (all were Protestant) and geographical origins (half were Glasgow-born), the trends mirrored that of male officers in this period. The first BAME and Sikh female officer in Glasgow, Sawarnjit Matharu, was appointed as a cadet in 1974.[61]

The model of the middle-class plainclothes statement-taker persisted across the interwar period in Scotland; female officers embraced it and there are examples that speak of their initiative, ability to gain the trust of witnesses, and capacity to take on the challenges of the criminal justice system. In 1930 Ellen Webster and Ellen Scollay were involved in the successful prosecution of Glasgow businessman Samuel Moorov for a series of indecent assaults on nineteen women whom he had interviewed for employment as assistants in his drapery firm. The assaults had taken place on the premises and when he and the women were alone. However, a legal principle was established and upheld (despite appeal) that single witnesses in individual crimes could be used as mutual corroboration if there was sufficient inter-relationship in time, place and circumstances between the incidents.[62] According to an account written retrospectively by a younger colleague:

> A civil servant from a local employment bureau called at the Central Police Office and asked to see a policewoman. She was interviewed by Miss Webster and to her she told of her disquiet regarding a clothing firm to whom she had sent a girl for interview.

The girl had disclosed a sexual assault, and the civil servant then connected it with the fact that she had sent other women to the same firm, and these women had either declined the job or not remained there for any length of time. Webster and Scollay 'decided to trace the girls who had either gone for interview or worked in the factory and amassed a file of uncorroborated statements all telling the same tale.'[63] Similarly, in 1937 two other Glasgow 'policewomen' were highly commended by Sillitoe for work which resulted in prison sentences for five men charged with serious sexual offences including rape.[64] Indeed, with the arrival of Sillitoe as new chief in December 1931, Glasgow's policewomen received strong backing; a supporter of the employment of policewomen, he increased their numerical strength from 11 to 15 in 1933.[65] Indeed, of the 37 'policewomen' in post across Scotland by the end of 1938, nearly half (15) were in Glasgow; two were in Aberdeen with the rest scattered in ones or twos across the towns and cities of the central belt, whilst the (invisible) contribution of police wives was still wholly taken for granted in rural areas.[66]

Women in Uniform 1939–75

Ideas about gender and policing were further challenged during the Second World War, as a result of significant campaigning and mobilisation. With war imminent in 1939 the Home Office and Scottish Office agreed that members of a newly created Women's Auxiliary Police Corps (WAPC) might be recruited by police forces in order to free up men for other key policing duties by undertaking altogether different work from that originally reserved for regular policewomen. This consisted of the driving and maintaining of vehicles, looking after equipment, clerical work and canteen work. In Glasgow, Sillitoe endorsed the setting up of a local WAPC in September 1939 with authorisation to recruit up to 220 women and with Baillie Violet Roberton acting as Commandant (indeed, Sillitoe's wife and daughter were also members). On 10 December 1940 a significant addition was made to the WAPC in Glasgow, with the appointment of fourteen uniformed patrols with powers of arrest to survey streets and railways stations, visit women's lodging houses in the city, carry out enquiries regarding female 'aliens', search women at the docks, and carry out observations of unlicensed dancehalls and shebeens.[67] Their work was the same as that which had been undertaken by uniformed 'women police' in London since the 1920s and was, thus, a decisive move into uniform for Glasgow policewomen.

As women's organisations were quick to point out, the war was highlighting significant social issues relating to women, children and adolescents on the Home Front (including the problem of 'camp followers' and 'good time girls' attracted to locations where soldiers were stationed or travelling through), which required the rejuvenation of the old 'patrol' idea. In 1940 a concerted UK-wide campaign was re-launched, in which groups such as the Women's Co-operative Guild, the Mothers' Union, the Young Women's Christian Association, the NVA, the Association of Head Mistresses, the National Association of Women Teachers, the National Council for Equal Citizenship, and the Salvation Army (amongst others) pressed for more policewomen. In Scotland this translated into more members of the WAPC rather than an increase in regular officers – but with expanded roles. At its numerical height 470 women were employed as paid WAPCs in Scotland – as well as 469 women in part-time unpaid policing work – although most were demobbed at war-end.[68]

A further crucial issue, around which women's organisations had long lobbied, came to fruition during wartime: the appointment of a woman as a nationally validated expert to assist HMICs in advising chief constables on the training and employment of women in police duties. This had been recommended by the Baird Committee back in 1920 but had never been taken up. In 1939, as the number of women employed in policing expanded incrementally, Edith Tancred wrote to the Home Office from her home in Prestwick, Ayrshire, offering to work with HMICs to co-ordinate the work of the WAPC (an offer that was politely declined).[69] In the spring of 1944 Home Secretary Herbert Morrison was still arguing that there was no justification for the appointment of a woman assistant to HMICs, but there was a *volte-face* by the summer given the sheer number of women being recruited as auxiliaries. Whilst women's groups in Scotland argued that a separate appointment should be made specifically for Scotland, the Scottish Office agreed it was efficient to share an appointment with other UK forces. The post was given to Barbara Denis de Vitré, who had not only served in Leicester but also in Sheffield and Kent, as well as training Egyptian policewomen in Cairo.[70] She took up the post of Police Staff Officer to support HMICs in 1945 (promoted to Assistant to HMIC in 1948). The appointment was received with considerable enthusiasm by women's organisations, who felt their campaigning work regarding women police had been completed. In 1961 Scotland finally gained its own Assistant to HMICS at the Scottish Office with the appointment of Janet Gray, formerly of Glasgow City Police (where she had served since 1931, having started her police career in Gloucestershire). From then until her retirement in 1970 Gray was the most senior policewoman in Scotland.[71]

The appointments of De Vitré and then Gray were crucial in the next phase of the development of policing as a 'modern career' for women in Scotland, albeit within a gender-related framework. De Vitré brought with her the model of the uniformed Policewomen's Department which had emerged in English cities, whilst recognising a wide portfolio of work that women might undertake in rural and semi-rural areas. Both De Vitré and then Gray worked closely with chief constables and local authorities, gradually nudging them to appoint more women and make more use of the ones they had. A core problem that they faced was a lack of understanding of how women might be appropriately deployed, and time after time they sought to educate chief constables when they found examples of women who were 'fed up ... because principally employed in typing and on office duties'.[72] Nevertheless, by the time of De Vitré's untimely death in 1960 there were female officers in all Scottish burghs, and only four counties had none. Ten years later when Gray retired, there were female officers in every Scottish force except Zetland. Whilst the impetus for women's move into policing had come from civil society organisations (external to government and policing), the vision for their new role in post-war Scotland came from senior police personnel within the Home Office (and from 1961, the Scottish Office). Moreover, insights into the experiences of female officers across Scotland in this period can be gleaned from their frank inspection reports, as well as from the retrospective personal testimony of former serving officers (including memoir and oral history).

On her first visit to Glasgow City Police in the summer of 1945 De Vitré recorded that Chief Constable McCulloch was 'supporting [female officers] well', and in 1946 the decision was made to double the number of regular policewomen to twenty-eight by retaining WAPCs who met the entry requirements in uniformed roles. One of De Vitré's goals as a moderniser was to ensure the systematic collation of information about women and children who had come to police attention. In Glasgow she ensured the introduction of a central index for this in 1946, despite some initial non-compliance from older plainclothes women on Divisions who 'fiercely oppose any change'.[73] Policewomen numbers in the city were further increased to 44 by 1955, 74 by 1960, and 87 by 1965, whilst female officers were organised through the Policewomen's Department.[74] In an oral history interview, Elsie – who was appointed initially as a uniformed WAPC in Glasgow in 1944 and successfully transferred to become a regular in 1946 – described the physical space occupied by the Policewomen's Department in the early 1960s. This had initially been a small room at Central Police Headquarters in Turnbull Street but, because this was very cramped, female officers lobbied for their own accommodation which they were finally allocated across the road:

Contained in this ground floor flat we had a front office, and there was always a policewoman behind it. The superintendent had a room, the inspectors had a room, the chief inspector had the next one down, and there was one where the sergeants were. We had a dining room, we had a proper kitchen with a cooker, washing facilities in it. On the other side of the corridor the two CID girls had a room, there was a little interview room for privacy and there was a drying room where they could take their wet coats and things in . . . We had our own car and our own driver, we were completely independent. We had no senior male officers . . . The woman superintendent, she answered to the Chief Constable. There was no male senior officers [who] interfered with us in any way and they had to ask when they wanted, perhaps, a policewoman.[75]

In addition to this self-contained unit, whose focus was cases involving women and children, two uniformed women were sent out to each Divisional station (where two plainclothes policewomen were already based). Nevertheless, the 'independent' structure or hub fostered a shared identity as 'policewomen' and it also projected a significant external image of a unit that was accessible and approachable.

In other cities, the model of the Policewomen's Department was replicated in the years after the Second World War. For example, in November 1950 Annie Ross was promoted to sergeant 'in the new women's unit being set up in Dundee constabulary', where numbers grew from five in 1953 to nine in 1961.[76] In Aberdeen, numbers rose from two in 1947 to ten by 1960, whilst Edinburgh's Policewomen's Department had swelled from one in 1945 to a very substantial forty by 1965.[77] The model of the specialist 'women's unit' nevertheless followed the existing paradigm that women's work in policing was gender-related, grounded in supporting and working with female and child victims of crime, looking for missing women and children, and taking statements when women and children were accused of offending. Women were organised into day and night shifts and, in urban areas, carried out their own uniform patrols of commercial or public spaces where teenage runaways or truants might be seeking shelter (railways stations, cafes, pubs, dancehalls or, in seaside towns, seafront shelters). It was stressed time and again that their work was largely about 'prevention' and it is undoubtedly the case that female officers were seen as a more approachable 'public' face to policing. Their effectiveness was measured less in terms of statistics and rather more so in terms of the relationships they built. There was still considerable overlap with the work of probation officers and other types of social work such as moral welfare and child protection, although ultimately female officers were responsible for investigating criminal cases if and when it was appropriate.

The following examples from Janet Gray's reports suggest something of the relationships that could be forged, of the responsive nature of interactions, and of the proactive role of parents in 'appealing' for or 'seeking' 'advice' and 'help'. Commenting on Aberdeen, she wrote in 1961 that female officers 'play a large part in reporting cases of child neglect, and in visiting the homes of difficult and wayward juveniles whose parents have sought the help of the police'. Similarly in 1963 she reported that they keep 'close watch on young girls who show signs of going astray and in assisting suitable cases to obtain employment'.[78] In relation to Dundee's Policewomen's Department, she wrote in 1961 that: 'They keep in touch with all girls who have appeared before the Court, and with those whose behaviour has necessitated the parents appealing to the police for advice and help.'[79] Arguably, surveillance was the primary purpose. Yet practical advice and support – the old model of 'befriending' – remained an important component. The separate entrance and counter in Glasgow's new Policewomen's Department made it relatively easy for women to walk in with queries, whether or not they could be resolved.

These dynamics were also apparent in small forces. Moira joined a county force in the late 1950s and was stationed in a small town on the edges of the Glasgow conurbation. She felt that policewomen 'were certainly well respected, and I think on some occasions, we were more trusted [than male officers]. Especially wives and mothers felt they could talk to us if they were having problems with their family.' The Canon in the local church was a good source of information regarding truancy or family difficulties and there was a sense in which they shared a pastoral role:

> He would say, 'Oh, Mrs so-and-so is getting a bad time from her husband', 'I haven't seen such and such a person's kids for a while. They are never there when I go up. I think they are tearaways.' We would maybe walk up, pop in and say, 'How are the kids?' because everyone knew us.[80]

In the case of one troubled family, with whom they worked regularly, an older daughter was going abroad but had had her passport hidden by her father: 'Eventually, we went, with her permission, to search the house and we found the passport underneath his bed.' Even after leaving the police to marry (on account of the marriage bar), Moira found that her previous role as a serving officer meant that neighbours sometimes turned to her for advice:

> A mother came across to tell me her daughter had gone missing and ask what she should do. She had gone to Ireland . . . I remember phoning the Garda and explaining who and what I was . . . This woman . . . knew I

had been a policewoman, but she felt able to come to me to ask what to do because she didn't want to go to the police.[81]

This example is a telling one, in that it clearly demonstrates that many families were reluctant to turn to police officers – whether male or female – who were seen as likely to exacerbate a problem rather than help. In this case a daughter might get into 'trouble' and a mother's parenting skills be questioned. Nevertheless, the skills, knowledge and confidence of those in the police service were valued. Those who were trusted to support, advise and resolve a problem informally were accepted as an important resource. These principles might apply whether individuals were still within or outwith the police, but what was crucial was the specific dynamic of trust that had to be won not assumed.

Indeed, in rural and county areas, where policewomen were appointed in small numbers and without a Policewomen's Department, they sometimes found themselves responsible for a much wider portfolio of work, including duties that were undertaken by male officers in other forces. For many years the only female officer in Caithness was widow Elizabeth (Betty) Orpin who had previously worked in the Metropolitan Police and moved to Wick during the Second World War. In June 1946 she was described as 'an excellent person', 'busy on a wide variety of outside duties' to the 'credit of the Chief Constable'.[82] By 1961 (when a second policewoman was appointed to cover Thurso given the expansion of population linked to Dounreay), Orpin not only looked after cases involving women and children but was also in charge of a whole series of departments – 'aliens, explosives, equipment, clothing, found property' – and was 'depute of the firearms section'. In addition, she was traffic warden for Wick, gave road safety talks, and 'as welfare officer to the force her assistance in soothing out difficulties between husbands and wives in isolated stations has been most successful'.[83] Gray's recommendation that she should be promoted to sergeant (given that many of these roles in other forces were undertaken by male sergeants) was initially turned down on the grounds that this was not possible because there were only two policewomen in Caithness (although it was finally granted a year later in 1962).

In Argyllshire on the west coast, the opposite problem had emerged: not enough work was being found because the police authority lacked imagination and preferred to rely on the unpaid work of police wives to search women taken into custody or to escort children who came to police attention. The county's first regular policewoman (previously a WAPC) was appointed in April 1946 and had been sent to Glasgow for training, but upon her return spent most of her time in the office undertaking clerical work in order to be on call for 'the special job when it comes along'. The solution as far as HMICS and the Chief Constable were concerned was to suggest the appointment of more policewomen to enable a wider range of duties to be covered, but the local police authority would only agree to do this 'on the grounds that they can carry out typing duties when not otherwise needed'. Matters came to a head with 'the refusal of the wives of the police to carry out escort duties' in Oban in 1948, forcing the police authority – already under sustained pressure from HMICS and the Chief Constable – to capitulate.[84]

The industrialisation, militarisation and economic regeneration of rural areas also led to the identification of a need for female officers. In 1961 the arrival of the US Navy Polaris and Poseidon nuclear submarine base in Holy Loch put pressure on policing in Dunoon, and Argyll County Council was now keen to appoint a further policewoman to work the area, given concerns about prostitution and moral protection. Janet Gray commented that '[t]here are eleven hotels, eight public houses and twelve cafes in Dunoon and these are frequented nightly by American servicemen and their girlfriends, with a small influx of women of doubtful character and morals from other areas.' Regular evening patrols were subsequently undertaken, a register was kept of women convicted of soliciting and trespass, and commercial premises were visited with the aim of safeguarding underage girls.[85] In Inverness-shire, where five women were in post by the mid-1960s, the growth of the tourist industry kept them occupied during the appropriate season. One policewoman was stationed at Kingussie to assist in duties at the ski slopes during the winter months (dealing with the perennial problem of 'lost' children) whilst another was posted to Mallaig to assist summer seaside visitors. By the early 1960s women serving in county forces felt that they performed a broad range of police functions; they worked as part of a male shift and were effectively generalists. As Moira put it: 'In a county force, you weren't limited. There were only so many of you and if there was work to be done, then all the police officers did it regardless of whether they were a policewoman or a policeman.'[86]

The prejudice of male colleagues was amongst the challenges that women faced when they arrived at a station (whether urban or rural) for the first time in the late 1940s and early 1950s. Sometimes this was rooted in reluctance to see women in roles that were anything other than clerical or secretarial. Often, too, it was reflective of paternalism that positioned women as in need of chivalric protection. Irene Livingstone joined Ayr Burgh Police in 1951, which at that time was 'the last plainclothes police force in Scotland'. She describes how male officers in higher ranks who joined in the 1920s 'weren't terribly keen on women joining', implying that attitudes were generational.[87] Indeed, Livingstone records how, when they were put into uniform in 1952, 'it was quite something'. Yet, when she suggested to the chief constable that the narrow skirt was impractical, he replied '"Miss Livingstone, you're not supposed to chase people up the High Street, remember you're a lady"'. She suggests he was outraged for similar reasons when he found out that she had typed up a statement relating to an indecent assault on a man that a male CID officer had passed on to her, and for which the officer was asked to apologise: 'the idea was that, as a lady, I wouldn't know about homosexual behaviour'.[88]

Moving to Glasgow in 1955, Livingstone enjoyed the opportunities it presented for 'a wider variety of work compared to Ayr' but nevertheless found similar patterns of prejudice when she was went out onto Division, away from the Policewomen's Department:

> The men were much more able to accept women in the job. But again you had the older men, the senior men, some of whom had joined in the '20s and '30s. When I first went to the Marine division the superintendent there didn't know what he had two CID women for, so what was he going to do with two uniformed girls? He didn't want us, and he made that perfectly plain.[89]

The strategy that was often adopted by women to develop their career in face of these restrictions was – tacitly and informally – to expand their remit, and to find male officers who were prepared to work with them below the radar. As Livingstone put it:

> We did as much in the way of police work as we possibly could, we got a row for it at times . . . the CID boss [on the Division] he used policewomen at every opportunity and we would do a lot of undercover jobs, plainclothes jobs.[90]

Janet Gray's annual inspection reports suggest that most (although not all) of these types of prejudice had been dispelled by the early 1960s as the interwar generation of senior male officers retired, and the model of the 'modern' policewoman (involved in an expanding portfolio of duties) gained acceptance.[91] Crucial to this acceptance, however, was the assumption that female officers were not competing with men for either appointment or promotion, had different conditions of employment, and were line-managed separately. Nevertheless, everyday sexism was part and parcel of police culture, along with the practice of 'station-stamping' new female recruits. In contrast to the 'social purity' ethos of the 1920s, policewomen had learnt to be pragmatists by the 1960s, internalising canteen culture: 'Sexist jokes were a thing, but you gave it back. There was no prudery. We didn't stand on our dignity and say "I will go to the Inspector" . . . You just dealt with it at the time.'[92]

In terms of recruitment, city and county forces faced different problems. Glasgow City tended to attract too many applicants for a limited number of places and, as a result, found it easy to turn away those who did not meet official recruitment criteria such as the minimum age of 22. Elsie had originally wanted to join the police in the mid-1930s:

> I had an interview with this old harridan of an inspector . . . and she said to me 'Away home and grow up'. So that kind of put me off, you know and it wasn't until the war and I thought 'I'll have another go again'.[93]

As small and rural forces in the Highlands and Islands began to appoint female officers in the years immediately after the Second World War, however, they struggled to attract more mature recruits and had to apply (to the Scottish Office) for exemptions in order to appoint keen young women. Mona Urquhart, who became the first 'WPC' in Inverness Burgh at the age of 19 in September 1947, had originally applied to Glasgow City but had been turned down on grounds of age. In 1946 she had secured a post as a typist at Inverness Police Headquarters where she was allowed to expand her role. At the point at which the Chief Constable requested an age exemption to employ her as a 'regular', she was 'already performing [a] police role': 'in the absence of the police matron, she has been able to handle female prisoners and children with absolute competency'.[94] The Scottish Office finally equalised the age restriction with male recruits in 1952.[95]

In the years immediately after the Second World War pay was also a problem that might deter recruits given that the salary of female officers was lower (by around 25 per cent) than that of men.[96] Despite debates about equal pay for equal work, both the Home Office and Scottish Office had decided to leave it up to individual forces to decide what to pay their policewomen in 1945. Indeed, the Scottish Office stated very revealingly: 'while we are far from minimising the value of moral force, we consider that police duties as a whole require a greater amount of physical force than it is reasonable to expect to find in a woman'.[97] Thus the rhetoric of gendered binaries was used once again to suggest that 'proper' police work was 'tough' physical policing (in line with the armed forces). Not only was women's work positioned as 'soft' policing, but the 'moral' and the 'physical' were viewed as contrasting categories. In 1953 it was, however, accepted that women's pay should be set at 90 per cent of male pay (justified in terms of the slightly shorter shifts women worked), an approach that was standardised across the UK (and reaffirmed by the Royal Commission of 1962) until full equal pay was finally achieved in 1974.[98]

Whilst the pay gap mirrored exactly that south of the border, the requirement that female officers must resign upon marriage continued to be a major and very significant discrepancy in women's conditions of employment. In 1946 the marriage bar for female officers was lifted in England and Wales (and allowance for maternity leave introduced) with the wide support of all constituencies within policing and in line with other public sector occupations. The proposal to follow suit in Scotland was opposed vociferously and unanimously (by chief constables, local authorities and the SPF) when the matter was discussed by the Scottish Police Council. Nevertheless, with an influx of younger women into policing by the 1950s, the problem of 'wastage' was becoming very apparent. Highly competent female officers, in whose training forces had invested, were leaving because they wished to marry and have a family (an aspiration that was held up as a norm for young women growing up in this decade) and the average length of service was diminishing to a few years. Barbara Denis de Vitré made her views about policewomen north of the border clear to the Scottish Office: 'they are, I believe, the only women so discriminated against, and I feel so strongly that we should establish the principle of their individual freedom'.[99] She suggested that 'Scottish girls were joining English forces largely because of the marriage bar' and that 'some of the younger policewomen in Scotland had a sense of grievance on the subject'. Increasingly, some chief constables had become frustrated by the directive and struggled to find a workaround. In Inverness Burgh, Urquhart, who had come top in her year (of both male and female officers) at Whitburn Training School in 1948, submitted her resignation to marry just two years' later.[100] With her Chief Constable's support she enrolled immediately afterwards as a Special Constable (a role she continued to perform for 30 years), as well as working in a paid capacity as a legal secretary.[101] The one policewoman employed in Stirling had had to resign in 1954 but, given that she still needed to work for financial reasons, was appointed as a civilian assistant; nevertheless, her duties were more limited and the Chief Constable lost the benefit of her training.

By 1955 opinion in Scotland was shifting, and the marriage bar faced criticism in parliament. The Scottish Office and county police authorities were keen to see it lifted. Its retention was defended by the Royal Burghs and by the SPF. Indeed, the latter view was shared by some female officers as well as male colleagues.[102] Elsie, who had chosen to develop a career as a policewoman and gained promotion to inspector, stated: 'When it was brought up at the Federation I fought it tooth and nail. It's not a job for a married woman.' The argument put forward by the SPF – and shared by Elsie – was that married women would be given special privileges (to specify their shift, or to take time off) causing 'discontent among their colleagues', whilst maternity leave would create further administrative problems, particularly in small forces.[103] Yet for Moira, who was required to resign in the early 1960s to marry, 'it was terrible': 'I couldn't bear to leave . . . The Chief Constable used to complain bitterly that he had just got a policewoman trained up to be of use and [she] had left. I desperately wanted to stay, but there was no way I could stay.' She became aware in later years that some senior policewomen 'were able to form partnerships as a gay couple – two policewomen living together. At that time, you talked about "sharing a flat", but in fact they were lesbians. It took me years to find that out'.[104] Despite (or perhaps because of) the emphasis on heterosexual marriage as a goal for women in the 1950s, same-sex relationships and strong friendships tended to pass under the radar and were rarely commented upon, discussed or named. The marriage bar remained contentious in Scotland but was not lifted until 1968, over 20 years after England and Wales.

In the years 1945–70 women's roles in Scottish policing were expanded from within, most crucially through the work of HMICS, and in particular Barbara Denis de Vitré and Janet Gray as tactful but persistent 'modernisers'. Yet women's roles continued to be shaped by structures, cultures and conditions of service that institutionalised gender difference. The hybrid identity of police/woman was formalised through the institution of the 'specialist' Policewoman's Department, which was highly influential in urban areas. Across the UK, it had become established policy for women officers (now present in all forces other than Zetland) to take all statements from adult women and children.[105] Nevertheless, female officers were quietly, gradually, but very effectively developing a broader profile of work that was generalist, and moving into areas that had previously been seen as the preserve of men. In the cities they worked next to men in Divisional stations. They were also joining other specialist units, such as scenes of crime teams for which they were trained in photographic work and fingerprinting, and they were incorporated into unit beat policing as members of mixed teams in the mid-1960s.[106] In more rural constabularies (where women were employed in very small numbers) there was yet more potential for them to become part of a male shift, working with male rather than female colleagues on duties that were not specifically linked to the essential fact of being a woman. Four women were seconded to the Scottish Crime Squad when it was set up in 1969. The initial prejudices of senior male officers had created problems in the late 1940s and early 1950s. However, the remarkable mission creep of the 1950s and 1960s was effected with little resistance because it was carefully contained – both within separate line management structures and through the persistence of the rhetoric of a 'particular' women's 'sphere' in policing – with the effect that female officers were not seen as competitors.[107]

Beyond 'Equality'?

In 1975 female officers in Scotland (as in England and Wales) were fully integrated with men in response to the Sex Discrimination Act of that year. The designation of 'WPC' (Woman Police Constable) disappeared overnight along with the institution of the Policewomen's Department. All were now 'police officers', subject to the same line management, recruitment and promotions processes, and conditions of service. In Scotland, the change took place at the same time as regionalisation, through one mass reorganisation process. For those who joined in the early 1970s integration felt a logical progression, since they had already experienced the expansion that had taken place in women's policing roles as a positive development. Yet there were significant negative effects of integration that were felt into the 1980s, including the loss of their important specialist and (community oriented) advisory role, complaints from male colleagues about women's lack of physical strength which did not help working relationships, and women's lack of visibility in senior roles.

Janet, who joined Glasgow City Police several years before formal 'integration', recounts that she felt 'more' than 'equal' from her first day in the job. Although recruited and trained as a 'policewoman' (which involved additional classes on sexual offences and child protection), she was seconded to the CID for further training following her probationary period. This enabled her to gain very broad experience:

> I did fraud squad, drug squad, flying squad, and general CID, stolen car squad . . . I had 6 months in each. I was very lucky. I was one of the first women to be allowed to do that . . . Then I went into general CID. A lot of us got a great respect from our male colleagues, if you were good at what you did . . . And very often [I] was referred to for advice, especially when I went into CID, because I think my woman police background and grounding in dealing with major crime and sexual offences and crimes against children [meant that] . . . when you went into CID you were actually given a lot of respect . . . Because we were specialist we were given a lot of respect by the men and I never felt unequal, ever . . . We were not only equal, we were more.[108]

Looking back, Janet's perception of male colleagues in the early 1970s is a very positive one: that they welcomed her as part of the team and recognised the particular strengths she brought as a specialist female officer. However, she saw the demise of the Policewomen's Department as leading to a concomitant loss of expertise (and failure to recognise its value): 'I often talked to women about it later, about how specialised we were and they could see where I was coming from . . . all my expertise, if you like, had gone.'

During the reorganisation of 1975 there was no discussion of how this specialist knowledge, built up over many decades, would be replicated. Indeed, the Third Report of the Edmund-Davies Committee, published in 1979, commented that across Great Britain integration 'had resulted in a serious loss of expertise in dealing with juveniles, missing persons and certain offences such as rape'.[109] The Policewomen's Departments had undoubtedly had their limitations. As this chapter has suggested and others have also argued, concerns about the wellbeing of young women had sometimes been blurred by 'moral purity' objectives, and protection had sometimes merged into control.[110] The work of female officers was restricted by the parameters of the law in defining categories of offences and the working of the courts as to what was seen as permissible evidence. The Moorov case of 1930 had been a significant moment in showing that legal assumptions could be challenged for the benefit of female complainants. Nevertheless, given the highlighting of the hidden incidence of past child abuse and exploitation through the recent series of enquiries in Scotland and other parts of the British Isles, the remit of the Policewomen's Departments (viewed with the benefit of hindsight) was limited in what it was able to achieve.[111] Back in 1925 Emily Miller had commented that only a small tip of the very large 'iceberg' that was the actual incidence of sexual offences against children was ever reported.[112] Those who are able to reflect back on their careers now have become aware that they were working 'in the dark'. In relation to some cases female officers have only realised retrospectively that they might have been returning teenage 'runaways' to abusive situations at home or in care. Until recent decades, too, there was little acknowledgement of the abuse of boys. As Janet explained: 'Society has become more aware of it, and we are learning now how to deal with it better' but 'at the time . . . it was investigated to the best of our abilities'.[113]

The 1979 Edmund-Davies Report also suggested that the abolition of Policewomen's Departments had led to an 'indefinable loss' of a 'social service role' and of 'community involvement': 'Mothers used to consult women officers about their problems, and about their children's problems, especially in the city centre areas where the need for help was greatest.'[114] The orientation of the Policewomen's Departments was towards preventive work (advising and helping) rather than invoking the letter of the law, which was the route of last resort. Of course, female officers, too, were often seen as the 'public face' of policing, as representatives of the version of police–community relations that the police service wished to publicise. Moreover, whilst female officers may well have facilitated effective police-community relationships, their number was small, and an overwhelming majority of the population would never have interacted with them in person. Given the development of Community Involvement Branches in Scotland (which made use of mixed teams) from 1971, the loss of Policewomen's Departments may have been offset earlier than in England and Wales. Nevertheless, it is notable that by the time of the 'discovery' of 'community policing' in the 1970s, the 'traditional' work of female colleagues was presented in this vein.

In his Annual Report of 1976 Chief HMICS David Gray articulated very different concerns about integration through essentialist arguments regarding biological sex, violence and physical force:

> Every effort has been made by the Chief Constables to implement the provisions of the Sex Discrimination Act . . . but with limited success . . . due solely to the physical unsuitability of women to cope with drunken violent hooligans, particularly in rough areas on night duty. Senior officers state

quite openly that they are not prepared to send 'slips of girls' to handle potentially violent situations. Beat sergeants and constables speak highly of the courage of the girls and of their willingness to play their part but say they feel bound to adopt a protective role towards the women who therefore become less effective than men.[115]

The realities of station life, including the infantilisation of women as 'slips of girls', the paternalistic approach of bosses, and the continued 'rough' and highly muscular nature of the encounters that made up urban policing in Scotland, are conveyed here. In 1977 Gray went on to argue that the Police Service, like the armed forces, should have been excluded from some sections of the Sex Discrimination Act.[116] This contrasted markedly with the inspectorate in England and Wales whose 1977 Annual Report discreetly stated that women's achievements in policing had 'done much to dispel many of the early misgivings about their involvement in every type of duty'.[117] Gray's rhetoric was referred to at the annual conference of the SPF in April 1978 in a speech made by the Federation's chair, who argued that the Sex Discrimination Act was 'impractical in the police service', that 'God made us differently and an act of Parliament cannot change it', and that '"slips of girls", as Her Majesty's Chief Inspector of Constabulary chose to call them . . . [were] not capable of coping with the ever-increasing violence and physical confrontation that society today is producing'.[118] This speech was widely reported in both the Scottish and UK press, which also recorded that it was met with a standing ovation from an assembled audience of over 200 rank-and-file delegates.[119]

By the late 1970s, the issue of female officers had become a tool in the dispute concerning police pay, which had not been improved since 1962. It was claimed that high quality female candidates had applied to the police service in 1975 and 1976, whilst the quality and volume of male applicants had fallen. This was because the police starting salary was considered high for women and low for men, given the wide gender pay gap generally. Back in 1974, the proportion of 'policewomen' within the Scottish police service had been capped at around 5 per cent. With 'integration' the cap was lifted and, by 1977, 16 per cent of probationers (those with less than two years' service) were female. Indeed, the Edmund-Davies Committee, whilst commenting on women's roles, was appointed to look specifically at police pay and recommended pay rises (which were implemented) in its First Report of 1978. Yet the Police Federations (of England and Wales as well as Scotland) undoubtedly used the occasion of the Edmund-Davies review – and the dispute about pay – to bolster the hegemonic view that male officers were key to the success of the service. Thus the Third Edmund-Davies Report of 1979 suggested that over-representation of women (feminisation) would lead to a decline in the status of policing: 'If the proportions were to increase greatly it is at least a possibility that the efficiency and perhaps the credibility of the police might be damaged . . . on the grounds of their physical ability to do certain police jobs.'[120]

There was clearly a significant and concerted backlash that aimed to ensure that women remained a small minority in the police service - by constructing them as a problem. Despite the initial spike in recruitment in 1976–7, the proportion of women in policing in Scotland flat-lined. In 1984 it was 5.5 per cent across Scotland, exactly the same as it had been in 1975 (compared to 9.2 per cent in England and Wales).[121] When the female Vice-Chair of the SPF was reported as proposing a motion at the 1987 annual conference calling for positive discrimination (in the form of a minimum target to be set for female recruits) the response from the floor was 'facetious', involving sexual innuendo about 'vital statistics' and women on 'top'.[122] Women still only constituted 8.6 per cent of the police strength in Scotland in 1990. It was not until the 1990s that more strategic equal opportunities policies were required for all police forces in relation to both gender and ethnicity, leading to the presentation of policing as an occupation requiring a diverse range of skills sets and, subsequently, a more significant rise in the proportion of female officers in Scotland to 16 per cent in 2000.[123]

Finally, despite 'equality', those women who made it into policing found it difficult to develop a career – in Scotland as in England and Wales – until the very end of the twentieth century. The proportion of women in promoted roles remained small: 8 per cent of all female officers in 1977, with a further drop to 6.4 per cent in 1990, whilst the proportion of male officers in promoted roles remained consistent at around 25 per cent. In large part this was because most female officers still left the service when they had children, and thus did not build up the length of service and, crucially, the experience that was necessary to gain promotion. In 1990, for example, only 14 per cent of female officers had more than 15 years of service compared to 45 per cent of men. In 1988 an independent team based at the University of Strathclyde examined the effect of the Sex Discrimination Act on the Scottish police service. They surveyed a representative sample of 3,800 police officers across seven out of the eight Scottish police forces; of these 71 per cent of male respondents indicated that they had children compared to only 7 per cent of female respondents.[124] There was no provision for flexible or part-time working, with the effect that women chose to resign rather than bring up a young family whilst working police shifts full-time. Moreover, both the 1988 study and a 1993 thematic report undertaken by HMICS suggested that female colleagues were deployed more narrowly than male counterparts, having 'less experience in criminal investigation and traffic functions, and much more in community involvement', which meant that they were seen as less qualified for senior roles.[125] According to the 1993 report, where women were employed in CIDs this tended either to be in drug squads or 'in the specialist units that had been set up to deal with sexual offences and child abuse' and had emerged to fill the vacuum left by the Policewomen's Departments as a result of heightened public concerns in the mid-1980s.[126] This work – and indeed, the work that women had undertaken for many years in the Policewomen's Departments prior to integration – tended to be seen as 'limited' in terms of experience and thus value when it came to the promotions competitions. In one unnamed force, the CID was characterised by a focus group as 'the last bastion of prejudice in the police service', suggesting the persistence here of a sexist 'detective' culture.[127] The 1993 report asserted that 'most female officers are capable of handling themselves in all situations' and advocated 'improved training and better equipment' as the way forward to enable all officers (irrespective of gender) to deal effectively with violent situations, shifting the debate away from physical strength.[128] Part-time working was also proposed, in recognition that working practices needed to change. Thus at the level of official rhetoric, the 1993 HMICS thematic report signified something of a paradigm shift.

It was not until 1995, some 20 years after the Sex Discrimination Act, that Sandra Hood became the first woman in Scotland to hold the rank of Chief Superintendent in charge of a police division. Norma Graham was appointed as Scotland's first female Deputy Chief Constable (for Fife) in 2005, and then Chief Constable from 2008 to 2012; this was some 12 years after the appointment of the first female chief in England (Pauline Clare in Lancashire in 1996). Yet unlike in England, no high-profile case of sexual discrimination or sexual harassment was brought by a female officer against her employers in Scotland.[129] Indeed, the 1993 report argued that female officers did 'not recognise the culture said to be prevalent' in England and Wales.[130] When it came to 'banter', 'female officers were clearly not inhibited from tackling colleagues who "over-stepped the mark"' and '"gave as good as they got"'. According to some female staff, 'Scottish women knew how to handle themselves and would not let matters get out of hand', whilst others suggested that the continued influence of 'Scottish religious traditions' acted as a check on male behaviours.[131] The fact that the marriage bar continued for so long in Scotland perhaps also suggests that socially conservative and paternalist views were persistent in shaping gender attitudes within Scottish police culture and thus, where discrimination occurred, it was more likely to be normalised as 'chivalric' and 'protective'.

CONCLUSIONS

The disputes about the gendering of policing, which emerged in the immediate wake of the Sex Disqualification Act, demonstrate the continued prevalence into the late twentieth century of long-established modes of thinking about policing as a manual occupation grounded in physical force and strength, delivered mainly by men. Equal opportunities frameworks and, importantly, the technological revolution of the last 30 years have enabled a radical overhaul in ideas about who might be a police officer and a refocusing on skill (including a range of emotional and intellectual skills) rather than strength. Many of the aims that are seen as core to community responsiveness in policing today – to safeguard children and young people and to enable disclosure, to protect the most vulnerable, to develop preventive and support functions – are recognisable (although articulated through rather different rhetoric) in the work of female police officers earlier in the twentieth century. A social work ethos was embedded directly in policing through the early work of female statement-takers and then the work of Policewomen's Departments. This was a direct result of the fact that this work was demanded by women's organisations – on behalf of women and children within local communities – at crucial moments of social change. This work was highly significant because of the recognition it gave victims/survivors of abuse, although it was ultimately limited in what it was able to deliver given the lack of resources and the restrictions of working within existing police cultures and structures. Across the twentieth century anecdotal evidence gives us glimpses of the ways in which female police officers were able to build relationships of trust with some women and children in what were hard-to-reach communities by establishing a familiar presence and offering advice and support; much of the work that they did could not be quantified. Nevertheless, female officers were aware, too, of the precarious nature of this trust, of its dependence on 'personality', and of the problem of balancing the roles of law enforcer and confidant.

Notes

1. PP, *HMICS ARs*: 1939, Cmd. 6193; 1950, Cmd. 6936; 1960, Cmnd. 1390; 1970, Cmnd. 4754.
2. *Scotsman*, 10 September 1915.
3. Glasgow City Museums, SP.2000.44, Rachel Hamilton (1829–75), http://www.theglasgowstory.com/image/?inum=TGSE00317 (last accessed 1 January 2020).
4. IWM, Emp. 43/102, WPS report on 'HM Explosives Factory, Gretna'.
5. Cree, '"Khaki fever"'; Wollacott, '"Khaki fever"'. On women patrols in the broader British context see Woodeson, 'First women police'; Levine, 'Walking the streets'.
6. IWM, Emp. 42.3/2 Report of the Women Patrols Committee for Scotland 1914–1920.
7. Ibid.
8. NRS, HH31/16/10, Scottish Office circular 780, 5 December 1914.
9. NRS, HH31/16/2, letter, Scottish Office to Home Office, 6 November 1914.
10. IWM, Emp. 42.3/2.
11. NRS, HH31/16 /4, quoted by CC Stevenson, Glasgow, 16 November 1914.
12. Cree, '"Khaki fever"'.

13. IWM, Emp. 42.5/51, leaflet, 'How women can help', Women Patrols Committee for Scotland, n.d.
14. Barbour, *Katherine Scott*, 27.
15. IWM, Emp. 42.5/58, Women Patrols Committee for Scotland, leaflet, November 1917.
16. Bland, *Banishing the Beast*.
17. Davidson, *Illicit and Unnatural*.
18. Cree, *Public Streets*, 23.
19. *Evening Telegraph and Post*, 1 December 1911 and 5 December 1911; *GH*, 6 December 1911.
20. *GH*, 10 September 1915; *Scotsman*, 10 September 1915.
21. IWM, Emp. 42.3/2.
22. TNA, HO 45/10806/309485.
23. NRS, HH55/347, deputation to the Scottish Secretary, 1918.
24. *Aberdeen Daily Journal*, 1 October 1913; 19 February 1918; 5 May 1921; 7 February 1922; NRS, HH31/16/10, letter from CC of Aberdeen, 7 December 1914.
25. PP, Committee on the Employment of Women on Police Duties (Baird Committee), *Minutes of Evidence*, (1921) Cmd. 1133, Q. 2078.
26. TNA, HO 45/19675, Second Report of the Scottish Training School, 1920.
27. PP, Cmd. 1133, Q. 1921.
28. Breitenbach and Wright, 'Women as active'.
29. PP, Cmd. 1133, Q. 1929. *Dundee Courier*, 30 May 1922.
30. Scottish Office, Whitehall, 1 August 1919–1775/277 Circular 1485, 'Policewomen'.
31. PP, Baird Committee, *Report*, (1920), Cmd. 877, paragraph 88.
32. *Dundee Courier*, 30 May 1922 and 15 August 1922; NRS, HH55/606.
33. *Standard*, 15 October 1937 and PP, Cmd. 1133, Q. 2008 which refers to a 'certain sphere of duty'.
34. Kent, *Making Peace*.
35. NRS, HH55/474.
36. PP, Cmd. 1133; PP, Departmental Committee on Sexual Offences against Children and Young People in Scotland, *Report* (1926), Cmd. 2592, and NRS, E878/73, Child Assault Committee: transcripts of evidence, 1925.
37. PP, Cmd. 1133, Q. 2079.
38. Ibid., Q. 2078.
39. PP, Cmd. 1133, Q. 2118–19.
40. Ibid., Q. 1956
41. NRS, E878/73, 673.
42. PP, Cmd. 1133, Q. 2055.
43. PP, Departmental Committee on Sexual Offences against Young Persons [England and Wales], *Report* (1925) Cmd. 2561.
44. PP, Cmd. 2592, paragraph 139.
45. Tancred, *Women Police*, 6.
46. They were also used for covert surveillance of 'Bolshevik, Communist and other political meetings' in the Northern Division in June 1921: GCA, SR22/63/18, letter of 25 June 1921.

47. NRS, E878/73, 971.
48. Ibid., 678.
49. PP, Cmd. 2592, paragraph 139.
50. NRS, E878/73, 556.
51. Ibid., 535.
52. Ibid., 971.
53. Ibid., 969.
54. *Scotsman*, 1 April 1926.
55. NRS, E878/68, Memorandum on moral welfare work by Miss Miller, 7 May 1925.
56. Ibid.
57. PP, Cmd. 1133, Q. 228–9.
58. NRS, E878/73, 524.
59. GCA, SR22/57/23, all records were retained for those in post or joining from 1926 onwards.
60. NRS, HH55/474.
61. Scottish Screen Archive, T0025; Sawarnjit Matharu, Colourful Heritage Online Archive, https://www.colourfulheritage.com/portfolio/sawarnjit-matharu/ (last accessed 11 May 2020).
62. Moorov v. H.M. Advocate, JC, 18 July 1930, 68–94.
63. NRS, HH55/1641, Irene Livingstone, 'In appreciation' (on death of Ellen Webster), typescript, 1972: refers to Webster's own notes as the source of information.
64. GCA, SR22/57/23.
65. Cockerill, *Percy Sillitoe*, 159.
66. PP, *HMICS AR*, 1938, Cmd. 5988.
67. Metropolitan Police Museum, Box 2, City of Glasgow Police, report of work done by woman patrols, 17 October 1941.
68. PP, *HMICS AR*, 1945, Cmd. 6936.
69. TNA, HO 45/19674, letter, Tancred to Sir Alexander Maxwell, 24 October 1939.
70. Jackson, *Women Police*, 27.
71. PP, *HMICS AR*, 1972, Cmnd. 5415.
72. NRS, HH55/494 Ayr County, Policewomen.
73. Metropolitan Police Museum, Papers of Miss K. M. Hill, handwritten inspection notes, 'Glasgow', July/August 1945, 1946 and 1947.
74. GCA, SR22/40, Glasgow, CC AR, 1955, 1960 and 1965.
75. Women's Library (London), 8WPC/A, Women Police Collection, Interview participant 34, Elsie (pseudonym).
76. *GH*, 17 November 1950.
77. PP, *HMICS AR*, 1960, Cmnd. 1390; 1965, Cmnd. 3032.
78. NRS, HH55/783.
79. NRS, HH55/606.
80. Interview with Moira (pseudonym), conducted by Davidson.
81. Ibid.
82. NRS, HH55/778.
83. Ibid.
84. NRS, HH55/777.

85. Ibid.
86. Interview with Moira.
87. Livingstone, 'Police Officer', 89.
88. Ibid., 90.
89. Ibid., 91.
90. Ibid.
91. For example, NRS, HH55/494.
92. Interview with Moira.
93. Women's Library, 8WPC/A, Interview 34.
94. NRS, HH55/790.
95. NRS, HH55/474.
96. NRS, HH55/774.
97. Ibid.
98. Ibid.
99. NRS, HH55/776, letter from Denis de Vitré to Charles C. Cunningham, 8 February 1954.
100. NRS, HH55/790.
101. *Scotsman*, 2 June 2016, 'Obituary: Mona Sutherland Mackenzie', http://www.scotsman.com/news/obituaries/obituary-mona-sutherland-mackenzie-pioneering-wpc-and-special-constable-1-4144957 (last accessed 1 January 2020).
102. Women were recognised as full members of the SPF in 1964, and as 'advisors' 1953–64: NRS, HH 55/1641.
103. NRS, HH55/776.
104. Interview with Moira.
105. Jackson, *Women Police*, 190.
106. PP, *HMICS AR*, 1963, Cmnd, 2368.
107. Ibid.
108. Women's Library, 8WPC/A, Interview 36, Janet (pseudonym).
109. PP, Committee of Inquiry on the Police (Edmund-Davies Committee), *Report III*, (1979), Cmnd. 7633, 87–8.
110. Cree, '"Khaki fever"'; Levine, '"Walking the streets"'; Jackson, *Women Police*.
111. For the Scottish Child Abuse Inquiry, see https://www.childabuseinquiry.scot/ (last accessed 1 January 2020).
112. NRS, E878/73, 525.
113. Women's Library, 8WPC/A, Interview 36.
114. PP, Cmnd. 7633, 87–8.
115. PP, *HMICS AR*, 1976, Cmnd. 6891.
116. PP, *HMICS AR*, 1977, Cmnd. 7306.
117. PP, *HMICS AR*, 1976, Paper number 414, 12.
118. *Scotsman*, 27 April 1978.
119. NRS, HH55/1641, press cuttings.
120. PP, Cmnd. 7633, 88.
121. HH55/1637.
122. *Scotsman* 24 April 1987.
123. HH55/1637; PP, *HMICS AR*, 2000, Cm. 4881.

124. HH55/1637, 'Effect of the Sex Discrimination Act on the police', University of Strathclyde, 1989, 16 and 12 (Strathclyde Police had declined to participate in the study).
125. Ibid., 8–9.
126. HMICS, *Thematic Inspection on Equal Opportunities* (Edinburgh, Scottish Office, 1993), 10.
127. Ibid., 11.
128. Ibid., 13
129. Jones, *Policewomen*; Brown and Heidensohn, *Gender and Policing*, 82–4.
130. HMICS, *Thematic Inspection*, 17–18.
131. HMICS, *Thematic Inspection*, 17–18.

7

CONCLUDING THE TWENTIETH CENTURY

This book has laid out a set of trajectories through which the relationship between police officers and communities can be charted across the twentieth century. We examined the ways in which modes of governance (the formal relationships between police officers, the state and local communities) were structured and articulated through public discourse, demarcating (in particular) a shift from municipal to (Scottish) national identity and accountability. We then used examples from contrasting social and geographical environments – the Glasgow conurbation and the Highlands and Islands as examples of 'urban' and 'rural' – to examine police styles, tactics, and interactions with a range of social and demographic groups across time. Finally, we charted the history of women's recruitment, highlighting the ways in which policing as an occupation was constructed, performed and embodied as explicitly male until the late twentieth century. In 1900, the practical job of the uniform beat officer was physically gruelling and dependent, in the most challenging urban locations, on the ability to demonstrate physical prowess when contested; uniforms, equipment and technology were rudimentary and officers were recruited from the white (probably Protestant) male manual labour force. By 2000, technological innovation, specialisation, professionalisation, and recognition of the benefits of diversity – in terms of social background as well as skills – were beginning to shift assumptions about who should be a police officer. It was a gradual but uneven route, in which the pace of change accelerated very significantly from the 1980s onwards. This book has focused on the period 1900–75 as that which has been least well-charted and is increasingly moving beyond living memory, but which also bears scrutiny as a period in which the predominant duties of constables – as the bulwark of policing – remained remarkably constant.

One of the central aims of this book has been to identify which factors (and dynamics) led to co-operation and trust, and which to conflict. Our study suggests that village constables in rural areas – and, to an extent, beat officers in smaller burghs – were more likely to be embedded within the social networks and everyday routines of the settled population. This was in large part because of their wider brief: as generalists carrying out a broad spectrum of duties from crime enquiries (often as first port of call) through to the administration of licence renewals and livestock checks. The relationship between officers and communities was personalised, with respect won through tact and diplomacy as individual officers were closely scrutinised upon arrival. High levels of autonomy and discretion created the capacity that led to both the most and least effective forms of policing, depending on the disposition of the officer concerned: from the point of view of the police authorities, building trust was only helpful if it ensured public order (rather than complaint) and was seen to reflect impartiality and regard towards the rule of law. Thus the policing model in the Highlands and Islands increasingly sought to balance propinquity with distancing, through the rotational system. Nevertheless, we suggest that accessibility, visibility, social familiarity and thus knowledge of local contexts – if combined with high levels of professionalisation (including training) and strong support mechanisms – can optimise police responsiveness to local need. These characteristics are likely to remain crucial, whether or not a physical base within communities is retained (given the information and communications revolutions of the twenty-first century).

Within the most urbanised of Scotland's environments, a strong group identity as 'police' undoubtedly enabled resilience within settings in which officers routinely encountered hostility in the first decades of the twentieth century. Yet in the longer term, this potentially reinforced, rather than eroded, distinctions between 'police' and 'policed' as oppositional groups. Beat constables were most likely to forge working relationships and alliances with the proprietors of small businesses that were often symbiotic (involving the exchange of services for information). The police box system enabled officers with a clear social work orientation to act as a point of advice, help and support for residents in poorer neighbourhoods. When there was an emergency (or an accident or death), the beat officer was either the bearer of news or the person to call on. These were not tasks that made their way into official audit figures, but they took up the majority of a beat officer's time and were analogous to many of the routine tasks carried out by rural officers. Where this role had been lacking – in housing schemes where local beat men had never been deployed – trust and confidence in the police was known to be very low in the 1960s. Yet trust had also been low earlier in the century in some areas of Glasgow that had been part of the 'traditional' beat system. Thus a complex set of dynamics was apparent, in which the co-existence of 'soft' policing tactics alongside 'hard' ones did not ensure that the former diffused the latter – particularly where different groups were targeted by different officers using different repertoires. It was this gap that the 'Community Involvement' initiatives of the 1970s aimed to fill, delivering social interventions in partnership with schools and other agencies to young people in areas of deprivation.

The reputation for 'toughness' that was a trademark of Glasgow City Police in the first decades of the twentieth century was in part forged through heavy-handed tactics, which sought to deal with high levels of conflict by matching or beating them. These tactics may have added to the status of the police within a predominantly masculine street culture, but they reinforced and exacerbated distrust and fear in some neighbourhoods when they did not accurately distinguish between the genuinely 'law-abiding' and 'trouble-making'. In the years after the Second World War, physical admonishment (for young men) gave way to heavy reliance on arrests for BoP, which was used as a 'proactive response' to discipline individuals even if no actual prosecution resulted.[1] The formal shift away from physical admonishment – the 'heavy-handed' approach – cannot be specifically dated. Rather it played out gradually as the politics and culture of deference were slowly replaced with greater inclusivity across the latter half of the twentieth century. Indeed, the general shift in cultures of discipline (of which it was part) was demonstrably slow, given that young offenders could be sentenced to birching (by a police officer at a police station) until 1948, and physical punishment was not banned in state schools until 1986.[2]

It is in relation to the policing of public protest (whether political demonstrations or industrial disputes) that the tensions within what is often described as the 'civil' model of policing (and its apparent distinction from 'military' or hybrid models) are most often exposed. On the one hand the 'civil' model (articulated, as we have seen, in Scotland) is grounded rhetorically and conceptually in consent and impartiality in applying the law. On the other hand, it rests ultimately on coercion and operates in practice through discretion, as police officers are required to make judgements as to whether making an arrest would be in the interests of maintaining the peace. As Weinberger states: 'the breadth and vagueness of the law itself, particularly in public order matters' is 'so imprecise' that 'virtually any public behaviour could be made an arrestable offence'.[3] It is in this context that fissures between the interests of the state (whether local or national) and those of its various citizens (and their competing rights) have, historically, been most exposed. This book has suggested that the legacy of such encounters was profound in some parts of Scotland. Whilst in the Western Isles the bitter conflict of the 1880s between crofters and law enforcement officers (both civil police and military) was not repeated in the twentieth century – as police in the Highlands and Islands sought to stress their independence – these experiences remained within living memory for several generations, leading to a residual attitude that the police represented the interests of large landowners. Similarly, memories and stories of the General Strike of 1926 were a reference point in areas of the west of Scotland into the 1960s, suggesting that the experience of interwar policing shaped perceptions in the post-war years. This is a salient reminder that 'history' is not sequential and linear, but sedimentary and multi-faceted. These narratives remained in play at the same time as the historical account of Scottish policing as a 'local service' protecting 'the common weal' was also under construction within the policy community. Yet in Glasgow itself there was remarkably little formal criticism of police methods in the first quarter of the twentieth century given the scale of protest and industrial disputes. Weinberger's argument that the official recognition that the Labour movement had achieved within local politics enabled dialogue and mediation (for example, around the policing of picketing) remains a convincing one.

Whilst the immediate post-war years can be associated with conscious attempts to build public trust (including through the JLS, youth work and community involvement schemes as well as through the press and media), the economic and political conditions of the 1970s–80s once again led to a series of flashpoints between police and protesters.[4] This culminated in the miners' strike of 1984–5, during which concerns about police intimidation and the significant erosion of civil liberties were raised by the Scottish Trades Union Congress, the SCCL, Scottish Labour MPs and local councillors (amongst others). These centred on what were new uses of BoP and obstruction charges – themselves dating back to the nineteenth century – to stop secondary picketing (at Ravenscraig steelworks and Hunterston terminal in particular). Critics argued that these tactics constituted harassment of travelling miners and denial of the right to freedom of movement. On 10 May 1984 buses containing miners had been stopped by Strathclyde Police on various major roads and requested to turn back, on the grounds that to continue would be 'likely' to lead to a BoP. Those who refused to do so were arrested in numbers and charged with obstructing the police in the course of their duties (which entailed prevention of the commission of offences).[5] Former Solicitor General, Labour's John McCluskey, argued at the time that the police would be 'seen to be taking sides', leading to a 'chasm between the police and large numbers of the public who normally have no quarrel' with them.[6] Conservative Secretary of State George Younger rejected the assertion of Labour MPs that the police had been acting 'politically' as well as the call for an inquiry into the Strathclyde actions.[7] As Jim Phillips has argued, a 'robust and partial approach was being taken by the police . . . in an increasingly violent and confrontational atmosphere'.[8]

Miners reported brutality by the police on picket lines and in the making of arrests, whilst it is apparent now that convictions for even minor charges led to years of blacklisting by employers. At the time, the police stressed the level of injury sustained by officers and emphasised the need to protect the rights of the small number of strike-breakers who chose to return.[9] Yet strike-breaking was anathema within the moral economy (value system) of close-knit mining communities, creating a scenario in which tensions with police were likely to be exacerbated.[10] In some cases, too, 'good understanding' between 'local' police and strike leaders were de-stabilised when officers from other forces were brought in as reinforcement under the 'mutual aid' system.[11]

It was incontrovertible that the strike was damaging relationships between police officers and those amongst whom they lived and worked. Labour MPs such as Alex Eadie (Midlothian) spoke of the 'damage which was being done to the police relationship with the community'.[12] In July 1984 Scotland's chief constables wrote in confidence to the Scottish Office of their 'serious concern' regarding 'lasting damage' that violence connected to the strike was causing:

> This confrontation, with the police as referees, if allowed to continue is likely to have a profound affect [sic] on the Police Service, not only in industrial situations but in the way in which it is able to fulfil its accepted role in the community.[13]

Yet the full consequences of these events await final evaluation. In September 2018 the Scottish government launched an independent review of the impact of policing on communities during the miners' strike, given that 'the scars from the experience still run deep'.[14] As Review Lead, John Scott QC Solicitor Advocate has commented, 'there is much material available on the 1984/85 Strike . . . but not much of that looks specifically at the impact on community relations of the policing of the strike'.[15] Personal testimony has been placed at its core. At the time of writing, the full report of findings had not yet been published. Over 30 years after the strike, the aim of the review is 'to bring a degree of closure – crucially, of a positive kind, through openness, disclosure and understanding'.[16] Some lessons have already been learned for policing. It can be argued that one of the major transformations of the late twentieth century has been the adoption of a 'community policing approach' which views protesters as 'a protest community' with whom the police might work in partnership, and the avoidance of 'tough policing measures'.[17]

The conflict that arose in Liverpool and London over 'proactive' use of stop-and-search and its targeting of Black youth was regarded 'as an "English" issue' in Scotland in the 1970s-80s.[18] Yet in Scotland the equivalent was the 'proactive' use of the BoP charge in relation to specific groups of white working-class males (including protesters, striking miners, and youth). As we have shown, it had long been a mainstay of the repertoire of Glasgow policing, but by the 1970s was increasingly challenged from a civil liberties' perspective. It was not that such methods were new, but that public expectations were changing. For psychologist Evelyn Schaffer, writing in 1980, hostility to police intervention was apparent in Scotland but simply less visible in the media: 'in a deprived area of Strathclyde a near riot developed after the police had arrested a local criminal . . . [but it was] not a subject for headline news' because 'all those involved' were white.[19] Whilst there were contentions around policing tactics, these were not framed through the experience of race and ethnicity, which took longer to become a priority. Indeed, community involvement and crime prevention initiatives of the 1970s-90s – including the Safer Cities programme launched in 1989 – tended to focus on white working-class communities rather than minority groups.[20] Writing in 1992, Bashir Maan suggested that, whilst Scots were perceived as comparatively 'more tolerant and more friendly', 'resignation and [thus] complacency about racial prejudice and discrimination' amongst first generation Asians had 'contributed to the "no problem here" concept'.[21]

The catalyst for change in approaches to race relations was the publication (in 2000) of the report into the police investigation of the murder of Sunjit Singh Chhokar. Alongside changes in equalities legislation (imposing a public sector duty to promote racial equality) and the need to respond to the 1999 Macpherson Report, this led to the development of a more strategic approach towards diversity.[22] In his report on the Chhokar case, Dr Raj Jandoo concluded that 'institutional racism had occurred' within Strathclyde Police because of a failure 'to meet equally the needs of all the people whom it serves, having regard to their racial, ethnic or cultural background'. Although policies had been developed since 1987, they had not been translated 'into action by every individual police officer'.[23] In its subsequent 2001 report, based on consultation with BAME community groups, HMICS recognised 'serious issues of confidence . . . among members of black and minority ethnic communities which should not be underestimated'. As previously, with the appointment of JLOs and other community liaison officers, good practice was not mainstreamed across policing but concentrated in the hands of a small number of 'champions'. Amongst BAME communities there were perceptions of being 'more likely . . . the subject of stop and search' and of the police not addressing 'their particular needs', as well as concerns about under-reporting of racist incidents because older generations were 'putting up with racism as an unavoidable way of life'.[24]

Whilst Scottish exceptionalism was presented as an absence of 'race issues', a probing of the history of relationships between police and communities makes it clear that this has long been otherwise.[25] Ethno-religious prejudice was apparent within the informal culture of some west-of-Scotland police forces, whilst antisemitic and racist tropes led to the stereotyping of minority groups in terms of criminality at various points across the first two-thirds of the twentieth century. Forms of racism that were present within a wider society clearly spilled over into policing and criminal justice, shaping approaches, responses, and assumptions. Yet across the century, officers sometimes acted as informal mediators between minority groups and majority populations including Travellers in rural areas. Nevertheless, the policy agenda that has developed since 2000 has very much 'shifted' the emphasis of the police approach towards the Gypsy/Traveller community away 'from a historical perspective of public order to the . . . less prescriptive dimension of race relations'.[26] A similar shift towards partnership working, consultation and access to justice is also apparent in the police approach to LGBTI communities.

The relationship between police and communities has also been evaluated here in terms of the demographic profile of who has become a police officer. Constables were positioned rhetorically as 'citizens, representing the rest of the community' in the years after the first World War. Yet as we have demonstrated, a particular type of 'citizen' was recruited in terms of religion, ethnicity, gender and physical build. In the west of Scotland 'highlanders' were valued as recruits in the first decades of the twentieth century because of assumptions about loyalty to the British state given their ethnic association with a martial tradition. In the highlands itself, forces overwhelmingly took on local recruits. It was in the last quarter of the twentieth century that assumptions about who, exactly, might be a police officer significantly shifted to accommodate the view that officers should directly reflect the composition of communities (and thus be representative of them as well as representing them). The full effects of this aspiration have yet to be realised. If the recruitment of women (who constituted 30 per cent of all officers in 2018) was gradual following the 1975 Sex Discrimination Act, it has been even slower in relation to the appointment of BAME officers. In 2000 there were a total of 77 BAME officers in post across the whole of Scotland, constituting 0.75 per cent of the establishment (compared to their presence as 2 per cent of the population of Scotland). This had increased to 1.4 per cent of the establishment in 2018 (compared to 2.6 per cent of the population).[27] As the experience of women's incorporation into policing has also shown, even where positive action is taken to promote the recruitment of groups poorly represented in policing, the pace of cultural change within institutions and their ability to attract 'non-traditional' applicants remains slow.

Further, in relation to ideas about how to build active links between the police and communities, the role of special constables has been signposted in recent years as an important intersection and 'true partnership'.[28] As this book has shown, however, special constables have been significantly underused in Scotland historically. Deployed only in emergencies (most obviously in wartime and the General Strike), there was little investment or training subsequently. Whilst chief constables saw the potential of the Special Constabulary in the 1950s, they were held back by the concerns of the SPF; and the 1967 Police (Scotland) Act repeated earlier restrictions. Rank-and-file officers who served in rural areas in the 1950s-60s demonstrated far more enthusiasm for special constables (seeing them as invaluable) than their city counterparts in Glasgow especially (who tended to shape SPF policy). This disparity was reflected in the distribution of special constables in the early 2000s, when the Highlands and Islands (as Northern Constabulary) contained 20 per cent of all specials.[29] Arguably the decline in numbers that has been noted since the 1960s was part of a broader trend of missed opportunities, which current policy seeks to turn round.

For much of the twentieth century the idea of democratic accountability through the local state remained hugely significant as the political context in which policing was debated. Eroded in part through regionalisation in 1975, it was more firmly severed as a result of further local government reorganisation in 1996 (which replaced regional councils with thirty-two unitary local authorities). The administrative logic behind the creation of the eight regional police forces was effectively lost, policing was 'more distanced from local government' as a result, and the disparities between the size of forces (most obviously Strathclyde compared to Dumfries and Galloway) left simply as anomalies.[30] At the same time, across the last 50 years, the emphasis has moved towards the idea of local community (and, indeed, pluralised 'communities') rather than the formality of local government, municipal boundaries and local officials. Although the eight 'regional' forces retained their cultural identities for a further 20 years, the concept and brand of the Scottish Police Service (shaped by chief constables through ACPOS and by HMICS) was gaining ever more traction, with the creation of Police Scotland in 2013 a logical next step in this regard.

We have suggested here that the trajectory of everyday policing in Scotland was broadly similar to other parts of Great Britain, with differences of nuance rather than substance. The Scots Law requirement for corroboration undoubtedly shaped police tactics on the ground in distinctive ways in both urban and rural areas across time. The role of an independent public prosecutor (PF), whilst important, concealed the presence of the 'police prosecutor' in some police courts well into the twentieth century, as well as the significance of sub-judicial and extra-legal procedures. The account we present problematises the argument that police officers across Scotland have ubiquitously sustained more harmonious relationships with local communities than in England and Wales. Rather, we argue, there have been many experiences, and the textures and dynamics of these encounters, like the landscapes they have traversed, have been distinctly variegated. Yet we have also demonstrated the creation of an identity as a police service for Scotland in the years since 1900, forged in relation to (and subsequently outliving) the proliferation of individual smaller forces that were the multiple predecessors to Police Scotland. This, in itself, might serve as a more useful foundational story and, indeed, one that appropriately embraces the diversity of experience that this journey reflects.

NOTES

1. Murray, 'Proactive turn', uses this term to talk about the increased use of stop and search in Scotland in the period 2005–10.
2. Jackson with Bartie, *Policing Youth*. In October 2019 the Scottish Parliament banned smacking in the home.
3. Weinberger, *Keeping the Peace?*, 2.
4. Phillips, '1972 miners' strike'.
5. *GH*, 10 May 1984.
6. *Scotsman*, 17 May 1984.
7. NRS, HH55/1949/1, notes and minutes, meeting of 23 May 1984, Scottish Secretary with Deputation of Labour MPs.
8. Phillips, *Collieries, Communities*, 94.
9. Ibid., 149–51; NRS, HH55/1940/1.
10. Phillips, *Collieries, Communities*, 131.
11. Ibid.; NRS, HH55/1940/1, Scottish Office memo, Solsgirth, 2 August 1984.
12. NRS, HH55/19491/1, minutes, meeting of 23 May 1984.
13. NRS, HH55/1940/1, letter from ACPOS, 5 July 1984.
14. Ministerial statement, 7 June 2018.
15. Interim Report to the Scottish Government, 'Policing during miners' strike: independent review' (2019) https://www.gov.scot/publications/miners-strike-review-interim-report/ (last accessed 25 March 2020).
16. Ministerial statement, 7 June 2018.
17. Donnelly, 'Policing the Scottish community', 220.
18. Murray, 'Proactive turn'; HMICS, *Pride and Prejudice: A Review of Police Race Relations in Scotland* (Scottish Executive, 2003), 70.
19. Schaffer, *Community*, 78.
20. Monaghan, 'Crime prevention'.
21. Maan, *New Scots*, 205.
22. See Murray, 'Proactive turn', 117–35 for more discussion.
23. R. Jandoo, *Report of the Inquiry into the Murder of Surjit Singh Chhokar* (Scottish Executive, 2001, SP Paper 424).
24. HMICS, *Without Prejudice? A Thematic Review of Race Relations in Scotland* (2001), 55.
25. Davidson, *No Problem Here*.
26. HMICS, *Pride and Prejudice: A Review of Police Race Relations in Scotland* (2003), 88.
27. Police Scotland, *Equalities and Diversity Mainstreaming & Outcomes Progress Report 2017–19*.
28. Fyfe, 'Policing crime', 192.
29. Ibid.
30. Dickson, 'Role of police', 427.

APPENDIX: THE ORIGINS OF POLICE RECRUITS IN SCOTLAND

GLASGOW CITY POLICE

The trends outlined here for new male recruits are based on anonymised samples of personnel records held by Glasgow City Archives (GCA) in the series SR22/55/20–28 City of Glasgow Police Registers of Police and SR22/57/22/G-K City of Glasgow Police Other Staff Records. The selection of years (and hence sampling strategy) takes into account the unevenness of recruitment in term of numbers across time (with almost no regular recruitment during the First and Second World Wars).

Table A.1 Birthplace of recruits to Glasgow City Police as a percentage of all in select years 1900–48. N=900.

Birthplace	1900–1	1904–5	1906	1909–10	1930–1	1934–5	1938–41	1946	1947	1948
Glasgow	2	1	4	5	44	26	38	46	43	56
West Central Scotland	5	11	8	16	18	30	32	23	24	24
Scottish Borders	0	1	1	1	0	4	0	2	1	1
Dumfries & Galloway	7	4	4	2	4	4	1	4	2	0
East Central Scotland	6	10	11	10	11	17	15	8	11	6
North East Scotland	30	18	29	26	9	7	5	3	0	2
Highlands	27	21	29	30	8	6	4	4	6	5
Ireland	21	29	13	9	1	1	1	0	1	1
England & Wales	2	3	1	1	4	5	3	8	10	2
Other	0	2	0	0	1	0	1	2	2	3

Table A.2 Former trades of recruits to Glasgow City Police as a percentage of all in select years 1900–48. N=1200.

Former Trade	1900–1	1904–5	1906–7	1910–11	1912–13	1919	1920–1	1924–5	1926	1930–1	1934–5	1938–41	1946	1947	1948
Agriculture	36	20	24	29	46	19	29	14	4	6	4	1	2	3	5
Industrial	32	50	38	33	24	38	38	46	64	36	43	35	42	45	43
Clerical	1	2	2	1	0	3	3	7	8	17	17	15	10	14	13
Service	16	16	20	20	16	24	16	22	20	25	15	40	25	21	16
Forces	15	12	16	17	14	15	14	10	2	10	16	6	10	16	21
Professions	0	0	0	0	0	0	0	1	0	0	0	0	0	0	0
Not given	0	0	0	0	0	1	0	0	2	6	5	3	11	1	2

Notes: We follow here the classification of trades used by the census in the first half of the century. 'Agriculture' includes forestry, fishing, farming and employment relating to livestock. 'Industrial' includes mining, construction, transport manufacture and maintenance, and manufacturing jobs (e.g. textiles, clothing). 'Clerical' includes banking, insurance, paralegal and public administration. 'Service' includes retail, food provisioning, domestic services and gardening, childcare, postal workers, transport services and entertainment industries. 'Forces' includes all police and armed services personnel (also fire and prison services) as well as transfers from other police forces. It only includes National Service in the army, navy or air force when no other previous occupation is specified.

Table A.3 Social class (or occupational status) of recruits to Glasgow City Police (as indicated by former trades) as a percentage of all in select years 1900–48. N=1200.

Social Class	1900-1	1904-5	1906-7	1910-11	1912-13	1919	1920-1	1924-5	1926	1930-1	1934-5	1938-41	1946	1947	1948
I	0	2	0	0	0	0	0	1	0	0	1	0	1	4	0
II	1	2	1	2	0	5	4	7	10	9	9	3	1	2	4
III	24	25	39	34	18	34	43	56	68	69	71	69	63	69	86
IV	50	48	50	54	70	47	40	30	16	12	12	18	19	10	3
V	25	23	10	10	12	14	13	6	6	10	7	10	16	15	7
Total	100	100	100	100	100	100	100	100	100	100	100	100	100	100	100

Notes: From 1911 onwards the census office classified occupations (within trades) by 'social class' (effectively allocating relative socio-economic status to each). I = professional and those of independent means; II = intermediate occupations; III = skilled manual; IV = semi-skilled manual; V = unskilled. The occupations listed in personnel records have been categorised using the following tools: N. A. Armstrong (1972) 'The use of information about occupations', in Cambridge Group for the History of Population and Social Structure, *Nineteenth-Century Society: Essays in the Use of Quantitative Methods for the Study of Social Data* (London), 203–23; Census 1951: Scotland Vol. 4, *Occupations and Industries* (Edinburgh, HMSO, 1956). Senior officers who transferred into Glasgow City Police are categorised under II.

Table A.4 Religion stated by recruits to Glasgow City Police as a percentage of all in select years 1930–48. N=600.

Religion	1930–1	1934–5	1938–41	1946	1947	1948
Presbyterian	90.0	93.0	94.0	78.0	81.0	85.4
Roman Catholic	5.0	3.0	2.0	13.0	10.0	10.4
Church of England	1.0	2.0	2.0	5.0	7.0	4.2
Other non-conformist	1.0	2.0	2.0	4.0	2.0	0.0
Unrecorded	3.0	0.0	0.0	0.0	0.0	0.0

Notes: Presbyterian = Protestant/Church of Scotland. Other non-conformist includes Episcopalian, Brethren and Methodist.

Ayr Burgh Police

The trends outlined here for new male recruits are based on anonymised samples (N=150) of personnel records held by GCA in the series SR22/71/1-2 Ayr Burgh Police, Personal Records.

Table A.5 Birthplace of recruits to Ayr Burgh Police as a percentage of all 1900–52.

Birthplace	1900–10	1911–20	1921–30	1931–9	1941–52
Ayr Town & South Ayrshire	25.0	47.8	36.4	30.0	42.0
East Ayrshire	4.2	0.0	9.1	5.0	10.0
North Ayrshire	8.3	0.0	0.0	5.0	4.0
Other West Central Scotland	4.2	0.0	27.3	30.0	14.0
East Central Scotland	8.3	4.4	9.1	15.0	4.0
Dumfries & Galloway	20.8	13.0	9.1	10.0	16.0
North East Scotland	16.7	21.7	6.1	5.0	2.0
Highlands	8.3	4.4	0.0	0.0	0.0
Borders	0.0	0.0	0.0	0.0	0.0
England & Wales	0.0	4.4	3.0	0.0	8.0
Ireland	4.2	4.4	0.0	0.0	0.0

Table A.6 Former trades of recruits to Ayr Burgh Police as a percentage of all 1900–52.

Former Trade	1900–10	1911–20	1921–30	1931–40	1941–52
Agricultural	37.5	56.6	12.1	5.0	6.0
Industrial	25.0	8.7	48.5	20.0	52.0
Clerical	0.0	8.7	18.2	25.0	12.0
Services	29.2	17.4	15.2	20.0	16.0
Forces	4.2	8.7	6.1	20.0	12.0
Professions	4.2	0.0	0.0	0.0	0.0
Not given	0.0	0.0	0.0	10.0	2.0

Note: See table A2.

Inverness County Police

The trends outlined here for new male recruits are based on a complete run of personnel records for all 233 officers recruited between 1901 and 1968, held by the Highland Archives, in the series R91/D/8/3/19 Inverness County Constabulary, Discharge Books and R91/D/8/2c, Personal Record Book.

Table A.7 Birthplace of recruits to Inverness County Police by county and number 1901–68.

Birthplace	1901–10	1911–12	1921–31	1931–40	1941–51	1951–60	1961–68	Total	% of Total
Inverness	6	16	11	5	15	30	18	101	43.3
Ross	5	8	2	4	6	12	6	43	18.5
Argyll			3	2	3	3		11	4.7
Sutherland	2			1	2	3		8	3.4
Caithness		1	1		4			6	2.6
Orkney			1					1	0.4
Nairn, Moray or Banff		1		1	1	5	1	9	3.9
Aberdeen or Perth				1	1	2	1	5	2.1
Fife or Lothians					3	2		5	2.1
Renfrew, Dumbarton or Stirling				1	1		1	3	1.3
Angus or Kincardine		1			1	1	1	4	1.7
Lanark			1		3	4	2	10	4.3
Ayr, Dumfries, Kircudbright or Wigton		1		1	1	2		5	2.1
England & Wales					3	2	1	6	2.6
Not given	2					1	13	16	6.9
Total	15	28	19	16	44	67	44	233	100.0

Note: Percentages shown to one decimal place only.

Table A.8 Former trades of recruits to Inverness County Police as a percentage of all 1936–68.

Former Trade	1936–45	1946–55	1956–68
Agricultural	9	14	18
Industrial	5	20	10
Clerical	24	14	22
Service	43	24	30
Forces	5	21	10
Professions	0	0	0
Not Given	14	7	10

Note: Information about occupation was only included from 1936 onwards. See also Table A.2.

Table A.9 Social class (or occupational status) of recruits to Inverness County Police (as indicated by former trades) as a percentage of all 1936–68.

Social Class	1936–45	1946–55	1956–68
I	0	0	0
II	5	5	4
III	67	66	63
IV	9	10	6
V	19	19	27

Note: see Table A3.

Table A.10 Religion stated by recruits to Inverness County Police as a percentage of all 1936–68.

Religion	1936–45	1946–55	1956–68	All
Presbyterian	76	89	88	87
Roman Catholic	0	4	5	3.6
Church of England	0	4	1	2.4
Other non-conformist	0	1	0	0.6
None	0	1	0	0.6
Unrecorded	24	1	6	5.9

Note: see Table A4.

INVERNESS BURGH POLICE

The trends outlined here for new male recruits are based on a complete run of personnel records for all 132 officers recruited between 1908 and 1965, held by the Highland Archives, in the series R91/D/A/8/1, Inverness Burgh Police, Personal Record Book.

Table A.11 Birthplace of recruits to Inverness Burgh Police by county and number 1908–65.

Birthplace	1908–27	1928–47	1948–65	Total	% of Total
Inverness	10	14	23	47	35.6
Ross	11	5	15	31	23.5
Argyll			3	3	2.3
Sutherland	1	2		3	2.3
Caithness	1		2	3	2.3
Nairn, Moray or Banff	1	2	6	9	6.8
Aberdeen or Perth	1	3	2	6	4.5
Fife or Lothians		5	1	6	4.5
Renfrew, Dumbarton or Stirling		1	1	2	1.5
Angus or Kincardine		1	1	2	1.5
Lanark		2	1	3	2.3
Roxburgh, Peebles or Selkirk	2		1	3	
Ayr, Dumfries, Kircudbright or Wigton		3		3	2.3
England & Wales	1	1	5	7	5.3
Dominions		2	1	3	2.3
No Information			1	1	0.8
Total	28	41	63	132	100.0

Note: Percentages shown to one decimal place only.

Table A.12 Former trades of recruits to Inverness Burgh Police as a percentage of all 1908–65.

Former Trade	1908–27	1928–47	1948–65
Agriculture	39	32	9
Industrial	14	10	32
Clerical	11	7	22
Service	4	32	22
Forces	32	15	8
Professions	0	2	2
Not given	0	2	5

Note: see Table A2.

SELECT BIBLIOGRAPHY

BOOKS AND ARTICLES

Alderson, J., *Policing Freedom* (Plymouth, 1979).
Anderson, M., *Scotland's Populations: From the 1850s to Today* (Oxford, 2018).
Anon., *Police Manual for Scotland* (Glasgow, 1893, 1910, and 1931).
Anon., *Scottish Criminal Law, Police Duties and Procedures* (Aberdeen, 1952 and 1980).
Armstrong, B., *A People without Prejudice?* (London, 1989).
Armstrong, G., and M. Wilson, 'Delinquency and some aspects of housing', in C. Ward (ed.), *Vandalism* (London, 1973), 64–84.
Armstrong, G., and M. Wilson, 'City politics and deviancy amplification', in I. Taylor and L. Taylor (eds), *Politics and Deviance* (Harmondsworth, 1973), 61–89.
Banton, M., *The Policeman in the Community* (London, 1964).
Barbour, G. F., *Katherine Scott: A Memoir* (Edinburgh, 1929).
Barrie, D. G., *Police in the Age of Improvement: Police Development and the Civic Tradition in Scotland, 1775–1865* (Cullompton, 2008).
Barrie, D. G., 'A typology of British police: locating the Scottish municipal police model in its British context, 1800–35, *British Journal of Criminology*, 50 (2010), 259–77.
Barrie, D. G., and S. Broomhall (eds), *A History of Police and Masculinities 1700–2010* (London, 2012).
Barrie, D. G., and S. Broomhall, *Police Courts in Nineteenth-Century Scotland*, 2 vols (Farnham, 2014).
Barrie, D. G., and S. Broomhall, 'Public men, private interests: the origins, structure and practice of police courts in Scotland, c. 1800–1833', *Continuity and Change*, 27 (2012), 83–123.

Barron, H. (ed.), *The Third Statistical Account of Scotland: The County of Inverness* (Edinburgh, 1985).

Bartie, A., 'Moral panics and Glasgow gangs: exploring the new wave of Glasgow hooliganism, 1965–1970', *Contemporary British History*, 24.3 (2010), 385–408.

Bartie, A., and A. Fraser, 'The Easterhouse Project: youth, social justice and the arts in Glasgow, 1968–1970, *Scottish Justice Matters*, 2.1 (2014), 38–9.

Bartie, A., and A. Fraser, '"It wasnae just Easterhouse": the politics of representation in the Glasgow gang phenomenon, c. 1965–1975', in M. Worley et al. (eds), *Youth Culture and Social Change* (London, 2017), 205–29.

Bartie, A., and L. A. Jackson, 'Youth crime and preventive policing in post-war Scotland (c. 1945–1971)', *Twentieth-Century British History*, 22 (2011), 79–102.

Bauman, Z., *Community: Seeking Safety in an Insecure World* (Cambridge, 2001).

Bland, L., *Banishing the Beast: English Feminism and Sexual Morality 1885–1914* (London, 1995).

Bourdieu, P., *The Logic of Practice* (Cambridge, 1992).

Braber, B., 'The trial of Oscar Slater (1909) and anti-Jewish prejudices in Edwardian Glasgow', *History*, 88 (2003), 262–279.

Breitenbach, E., and V. Wright, 'Women as active citizens: Glasgow and Edinburgh c. 1918–1939', *Women's History Review*, 23 (2014), 401–20.

Brewer, J. D., *The Royal Irish Constabulary: An Oral History* (Belfast, 1990).

Brogden, M., *On the Mersey Beat: Policing Liverpool Between the Wars* (Oxford, 1991).

Brogden, M., and P. Nijhar, *Community Policing: National and International Approaches* (Cullompton, 2005).

Brown, J., and F. Heidensohn, *Gender and Policing* (Basingstoke, 2000).

Burke, M., *Coming Out of the Blue* (London, 1993).

Burke, M., 'Homosexuality as deviance: the case of the gay police officer', *British Journal of Criminology*, 34 (1994), 192–203.

Cain, M., 'Role conflict among police juvenile liaison officers', *British Journal of Criminology*, 8 (1968), 366–83.

Calhoun, C. J., 'Civil society/public sphere': history of the concept(s)', in *International Encyclopedia of the Social and Behavioural Sciences* (Amsterdam, 2001).

Calhoun, C. J., 'Community: toward a variable conceptualization for comparative research', *Social History*, 5 (1980), 105–121.

Cameron, E. A., 'Internal policing and public order, c. 1797–1900', in Spiers et al. (eds), *Military History*, 436–57.

Cameron, E. A., *Land for the People: The British Government and the Scottish Highlands c. 1880–1930* (East Linton, 1996).

Cameron, E. A., 'The seven men of Knoydart and the Scottish highlands in the 1940s', *Transactions of the Gaelic Society of Inverness*, LXII (2001), 156–83.

Cant, B. (ed.), *Footsteps & Witnesses: Lesbian and Gay Lifestories from Scotland* (Edinburgh, 1993).

Carson, K., and H. Idzikowska, 'The social production of Scottish Policing, 1795–1900', in D. Hay and F. Snyder (eds), *Policing and Prosecution in Britain, 1750–1850* (Oxford, 1989), 286–8.

Carson, W. G., 'Policing the periphery: the development of Scottish policing, 1795–1800', *Australian and New Zealand Journal of Criminology*, Part I, 17 (1984), 207–32; Part II, 18 (1985), 3–16.

Chand, A., *Masculinities on Clydeside: Men in Reserved Occupations during the Second World War* (Edinburgh, 2016).

Churchill, D., *Crime Control and Everyday Life in the Victorian City* (Oxford, 2017).

City of Glasgow Police, *Instruction Book* (Glasgow, 1892, 1912 and 1923).

Clark, C., 'Sites, welfare and "barefoot begging": Roma and Gypsy/Traveller experiences of racism in Scotland', in Davidson et al., *No Problem Here*, 145–61.

Clarke, J., 'Sincere and reasonable men: the origins of the National Council for Civil Liberties', *Twentieth Century British History*, 20 (2009), 513–37.

Clarke, J., *The National Council for Civil Liberties and the Policing of Interwar Politics* (Manchester, 2012).

Cockerill, A. W., *Sir Percy Sillitoe* (London, 1975).

Cohen, S., *Folk Devils and Moral Panics* (London, 2011, 1st edn 1972).

Colquhoun, R., *Life Begins at Midnight* (London, 1962).

Corfield, P., *Time and the Shape of History* (New Haven, 2007).

Crang, J. A., 'The Second World War', in Spiers et al. (eds), *Military History*, 559–99.

Cree, V., *From Public Streets to Private Lives* (Aldershot, 1985).

Cree, V., '"Khaki fever" during the First World War: a historical case study of social work's approach towards young women, sex and moral danger', *British Journal of Social Work*, 46 (2015), 1839–54.

Cunnison, J., and J. B. S. Gilfillan (eds), *Third Statistical Account for Scotland: City of Glasgow* (Glasgow, 1958).

Damer, S., *From Moorepark to 'Wine Alley': The Rise and Fall of a Glasgow Housing Scheme* (Edinburgh, 1989).

Damer, S., *Glasgow: Going for a Song* (London, 1990).

Davidson, N., M. Liinpää, M. McBride and S. Virdee, *No Problem Here: Understanding Racism in Scotland* (2018, Edinburgh).

Davidson, R., *Illicit and Unnatural Practices: The Law, Sex and Society in Scotland since 1900* (Edinburgh, 2018).

Davidson, R., and G. Davis, *The Sexual State: Sexuality and Scottish Governance 1950–1980* (Edinburgh, 2012).

Davies, A., *City of Gangs: Glasgow and the Rise of the British Gangster* (London, 2013).

Davies, A., 'Police violence and judicial bias in the age of mass democracy: Glasgow, 1933–1935', *Social History*, 44 (2019), 57–85.

Davies, A., '"Sillitoe's Cossacks": policing the Glasgow gangs in the 1930s', in R. Bessel and C. Emsley (eds), *Patterns of Provocation* (Oxford, 2000), 41–62.

Davies, A., 'Street gangs, crime and policing in Glasgow in the 1930s: the case of the Beehive Boys', *Social History*, 23 (1998), 251–67.

Davies, A., '"They sing that song": football and sectarianism in Glasgow during the 1920s and 1930s', in J. Flint and J. Kelly (eds), *Bigotry, Football and Scotland* (Edinburgh, 2013), 50–65.

Delanty, G., *Community* (London, 2003).

Dempsey, B., *Thon Wey; Aspects of Scottish Lesbian and Gay Activism 1968 to 1992* (Edinburgh, 1995).
Devon, J., *The Criminal & The Community* (London, 1912).
Devon, J., 'Some causes of crime', *Transactions of the Royal Philosophical Society of Glasgow*, XL (1908–9), 29–52.
Dickson, M., 'The role of the police in modern Scotland – myths and realities', in Donnelly and Scott, *Policing Scotland*, 427–50.
Dinsmor, A., and A. Goldsmith, 'Scottish policing – a historical perspective', in Donnelly and Scott (eds), *Policing Scotland*, 47–71.
Dodsworth, F., '"Civic" police and the conditions of liberty: the rationality of governance in eighteenth-century England', *Social History*, 29 (2004), 199–216.
Dodsworth, F., 'Review of David G. Barrie, *Police and the Age of Improvement*', *British Journal of Criminology*, 20 (2009), 580–2.
Donnelly, D., *Municipal Policing in Scotland* (Dundee, 2008).
Donnelly, D., 'Policing the Scottish Community', in Donnelly and Scott (eds), *Policing Scotland*, 201–27.
Donnelly, D., and K. Scott (eds), *Policing Scotland* (Abingdon, 2010).
Donnelly, D., and K. Scott, 'Policing in Scotland', in Newburn (ed.), *Handbook of Policing*, 182–203.
Duncan, R., and A. J. McIvor (eds), *Militant Workers: Labour and Class Conflict on the Clyde, 1900–50* (Edinburgh, 1992).
Emsley, C., *The English Police: A Political and Social History* (London, 1996).
Emsley, C., *Hard Men: Violence in England since 1750* (London, 2005).
Emsley, C., '"Mother, what *did* policemen do when there weren't any motors?" The law, the police and the regulation of motor traffic in England, 1900–1939', *Historical Journal*, 36 (1993), 357–81.
Englander, D., 'Police and public order in Britain 1914–1918', in C. Emsley and B. Weinberger (eds), *Policing Western Europe, 1850–1940* (Westport, 1991), 90–138.
Evans, M., *An Inside Job* (Oxford, 1991).
Farmer, L., *Criminal Law, Tradition and Legal Order: Crime and the Genius of Scots Law 1747 to the Present* (Cambridge, 1997).
Fenwick, T., 'Learning policing in rural spaces: "covering 12 foot rooms with 8 foot carpets"', *Policing*, 9 (2015), 234–41.
Fielding, N., 'Theorising community policing', *British Journal of Criminology*, 42 (2002), 147–63.
Floud, R., R. W. Fogel, B. Harris and S. C. Hung, *The Changing Body* (Cambridge, 2012).
Francis, M., *The Flyer: British Culture and the Air Force 1939–45* (Oxford, 2008).
Fraser, M., *Policing the Home Front 1914–18* (London, 2019).
Fraser, W., 'Post-war police developments: retrospect and reflections' [James Smart lecture] (Glasgow, 1981).
Fyfe, N. R., 'Policing crime and disorder in Scotland', in Donnelly and Scot, *Policing Scotland*, 175–200.
Fyfe, N., R., S. Anderson, N. Bland, A. Goulding, J. Mitchell and S. Reid, 'Experiencing organizational change during an era of reform. Police Scotland, narratives of

localism, and perceptions from the "frontline"', *Policing*, August (2018), https://doi.org/10.1093/police/pay052 (last accessed 1 January 2020).
Goldsmith, A. J. (ed.), *Complaints Against the Police: The Trend to External Review* (Oxford, 1991).
Gordon, P., *Policing Scotland* (Glasgow, 1980).
Gorringe, H., and M. Rosie, 'The Scottish approach? The discursive construction of a national police force', *Sociological Review*, 58 (2010), 65–83.
Halfacree, K., 'Still "Out of place in the country"? Travellers and the post-productivist rural', in Mawby and Yarwood (eds), *Rural Policing*, 123–36.
Henderson, M., *Finding Peggy* (Ealing, 1994).
Hobbs, H., *Doing the Business: Entrepreneurship, the Working Class and Detectives in the East End of London* (Oxford, 1989).
Houlbrook, M., 'The man with the powder puff in interwar London', *Historical Journal*, 50 (2007), 145–71.
Hughes, A., *Gender and Political Identities in Scotland, 1919–1939* (Edinburgh, 2010).
Hutchison, D., 'The history of the press', in N. Blain and D. Hutchinson (eds), *The Media in Scotland* (Edinburgh, 2008), 55–70.
Jackson, L. A., *Women Police: Gender, Welfare and Surveillance in the Twentieth Century* (Manchester, 2006).
Jackson, L. A., with A. Bartie, *Policing Youth: Britain, 1945–1970* (Manchester, 2014).
Jenkinson, J., 'Black sailors on Red Clydeside: rioting, reactionary trade unionism and conflicting notions of "Britishness" following the First World War', *Twentieth-Century British History*, 19 (2008), 29–60.
Johansen, A., 'Police-public relations: interpretations of policing and democratic governance', in P. Knepper and A. Johansen (eds), *The Oxford Handbook of the History of Crime and Criminal Justice* (Oxford, 2016).
Johnston, R., and A. McIvor, 'Dangerous work, hard men and broken bodies: masculinity in the Clydeside heavy industries, c. 1930–1970s', *Labour History* Review, 69 (2004), 135–52.
Johnston, T., *Memories* (London, 1952).
Jones, D. J. V., *Crime and Policing in the Twentieth Century: The South Wales Experience* (Cardiff, 1996).
Jones, S., *Policewomen and Equality* (Basingstoke, 1986).
Kent, S. K., *Making Peace: The Reconstruction of Gender in Interwar Britain* (Princeton, 1993).
Klein, J., *Invisible Men: The Secret Lives of Police Constables in Liverpool, Manchester and Birmingham, 1900–1939* (Liverpool, 2010).
Klein, J., 'Quiet and determined servants and guardians: creating ideal English police officers, 1900–1945', in Barrie and Broomhall (eds), *History of Police*, 201–16.
Knox, B., *Court of Murder* (London, 1968).
Knox, W., *Scottish Labour Leaders 1918–1939* (Edinburgh, 1984).
Knox, W. W. J., and A. McKinlay, 'Crime, protest and policing in nineteenth-century Scotland', in T. Griffiths and G. Morton (eds), *A History of Everyday Life in Scotland 1800–1900* (Edinburgh, 2010), 196–224.

Lawrence, P., '"Scoundrels and scallywags, and some honest men . . .": memoirs and the self-image of French and English policemen c.1870–1939', in B. Godfrey, C. Emsley and G. Dunstall (eds), *Comparative Histories of Crime* (Cullompton, 2003), 125–44.
Leitch, R. (ed.), *The Book of Sandy Stewart* (Edinburgh, 1988).
Levine, P., 'Walking the streets in a way no decent woman should', *Journal of Modern History*, 66 (1994), 34–78.
Livingstone, I., 'Police Officer', in C. Bell (ed.), *Scotland's Century* (Glasgow, 1999), 87–96.
Loader, I., and A. Mulcahy, *Policing and the Condition of England* (Oxford, 2003).
Lowe, W. J., and E. L. Malcolm, 'The domestication of the Royal Irish Constabulary, 1836–1922', *Irish Economic and Social History*, 19 (1992), 27–48.
Maan, B., *The New Scots* (Edinburgh, 1992).
McArthur, A., and H. Kingsley Long, *No Mean City* (London, 1935).
McCrone, D., *Understanding Scotland: The Sociology of a Stateless Nation* (London, 1992).
Macfarlane, C., *Gorbals Diehards* (Edinburgh, 2010).
MacGill, P., *Children of the Dead End* (Edinburgh, 1999 [1914]).
McGovern, J., *Neither Fear nor Favour* (London, 1960).
Mack, J. A., 'Full-time miscreants, delinquent neighbourhoods and criminal networks', *British Journal of Sociology*, 15 (1964), 38–53.
Mack, J. A., *Police Juvenile Liaison: Practice and Evaluation* (Glasgow, 1968).
Mack, J. A., 'Police Juvenile Liaison Schemes', *British Journal of Criminology* 3.4 (1962–3), 361–75.
Mackenzie, S., and A. Henry, *Community Police: a Review of the Evidence* (Edinburgh, 2009).
McLaughlin, B., *Crimestopper* (Edinburgh, 2012).
McLaughlin, E., "Last one out, turn off the 'blue lamp'": the geographical "placing" of police performance management', *Policing*, 2 (2008), 266–75.
McLean, I., *The Legend of Red Clydeside* (Edinburgh, 1983).
McNee, D., *McNee's Law* (London, 1983).
McNeill, F., 'Remembering probation in Scotland', *Probation Journal*, 52 (2005), 23–38.
Mavor, I., *Glasgow* (Edinburgh, 2000).
Mawby, R. I., and A. Wright, 'Police accountability in the UK', Paper for Commonwealth Human Rights Initiative, 2005, http://www.humanrightsinitiative.org/programs/aj/police/res_mat/police_accountability_in_uk.pdf (last accessed 1 January 2020).
Mawby, R. I., and R. Yarwood (eds), *Rural Policing and Policing the Rural* (Aldershot, 2011).
Mays, J. B., *Growing Up in the City* (Liverpool, 1954).
Meek, J., *Queer Voices in Post-war Scotland: Male Homosexuality, Religion and Society* (London, 2015).
Mendel, J., N. R. Fyfe and G. den Heyer, 'Does size matter? A review of the evidence regarding restructuring police organizations', *Police Practice and Research*, 18 (2016), 3–14.

Merrilees, W., *The Short Arm of the Law* (London, 1966).
Miller, J., *The Dam Builders* (Edinburgh, 2007).
Mina, D., *The Long Drop* (London, 2017).
Monaghan, B., 'Crime prevention in Scotland', *International Journal of the Sociology of Law*, 25 (1997), 21–44.
Moores, C., 'The progressive professionals: the National Council for Civil Liberties and the politics of activism in the 1960s', *Twentieth Century British History*, 20 (2009), 538–53.
Morrison, N., *My Story* (Inverness, 1937).
Morton, G., 'Civil society, municipal government and the state: enshrinement, empowerment and legitimacy. Scotland, 1800–1929', *Urban History*, 25 (1998), 348–67.
Muncie, W., *The Crime Pond* (Edinburgh, 1979).
Neat, T., *The Summer Walkers* (Edinburgh, 1997).
Newburn, T. (ed.), *Handbook of Policing* (London, 2008).
Pacione, M., *Glasgow: The Socio-Spatial Development of the City* (Chichester, 1995).
Pattinson, J., A. McIvor and L. Robb, *Men in Reserve: British Civilian Masculinities in the Second World War* (Manchester, 2017).
Perchard, A., *Aluminiumville: Government, Global Business and the Scottish Highlands* (Lancaster, 2012).
Perchard, A., and N. Mackenzie, '"Too much on the Highlands": recasting the economic history of the Highlands and Islands', *Northern Scotland*, 4 (2013), 3–22.
Phillips, J., 'The 1972 miners' strike: popular agency and industrial politics in Britain', *Contemporary British History*, 20 (2006), 187–207.
Phillips, J., *Collieries, Communities and the Miners' Strike in Scotland* (Manchester, 2012).
Pieri, J., *The Big Men: Personal Memories of Glasgow's Police* (Glasgow, 2010, 1st edn 2001).
Pugh, M., 'Centralism versus localism? Democracy versus efficiency? The perennial challenges of Scottish local government organisation', *History & Policy* (2014), http://www.historyandpolicy.org/policy-papers/papers/the-perennial-challenges-of-scottish-local-government-organisation (last accessed 1 January 2019).
Ralston, A. G., *The Real Taggarts* (Edinburgh, 2017).
Reiner, R., *The Blue-Coated Worker* (Cambridge, 1978).
Reiner, R., *The Politics of the Police* (Oxford, 1st edn 1985, 4th edn 2010).
Ritchie, M., and J. A. Mack, *Police Warnings* (Glasgow, 1974).
Rose, S. O., *Which People's War? National Identity and Citizenship in Wartime Britain 1939–1945* (Oxford, 2004).
Rosenbaum, D. R. *The Challenge of Community Policing* (London, 1994).
Royle, T., *A Time of Tyrants: Scotland and the Second World War* (Edinburgh, 2013).
Schaffer, E. B., *Community Policing* (London, 1980).
Scott, J. C., *Domination and the Arts of Resistance* (New Haven, 1990).
Scott, K., 'The police and criminal justice in Scotland', in Donnelly and Scott (eds), *Policing Scotland*, 355–74.
Settle, L., *Sex for Sale in Scotland: Prostitution in Edinburgh and Glasgow, 1900–1939* (Edinburgh, 2016).

Shanks, N. J., *Police Community Involvement in Scotland* (Edinburgh, 1980).
Sherwood, M., *The British Honduran Forestry Unit in Scotland 1941–43* (London, 1982).
Shields, J. V. M., and J. A. Duncan, *The State of Crime in Scotland* (London, 1964).
Shpayer-Makov, H., 'The appeal of country workers: the case of the Metropolitan Police', *Historical Research*, 64 (1991), 186–203.
Shpayer-Makov, H., *The Making of a Policeman: A Social History of a Labour Force in Metropolitan London, 1829–1914* (London, 2002).
Sibley, D., *Geographies of Exclusion* (London, 1995).
Sillitoe, S., *Cloak without Dagger* (London, 1956).
Smale, D. M., 'Alfred John List and the development of policing in the counties of Scotland, c. 1832–77', *Journal of Scottish Historical Studies*, 33 (2013), 52–80.
Smale, D. M., 'The First World War and policing in the Scottish Borders', *History Scotland*, Part I, 18.1 (2018), 32–9; Part II, 18.2 (2018), 36–42.
Smith, D., 'Juvenile delinquency in Britain in the First World War', *Criminal Justice History*, 11 (1990), 119–56.
Smith, D., 'Official responses to juvenile delinquency in Scotland during the Second World War', *Twentieth Century British History*, 18 (2007), 78–105.
Smyth, J. J., *Labour in Glasgow 1896–1936: Socialism, Suffrage, Sectarianism* (East Linton, 2000).
Spiers, E. M., J. Crang, and M. J. Strickland (eds), *A Military History of Scotland* (Edinburgh, 2012).
Stallion, M., *A Life of Crime: A Bibliography of British Police Officers' Memoirs and Biographies* (Braintree, 2013).
Stallion, M., and D. Wall, *The British Police Forces and Chief Officers 1829–2012* (Hook, 2011).
Stewart, S., *A Traveller's Life* (Edinburgh, 2011).
Streets, H., 'Identity in the Highland regiments in the nineteenth century', in S. Murdoch and A. Mackillop (eds), *Fighting for Identity* (Leiden, 2002), 213–26.
Summerfield, P., 'Culture and composure: creating narratives of the gendered self in oral history interviews', *Social and Cultural History*, 1 (2004), 65–93.
Swinson, A., *Scotch on the Rocks* (Edinburgh, 2005, 1st edn 1963).
Tancred, E., *Women Police 1914–1950* (London, 1951).
Taylor, H., 'Rationing crime: the political economy of criminal statistics since the 1850s', *Economic History Review*, LI (1998), 569–90.
Tilley, N., 'Modern approaches to policing: community, problem-oriented and intelligence-led', in Newburn (ed.), *Handbook of Policing*, 373–403.
Ugolini, W., and J. Pattinson, 'Negotiating identities in multinational Britain during the Second World War', in Ugolini and Pattinson (eds), *Fighting for Britain* (Bern, 2015), 1–24.
Van Slingelandt, N., and I. Macdonald (eds), *A Long Way from Lochaber: The Life Story of Charles Cameron Macdonald 1903–1990* (Elgin, 2000).
Vinven, R., *National Service: A Generation in Uniform 1945–1963* (Harmondsworth, 2015).
Waddington, P., 'Police (canteen) sub-culture: an appreciation', *British Journal of Criminology*, 39 (1999), 287–309.

Weber, M., 'Bureaucracy and law', in H. H. Gerth and C. Wright Mills (eds and trans.), *From Max Weber: Essays in Sociology* (London, 1982).
Weinberger, B., *The Best Police in the World: An Oral History of English Policing from the 1930s to the 1960s* (Aldershot, 1995).
Weinberger, B., *Keeping the Peace? Policing Strikes in Britain, 1906–1926* (Oxford, 1991).
White, M., and A. Hunt (2000) 'Citizenship: care of the self, character and personality', *Citizenship Studies*, 4 (2000), 93–116.
Williams, C. A., J. Patterson and J. Taylor, 'Police filming English streets in 1935: the limits of mediated identification', *Surveillance & Society*, 6.1 (2009), 3–9.
Williamson, D., *The Horsieman: Memoirs of a Traveller* (Edinburgh, 2008).
Withers, C. W. J., '"The long arm of the law": migration of highland-born policemen to Glasgow, 1826–1891', *Local Historian*, 18 (1988), 127–35.
Wolcott, D. B., *Cops and Kids: Policing Juvenile Delinquency in Urban America 1890–1940* (Athens, OH, 2005).
Wollacott, A., '"Khaki fever" and its control: gender, class, age and sexual morality on the British homefront in the First World War', *Journal of Contemporary History*, 29 (1994), 325–47.
Wood, E., *The Hydro Boys* (Edinburgh, 2002).
Wood, I. S., 'Internal policing and public order, c. 1900–94', in Spiers et al. (eds), *Military History*, 536–58.
Wood, J. C., 'Press, politics and the "police and public" debates in late-1920s Britain', *Crime, Histoire & Sociétés*, 16.1 (2012), 75–98.
Wood, J. C., '"The third degree": press reporting, crime fiction and police powers in 1920s Britain', *Twentieth Century British History*, 21 (2010), 464–85.
Woodeson, A., 'The first women police: a force for equality or infringement,' *Women's History Review*, 2 (1993), 217–32.
Young, H., 'Hard man, new man: re-/composing masculinities in Glasgow, c. 1950–2000', *Oral History*, 35 (2007), 71–81.
Young, M., *In the Sticks: Cultural Identity in a Rural Police Force* (Oxford, 1993).

Theses and Dissertations

Barrie, D. G., 'Britain's oldest police? A political and social history of policing in Glasgow 1779–1846', PhD thesis, University of Strathclyde, 2000.
Ewen, S., 'Power and administration in two midland cities, c. 1870–1938', PhD thesis, University of Leicester, 2003.
Goldsmith, A., 'The development of the City of Glasgow Police c. 1800–1939', PhD thesis, University of Strathclyde, 2002.
Goodwin, E. G., 'The police in Edinburgh during the Second World War: organisational and operational demands', PhD thesis, University of Edinburgh, 2016.
Murray, K., '"The proactive turn": stop and search in Scotland', PhD thesis, University of Edinburgh, 2014.
Ritchie, D., '"They do not become good Scotsmen": a political history of the anti-Irish campaign in Scotland 1919–1939', PhD thesis, Edinburgh, 2012.

Smale, D. M., 'The development of the new police in the Scottish Borders c. 1840–1890', PhD thesis, The Open University, 2008.

Smale, D. M., 'To what extent did the Second World War impact on policing in the Scottish Borders?', MSc Dissertation, University of Edinburgh, 2013.

INDEX

Note: n refers to notes, t refers to tables

Aberdeen City Police, 64
   female officers, 180, 191, 192
   General Strike 1926, 33
   instruction manuals, 25
   manpower, 55
   street soliciting, 107
   warnings system, 118
Aberdeen, first, 16
'Aberdeen system', 55
abortion cases, 101
ACPOS, 116, 216
Adair, James, 112, 114–15, 134n
Allen, Mary, 176
Anderson, James, 123
antisemitism, 110, 112, 215
Ardersier
   military populations, 166
   occurrence books, 148
   police stations, 142, 169
   vagrants, 157–8
   village constable, 139, 146
Ardwall, Lord, 109
Argyll County Council, 194
Argyll County Police, 71, 120
Argyllshire, 159, 169, 193–4

Armstrong, Gail, 122–5
Asian officers, 59, 187
Asian communities, 59, 214
Atholl, Duchess of, 181
Ayr Burgh Council, 21–2
Ayr Burgh Police, 54, 56, 105, 180, 194–5, 221–2, 221t, 222t
Ayrshire, 169

Baird, John, 182
Baird Committee (on the employment of Women on Police Duties) 1920, 182–3, 189
Ballantyne, Agnes (Nancy), 41, 126
BAME
   black youth, 41, 213
   community groups, 214
   female officers, 187
   officers, 59, 93n, 187, 215
   prejudice, 112–13, 167
Banton, Michael, 4, 68–70, 73–8, 90–1, 100
Barnard, Asher, 112
Barnes, George, 108
Barra, 140, 149
Barras, Glasgow, 74

235

Barrie, David, 3, 31
Bartie, Angela, 122, 123
batons, 5, 28, 33, 43, 81, 87, 124, 163–4
BBC, 122
beat men, 7, 53, 67–78, 100, 131n, 210–11
Beaton, John, 38
Beauly 141–3, 146–7, 169
'Beehive Boys', 80
Bettyhill police station, 141, 169
Birmingham, 92n
Birnam, Lord, 21–2
'Black Marias', 75, 82
black youth, 41, 213
Blackhill, Glasgow, 67, 75
Blair, Helen, 185–6
'Bloody Friday' 31 January 1919, 5, 73
Board of Trustees, 123
Bourdieu, Pierre, 63
Boys' Brigade, 118–19, 134n
Braber, Ben, 110–11
'breach of the peace' (BoP), 55, 83–8, 84t, 90, 124–5, 211–14
Bristol, 180–1
British Aluminium Company, 162
British Honduran Forestry Unit, 167
Brixton riots 1981, 42
Brogden, Mike, 4, 68
Broomhall, Susan, 31
brothel-keeping, 112–13
Brown, Jessie, 108–9, 111
'brutality', 79–80
Buchanan-Smith, Alick, 41
Burgh Police (Amendment) Act 1911, 133n
Burgh Police (Scotland) Act 1833, 16
Burgh Police (Scotland) Act 1892, 7, 17, 106–7, 132n
Burke, Marc, 116
buses, 69

Cain, Maureen, 121
Cairo, 189
Caithness, 170n
  complaints, 154
  female officers, 193
  localised policing, 154–5
  poaching, 151
  recruits, 139, 140
  Scottish Travellers, 161
  Thurso Tribunal, 34–5, 80

Caithness County Council, 160
Callaghan, James, 35
Calvinism, 110, 112
campaigns, 110–11
  for female officers, 176–82
  for reform, 40–5
Cannich, 139, 146
Carmichael, John, 180
Carnegie Trust, 121, 180–1
Carson, W. G., 3
Castle Bay, Barra, 141
Castlemilk housing scheme, Glasgow, 85, 125
'Cat and Mouse Act', 43
Central Clydeside Conurbation, 8
Central Office of Information, 39–40
Chhokar, Sunjit Singh, 42, 214
Chief Constables (Scotland) Association (CC(S)A), 24, 25, 39
Chief Constables (Scotland) Club, 24, 25
Children Act 1908, 159–160
children and young people, 68, 80–1, 87–8, 117–29, 185
  protection of, 115, 178–9, 183–7
  see also youth
Children Hearings, 121, 128
Christianity, muscular, 112, 119
Church of Scotland, 58–9
  Mission Committee, 160
  Police Court Missionary, 108
CID
  and criminal networks, 102–3
  female officers, 175, 179, 182, 186, 191, 195, 199, 202–3
  and 'homosexual offences', 114
  and information or informants, 71, 101–2
  and the JLO, 119
  and the press, 104
  and village constables, 147
  women statement takers, 175, 179, 182
cine-film footage, 106, 132n
citizenship, 26–7, 215
civil rights, 41, 120–1, 212, 214
Clare, Pauline, 203
Coatbridge, 118
Coatbridge Burgh Police, 66, 120
Cohen, Stanley, 122
Collins, Godfrey, 82
Colquhoun, Robert, 53, 65, 73, 79, 101–2, 104, 134n
'come-back', 55, 83, 124–5, 127

Committee on Children and Young Persons 1961–4 (Kilbrandon Committee), 121
Committee on Sexual Offences against Children 1925, 185
Committee on the Police Service of England, Wales and Scotland 1919 (Desborough Committee), 23, 25–7, 38
Community Improvement Scheme (CIS), 120
Community Involvement Branches, 7, 100, 128, 130, 200, 211, 214
'community policing', 6–7, 121, 200, 213
complaints, 15, 32–42, 50–1n, 82–3, 108–9, 111, 126–8, 132n
'conference points', 145–6
Conservative Manifesto for Scotland 1979, 42
construction work, 161–5
Convention of Royal Burghs, 19, 21
corroboration
   'breach of the peace' (BoP), 83–8
   complaints, 37–8
   Discipline Code, 40
   fingerprinting, 79
   homosexuality, 113
   JLO, 121
   rural policing, 147, 149, 151, 156, 168
   Scots Law, 2, 55, 216
   street soliciting, 107, 112
   street soliciting and homosexuality, 104, 130
   Thurso Tribunal, 34
   women statement takers, 188
County and Burgh Police (Scotland) Act 1857, 16–17
Court of Session, 111
Cree, Viviene, 179
Criminal Law Amendment Act 1885, 113, 133n
Criminal Law Amendment Act 1912, 112, 179
Crofters' Wars 1880s, 32, 149, 211–12
Crown Office, Edinburgh, 29, 37
Cunningham, Charles Craik, 22

Dalcross aerodrome, 142
Damer, Seán, 73
Danube Street, Stockbridge, 112
Davidson, Roger, 101, 112–13, 113
Davies, Andrew, 4, 67, 72–3, 79–82, 87
Daviot, 139
Dawson, Margaret Damer, 176
De Vitré, Barbara Denis, 189–90, 197, 198

Defence (Amalgamation) Regulations, 19
Defence of the Realm Acts, 9–10, 17, 165
Defence of the Realm Regulations, 40, 50n
Departmental Committee on Tinkers in Scotland 1918, 159
Departmental Committee on Sexual Offences against Children and Young People in Scotland 1924–6 (Child Assault Committee), 183–7
Departmental Committee on the Employment of Women on Police Duties 1920 (Baird Committee), 182
Desborough, Lord, 23
Desborough Committee 1919 (on the Police Service of England, Wales and Scotland), 38
Desborough Report, 23, 25, 26–7
detectives, 99–104
   assault, 83
   beat men, 71
   female, 179
   rural policing, 147
   sexism, 203
   young people, 126
Devon, James, 29–30, 30, 72
Discipline Code, 35–8, 40, 50n
'discretion', 6, 11, 32, 210–11
   beat men, 63
   'breach of the peace' (BoP) proceedings, 86
   children and young people, 117
   Glasgow, 31
   instruction manuals, 77
   plainclothes, 129
   rural policing, 143, 148–56, 168–9
   street betting, 105
   warnings system, 109
Dollan, Patrick, 33, 43–4, 73
domestic violence cases, 74, 86–7
Drumchapel, Glasgow, 54, 125
drunk-drivers, 155
drunkenness, 36, 50n, 61–2, 154, 166, 173n
Dudgeon, Brigadier-General Robert Maxwell, 14–15, 19, 25, 27, 32–3
Duke Street Prison, Glasgow, 29–30, 72
Dumbarton, 54
Dunbartonshire, 8, 88
Duncan, Judith A., 54, 91n, 164
Duncan, Phoebe, 184, 185

Dundee City Police
  female officers, 180–4
  manpower, 91n
  Policewomen's Departments, 191–2
  racism, 112
  warnings system, 118
  women patrols, 178
  youth gangs, 84
Dundee
  first constabulary, 16
  'Poor Agents' system, 31
Dunoon, 194
Dunvegan, Skye, 143, 159

Eadie, Alex, 213
Easterhouse, Glasgow, 54, 122, 124–5
Easterhouse Project, 123–4, 128, 130
Eastriggs, 176–7
'Echo 10' team, 124, 125
Edinburgh City Police
  beat men, 68
  'breach of the peace' (BoP), 83–4
  'cleansing' bylaws, 114
  complaints, 37, 50–1n
  General Strike 1926, 33
  manpower, 91n
  masculinity, 115
  Policewomen's Departments, 191
  recruits, 56, 92n
  Scottish Office, 18
  'social work', 75, 76–7
  street soliciting, 107–9, 111–12
  training schools, 25
  'troublemakers', 78
  'vice squad', 106women patrols, 178–9
Edinburgh
  first constabulary, 16
  'Poor Agents' system, 31
Edmund-Davies Committee (on the Police) Third Report 1979, 199–202
Emergency Powers Act 1920, 10
Emsley, Clive, 4, 79
England and Wales
  black communities, 41
  children and young people, 185
  crime rates, 91n
  female officers, 201
  homosexuality, 113, 130
  lack of equality for Scottish police, 23
  legal system, 29
  marriage bar, 196, 198
  oath to monarch, 26
  organisation of policing, 2, 19
  Police Complaints Board, 41–2
  Royal Commission on Police Powers and Procedures 1928–9, 34
  Sex Discrimination Act 1975, 198
  special constables, 88
  street soliciting, 107
entrapment, 116, 129
Evening Citizen, 125–6
evening patrols, 146–7, 194

Faculty of Advocates, 39–40
Farmer, Lindsay, 29, 72
farms, 144–6
female officers, 175–208
  Aberdeen, 108, 191, 192
  BAME, 187
  Caithness, 193
  campaigns for, 176–82
  Dundee, 180–4
  England and Wales, 201
  Glasgow, 175, 180–2, 184–91, 199
  Gray, David, 193, 200–1
  HMIC, 189–90, 193–4, 198, 200–3
  Inverness, 196, 197
  McCulloch, Malcolm, 190
  Metropolitan Police, London, 181, 193
  Scottish Office, 180–1, 185, 188–90
  Scottish Secretary, 177–8, 181–2
  Second World War, 9, 188–9
  Sillitoe, Sir Percy, 188
  'social work', 178–9, 183–5, 187, 189, 192–3, 199–200
  'special sphere' of usefulness, 182–8
  SPF, 201, 202
  see also Policewomen's Departments; women
Ferguson, Lieutenant-Colonel Sir Arthur George, 47n, 157
First World War, 9–10, 17, 23, 107, 146–7, 156, 166
Flotta oil terminal, 164
Fort George barracks, 166
Fort William, 162
Forward, 43–4
Fraser, Sir William, 1, 4, 41
Free Church, 140, 146

INDEX

Gaelic, 151–2, 158
Gallowgate Glasgow, 74
'gang culture', 4, 54, 79–80, 84–5, 122–4
gangsters, 79–80
Garngad, 82
Garscube Road, Glasgow, 78, 83, 85
General Police and Improvements (Scotland) Act 1862, 132n
General Strike 1926, 5, 32–3, 43–4, 56, 73, 74, 212
Gilchrist, Marion, 110–11
Glasgow City Police
  beat men, 53–98
  birthplace of recruits, 218t
  'breach of the peace' (BoP) proceedings, 214
  campaigns, 43
  Chief Constables, 45, 92n
  CID, 71, 99, 101–4
  culture and identity, 59–67
  detectives, 71, 99, 101–4, 126
  Discipline Code, 36, 50n
  female officers, 175, 180–2, 184–91, 199
  female recruits, 195–6
  'gangs', 4, 79, 122–4
  General Strike 1926, 5, 33, 43, 56, 73–4
  habitus, 62–5, 89
  highest crime rates, 8, 54
  homosexuality, 113, 115–16
  Instruction Book, 25, 77
  JLS, 128
  justice system, 29–31
  Marine Division, 30, 118
  the 'ned', 78–88
  plainclothes, 101–3
  'Police Fiscal', 29
  police strike 1919, 23
  Policewomen's Departments, 192–3
  prejudice against policewomen, 195
  probation, 120
  recruits, 56, 58, 139, 218–21, 219t, 220t, 221t
  Regulations 1857, 71
  specialist policing, 99–100
  Strathclyde Police, 128, 169
  street betting, 105
  street soliciting, 106–12
  'toughness', 211
  Traffic Department, 99
  'Untouchables', 122, 124–8

'vice squad', 105, 109–10, 114
  warnings system, 117–18
  women patrols, 178–9
Glasgow City Police Training School (Oxford Street), 25, 62–3
Glasgow, first constabulary, 16
Glasgow Corporation, 29, 73, 83, 180–1
Glasgow Evening News, 104
Glasgow Green, 82, 114
Glasgow Herald, 43
Glasgow Juvenile Court, 119, 134n
Glasgow Police Act 1892, 72
Glasgow Police Acts, 72, 79
Glasgow Vigilance Association, 178–9
Goldsmith, Alistair, 3
Goodwin, Edward, 10
Gorbals, 58, 75, 108, 134n
Gordon, Paul, 35, 42–3
Gordon, Robert B., 65
Govan, 68
Govan Burgh Police, 56
Graham, Norma, 203
Grantham Borough Police, 180
Gray, David
  career police officers, 28
  'community policing', 7
  complaints system, 41–2
  female officers, 193, 200–1
  JLS, 119–21
  recruits, 90
  Special Constabulary, 88
  'Untouchables', 128
Gray, Janet, 189–90, 192, 194, 196, 198
Great Glen, 165
Greenock Burgh Police, 7, 36, 50n, 54, 100, 119
Greenock Social Services Association, 'Youth Committee', 120
Gretna, 176–7
Gretna Special Police Area, 18–19
'gross indecency', 113–14, 133n
Guthrie, Lord, 110–11
Gypsy/Traveller communities, 158–61, 215

Haldane, Christine, 108
Hamilton, 54, 65, 88
Hamilton, Rachel, 176
Hammill, Patrick, 67
harassment, 124–7
Hatton, Bill, 41, 87–8, 125–8

239

Heath, Edward, 41
height of police officers, 57, 62, 92n, 115, 176
Henderson, Hamish, 160
Henderson, Meg, 67
Her Majesty's Inspector of Constabulary for Scotland (HMICS), 17–18
   BAME community groups, 214
   BAME officers, 59
   beat men, 100
   career police officers, 28
   'community policing', 121
   complaints system, 40, 42–3
   Discipline Code, 36–7
   Easterhouse Project, 125
   female officers, 189–90, 193–4, 198, 200–3
   localised policing, 154–5
   'national' police service for Scotland, 22
   police and public, 32–3, 39
   police stations, 140–1
   professionalisation, 25
   Scottish Police Service, 216
   vagrants, 157
High Court of Justiciary, 29, 31, 101, 108, 113
'highland bobby', 138, 153
Highland Brigade Depot, Fort George 166
Highlanders, 56–7, 91–2n, 92n, 215
HM Gretna Munitions Factory, 176–7
Holy Loch, 194
Home Office, 118, 180, 183, 188–90, 196
homosexuality, 113–17, 195–6
Hood, Sandra, 203
House of Commons, 108
Hunterton, 212

ice-cream shops, 111, 186
Immoral Traffic (Scotland) Act 1902, 112
Independent Labour Party (ILP), 5, 44, 52n, 82
Indian pedlars, 165
Instruction Book, 25, 77
instruction manuals, 25–8, 45
Inverness Burgh Police, 19, 22
   female officers, 196, 197
   JLS, 120
   recruits, 56, 224, 224t
Inverness County Police, 19, 170n
   construction work, 162

Crofters' Wars 1880s, 149
police stations, 140, 141
recruits, 139, 222t, 223, 223t
rural policing, 137
village constable, 139
Inverness Courier, 19
Inverness-shire, 160, 194
Investigation Bureau, 99
Irish
   'navvies', 161–2
   recruits, 56, 58, 91n
Irish Catholics, 58–9, 65–7
Irish Home Rule, 176
Irish Republican Army (IRA), 58
Irish War of Independence 1919–21, 58
'Italians', 186
Ivory, William, 32, 38, 149

Jandoo, Dr Raj, 214
Jewish community, 58
Johansen, Anja, 16, 27
'Johnston, Mrs Thomas', 177, 181
Johnston, Thomas (Tom), 18, 19, 43
Joint Working Party on the Handling of Complaints Against the Police 1974, 41
Jones, David, 4
Joynson-Hicks, William, 33
Juvenile Bureaux, 119
juvenile courts, 118, 119, 134n
'juvenile delinquency', 117–22
Juvenile Liaison Officer (JLO), 119–22, 214
Juvenile Liaison Schemes (JLS), 100, 117–22, 128, 130

Kelso, James, 125–6
Kent, 189
'khadi justice', 32
'khaki fever', 177, 178
Kilbrandon, Lord, 121
Kilbrandon Report 1961–4 (on Children and Young Persons), 121
Kilmarnock, 34, 118, 120
Kingussie, 194
Kinlochbeg, 162
Kinlochleven, 162–3, 165
Kinlochmore, 162–3
Kinnear, Sydney, 28, 33, 49n, 100, 125, 154–5
Kirkhill, 147
Kirkwall, 166

INDEX

Kissen, Manuel, 39
Klein, Joanna, 4, 25–8
Knox, Bill, 104
Knoydart peninsula, 149
Kosmo dance club, Edinburgh, 112
Kyleakin, 140

labour camps, 163–4
Labour Party, 17, 21, 34, 44, 52n, 122, 181
Lairds, 17
Lanark County Police, 21
Lanarkshire, 8, 65, 69–70, 88, 169
Lancashire, 121
Law Society, 39–40
Lawrence, Stephen, 42
legitimacy, 26, 104, 138, 145, 149–56, 167
Leicester, 189
Leith, 106
Lerwick, 166
Lesbian and Gay Police Association, 116
Lewis, 32, 71, 149
LGBTI communities, 115–16, 116, 215
Licensing Department, 99, 108
List, Alfred, 157
Liverpool, 68, 91n, 119, 180, 213
Livingstone, Irene, 194–5
Local Government (Scotland) Act 1889, 157
Local Government (Scotland) Act 1908, 157–8
Local Government (Scotland) Bill, 22
'localism', 2, 6–7, 17, 22
'Lochaber Project', 162
London, 107, 213
London Gay Pride March, 116
Lord Advocate, 29, 34, 42, 113, 132n
Lovat Scouts, 56

Maan, Bashir, 59, 128, 165, 214
McCluskey, John, 212
McCulloch, Malcolm, 92n
  '999' system, 73, 75
  complaints, 83
  female officers, 190
  Highland recruitment, 56
  Investigation Bureau, 99
  Special Constabulary, 88–9
Macdonald, Charles Cameron, 30, 56, 118
MacGill, Patrick, 163
  Children of the Dead End, 162, 165

McGovern, John, 44, 52n, 82–3
McIvor, Arthur, 60
Mack, John Anderson, 102–3, 121, 128
Mackay, Samuel, 102–3
Mackenzie, Compton, *Whisky Galore*, 151
McLauchlan, Daniel, 118
Maclay, John, 35
McLeod, Georgina W,, 181
'MacNab, John', 151
McNee, David, 92n
  Boys' Brigade, 134n
  children and young people, 68
  drunkenness, 62
  police culture, 90
  Roman Catholicism, 67
  street football, 77
  'Untouchables', 126, 128
  'vice squad', 105, 109–10
McNeill, Fergus, 120
Macpherson, Charles Angus, 107–8
Macpherson Inquiry 1997–8 (into the Matters Arising from the Death of Stephen Lawrence), 42
Macpherson Report 1999, 214
Maitland, Dorothy, 180
Mallaig, 194
Manchester, 91n, 92n
Manuel, Peter, 102–3, 131n
marriage bar, 196–8
Maryhill Division, Glasgow, 74
masculinity
  Dudgeon, Brigadier-General Robert Maxwell, 14
  'gang culture', 79
  hyper-masculinity, 60–2
  and legitimacy, 25–6, 27, 45
  'troublemakers', 102
  'vice squad', 104
Matharu, Sawarnjit, 187
Mawby, Rob, 15–16
Maximes club, Edinburgh, 115
Meek, Jeffrey, 113–14
Meldrum, Andrew, 28, 49n
Melvich, Sutherland, 141
Memorandum on the Social Evil in Glasgow, Motion, James, 111, 113
Merrilees, William, 106, 108, 109, 111–12, 114–15, 134n

241

Metropolitan Police, London
  corruption allegations, 33
  female officers, 181, 193
  juvenile courts, 118
  manpower, 2
  recruits, 57, 92n
  warnings system, 107
Midlothian, 112
migrant communities, 156–67
migrant labour, 161–5
military populations, 165–7
Miller, Emily, 175, 179, 180, 184–7, 200
Miners' strike 1984–5, 212–13
Ministry of Munitions, 18–19, 176–7
Money, Sir Leo Chiozza, 33
Moorov, Samuel, 187–8, 200
Morrison, Herbert, 189
Morrison, Norman, 23, 24, 71, 145–6, 165
Motherwell and Wishaw, 19–21
Motherwell Times, 21
Motion, James, *Memorandum on the Social Evil in Glasgow*, 111
motor
  offences, 37, 39, 83, 84, 87
  patrol units, 55, 79, 99
  police vehicles, 7, 10, 53, 89, 125, 168
Muncie, William, 105–6, 131n
Municipal Corporations Act 1835, 16
Munro, David, 24, 25, 32, 47n

Napier Commission 1883–4, 149
National Council for Civil Liberties (NCCL), 39–40
National Unemployed Workers Movement (NUWM), 33, 40, 44, 82
National Union of Women Workers (NUWW), 177, 180
National Vigilance Association (NVA), 178–9, 181
navvies, 161–2
Newfoundland Overseas Forestry Unit, 167
newspapers, 42–4, 103, 104, 111, 122–3, 125–6, 167
'999' system, 75
No Mean City, 60
North Ballachulish, 163
Northern Constabulary, 8, 168–9, 169n, 216
Noyce, Dora, 112

'obstruction', 68, 78, 212
occurrence books, 8, 142–4, 147–9, 157–60, 166
Ogg, Derek, 116
Onich, 163
Orange Order, 176
Orkney, 139, 140, 152–5, 164–5, 168
Ormidale Committee 1933 (on Police Consolidation in Scotland), 19, 21
Orpin, Elizabeth (Betty), 193

Paisley Burgh Police, 54, 60, 66–7
Paisley, first constabulary, 16
Pankhurst, Emmeline, 43
Partick Cross riots, Glasgow, 176
Pattinson, Juliette, 60
'peace officers', 76–7, 100
pedlar's certificate, 158
'people's war', 73
'permit camps', 160
Perth, first constabulary, 16
Perthshire, 160
Perthshire and Kinross, 120
Phillips, Jim, 212
Pieri, Joe, *The Big Men*, 60, 93n
plainclothes, 99–136, 179, 182, 186
poaching, 150–1
Police (Scotland) Act 1857, 26
Police (Scotland) Act 1862, 157
Police (Scotland) Act 1946, 19
Police (Scotland) Act 1956, 89
Police (Scotland) Act 1967, 3, 40, 216
Police (Women) Regulations 1931 & 1934, 183, 187
Police Act 1919, 23–4
police boxes, 69, 85
Police College, 25
Police Complaints Authority, 52n
Police Complaints Board, 41–2, 52n
Police Complaints Commissioner for Scotland (PCCS), 42
Police Consolidation (Scotland) Committee 1933 (Ormidale), 19
police courts, 29–31, 34, 49n, 107, 216
Police Federation, 24, 201–2
police houses, 69–70, 140–2
Police Manual, 25
'police prosecutor', 216
Police Review, 23, 35
Police Scotland, 2, 45, 169, 216–17

INDEX

police stations, 69–70, 140–2, 169
  electrification of, 141
police strike 1919, 23
Police Union, 23
police wives, 142, 176, 188, 193
Policewomen's Departments, 100, 190–3, 196, 198–200, 203, 204; *see also* female officers; women
Polkemmet House, West Lothian, 25
'Poor Agents' system, 31
Port Charlotte, Islay, 145–6
prejudice
  ethno-religious, 214–15
  against policewomen, 186–7, 194–5
press relations, 42–4, 103, 104, 111, 122–3, 125–6, 167
Prevention of Crime Act 1953, 122
probation, 100, 120–1, 180, 183–4, 191
Probation of Offenders (Scotland) Act 1931, 120
Procurator Fiscal (PF), 29–30, 34, 37–8, 41, 50–1n, 107–8, 112–13, 147
professionalisation, 25, 28
Progressive Alliance, 122–3
Progressive Party, 21, 83
Protestantism, 65–7, 140, 170n

racism, 42, 58, 65, 110, 112–13, 167, 214–15
RAF, 60, 63
railways, 161–2
Ralston, Andrew, 104
Ratcliff, William, 86
Ravenscraig, 212
recruitment, 195–6, 202
recruits, 56–9, 63–4
  Ayr Burgh Police, 221t, 222t
  birthplace, 218t, 221t, 222t, 224t
  former trades, 219t, 222t, 223t, 224t
  Glasgow City Police, 218t, 219t, 220t, 221t
  Inverness Burgh Police, 224t
  Inverness County Police, 222t, 223t
  religion, 221t, 223t
  social class, 220t, 223t
'Red Clydeside', 4–5, 56
religious identity, 65–7
'remote rural', 8, 169n
Renfrew, Thomas, 28, 79n
Renfrewshire, 8
Representation of the People Act 1918, 26–7
Rhiconich, Sutherland, 158

Ritchie, Margaret, 121, 128
Road Traffic Act 1930, 99
road-building, 162
Robb, Linsey, 60
Robertson, Baillie Violet, 188–9
Robertson, James A., 92n, 122–4
Robertson, James Ronald, 83
Robertson, Sir David, 34, 44, 50n
Roman Catholic Boys' Guild, 120
Roman Catholicism, 65–7, 93n, 120, 140
Ross, Annie, 182, 191
Ross, Willie, 122
Ross and Cromarty, 151, 156
'rough justice', 32, 111–12
'rough-handling', 80–2
Royal Commission on Betting, Lotteries and Gaming 1950, 105
Royal Commission on Police Powers and Procedures 1928–9, 34, 38
Royal Commission on Police Powers and Procedures 1960–2, 34–5, 37–8
Royal Commission on Police Powers and Procedures Report 1962, 22, 30, 38–40
Royal Irish Constabulary (RIC), 22, 48n, 58, 92n
Runnymede Trust, 65
rural policing, 137–74

Sabbatarianism, 111, 140, 151
Safer Cities programme, 214
Saracen Cross, Glasgow, 78
Sauchiehall Street, Glasgow, 124
Savidge, Irene, 33–4
Scarman Inquiry 1981 (Brixton Riots), 42
Schaffer, Evelyn, 214
Scollay, Ellen, 187–8
Scots Law, 2, 32, 83, 86, 104, 216
The Scotsman, 34, 157, 167
Scott, John, 213
Scott, Lady Katherine, 178
Scottish Association of Superintendents and Lieutenants, 24
Scottish Borders, 22, 157, 161–2, 167
Scottish Co-operative Women's Guild, 181
Scottish Council for Civil Liberties (SCCL), 40–5
Scottish 'Council of State,' 18
Scottish Crime Squad, 198
Scottish Criminal Law, Police Duties and Procedures, 25–6, 115–16

243

Scottish Executive, 42
Scottish Homosexual Reform Group, 114, 116
Scottish Household Survey, 169n
Scottish Minorities Group, 114
Scottish National Party (SNP), 21
Scottish Office
   Community Involvement Branches, 121
   'community policing', 7
   Discipline Code, 37–8
   female officers, 180–1, 185, 188–90, 196
   localised policing, 18–22
   marriage bar, 196–7
   miners, 213
   police courts, 30
   Scottish Police Service, 24
   training schools, 25
   warnings system, 118
   women patrols, 177–8
Scottish Police College, 73–4
Scottish Police Council, 24, 141, 197
Scottish Police Federation (SPF)
   female officers, 201
   female recruits, 202
   marriage bar, 197
   'nationalisation', 23
   police and public, 73
   police stations, 140–1
   Police Union, 24
   Special Constabulary, 216
   street betting, 105
   Thurso Tribunal, 35
Scottish Police Service, 2–3, 24, 216
Scottish Police Union, 38
Scottish Presbyterian churches, 58
Scottish Secretary, 18
   complaints, 37
   construction work, 163
   female officers, 177–8, 181–2
   Garngad, 82
   Police Union, 24
   Thurso Tribunal, 35
Scottish Training school, 25
Scottish Training School for Women Police, 180–2
Scottish Travellers, 158–61
Scottish Union of Women Workers (SUWW), 177–81
seafaring populations, 166
Second World War
   CID, 99, 146–7

England and Wales, 19
female officers, 9, 188–9
instruction manuals, 25
intelligence duties, 10
lawlessness, 54
military populations, 165
military service, 58, 59–60
'people's war', 73
police and public, 33
Scottish Office, 18
Special Constabulary, 88–90
Secretary of State for Scotland *see* Scottish Secretary
Select Committee on Race Relations and Immigration, 41
Settle, Louise, 106, 108, 109, 112
Sex Discrimination Act 1975, 198, 200–1, 203–4
Sex Disqualification (Removal) Act 1919, 182
Sexual Offences Act 1967, 113
Sheffield City Police, 45, 189
Sheriffs-Substitute Association, 30
Sherwood, Marika, 166–7
Shetland/Zetland, 138–9, 140, 154–5, 168, 190, 198
Shields, J. V. M., 54, 91n, 164
Shortt, Edward, 23
Shpayer-Makov, Haia, 57
Sikh officers, 59, 187
Sillitoe, Sir Percy, 92n
   compulsory retirement, 57
   female officers, 188
   Sheffield City Police, 45
   'toughness', 79–80, 82, 90
   Traffic Department, 99
Singh, Dilawer, 59
Skye, 32, 38, 140, 142, 149–51, 159
Slater, Oscar, 110–11
Smale, David, 3, 157, 166–7
Smith, Andrew D., 92n, 106
Smith, Edith, 180
Smith, Reverend Angus, 140
'social purity', 178–9, 187, 194
'social work', 75–8, 100, 129–30
   beat men, 90–1
   female officers, 178–9, 183–5, 187, 189, 192–3, 199–200
   JLS, 120–1
   'peace officers', 76–7, 100
Solicitor-General for Scotland, 108

South Uist, 140, 149
Southern Police Court, Glasgow, 108
Special Constabulary, 59, 88–9, 156, 197, 216
specialist policing, 99–136
SS *Politician*, 151
St Rollox Division, Glasgow, 79
stereotypes
　ethno-religious, 66, 112, 215
　Glasgow, 72
　homosexuality, 114–16
　street soliciting, 108
　'troublemakers', 102
Stevenson, Edward, 58
Stevenson, James V., 29, 38, 57, 71, 92n, 106, 111, 179
Stewart, Belle, 160
Stewart, John, 159
Stewart, Sheila, 160–1
Stirling, 197
Stirling and Clackmannan, 120
stop and search, 41, 79, 122, 125–6, 213–14
Strathclyde Police, 8, 23, 62, 128, 169, 212, 214
street betting, 105–6
street football, 77
Street Offences Act 1959, 110
street soliciting, 106–13, 132n
strikes, 4–5, 212–13
Stuart, Charles, 22
suicide, 147
Summary Jurisdiction (Scotland) Act, 31
Sunday observance, 111, 140, 151
Sutherland, 140–1, 150
Sutherland Constabulary, 170n
Sutherland County Police, 137–8, 141, 144–7, 153, 164
Swinson, Arthur, 151

Tancred, Edith, 181, 182, 184, 189
telephones, 141, 145
Thomson, Jean, 180, 182, 183–4
Thurso Tribunal, 34–5, 37–8, 44, 46, 50–1n, 80, 83
Tomnacross, Inverness-shire, 146
Tongue, Sutherland, 140–1
'toughness'
　detectives, 103
　Glasgow City Police, 60–5, 86, 89–91, 211

migrant labour, 164–5, 167
'the ned', 78, 79
and Special Constabulary, 88
Town Council (Scotland) Act 1900, 7, 17
Toxteth riots 1981, 42
Trades Dispersal Act 1906, 5
training schools, 25, 28, 45, 62–3, 152–3
Tribunal of Inquiry, 33–4, 83
Tribunal of Inquiry (Evidence) Act 1921, 33
'troublemakers', 80–2, 87–8, 91
Tulliallan Castle, 25, 28, 116, 121
24 Hours, 122

Unit Beat Policing, 55
United Free Church of Scotland, 111
University of Strathclyde, 202
'Untouchables', 122–9
Urquhart, Mona, 196, 197

vagrants, 157–8, 166
Vaughan, Frankie, 122–3
'vice squad', 99, 100, 104, 129
village constables, 7, 169
　as mediator, 148–9, 160–1
　and police life, 139–44
　warnings system, 107–8, 117–22
Waterloo Place, Edinburgh, 106
'weapons amnesty', 122–3
Weber, Max, 32
Webster, Ellen, 187–8
weights and measures, 145
Weinberger, Barbara, 4, 5, 10, 17, 24, 142, 211
Weir Street/Gibbshill area, Greenock, 119–20
West Highland Free Press, 44
Western Isles, 149–52
Whitburn Police Training College, 25, 62–3, 197
'white slave trade', 110–11, 178–9
Whitehead, Philip, 41
Wick, 193
Williamson, Duncan, 160
Wilson, Mary, 122–5
Wolfenden Committee 1953–7 (on Homosexual Offences and Street Prostitution), 113–14, 134n

245

women, 175–208
  CID, 186, 195, 199, 202–3
  detectives, 179
  First World War, 9
  marriage bar, 196–7
  patrols, 177–9
  pay, 196, 201–2
  prejudice against, 186–7, 194–5
  recruits, 195–6, 215
  statement takers, 34, 175, 179, 182, 188
  see also female officers; Policewomen's Departments
Women Police Service (WPS), 176–7
Women's Auxiliary Police Corps (WAPC), 188–9, 190–1

Women's Citizens' Associations, 181
Wood, John Carter, 33–4
Woodburn, Arthur, 22
Wright, Alan, 15–16

Young, Malcolm, 168
Young Women's Christian Association, London, 178
Younger, George, 212
youth, 117–29
  black, 41, 213
  gangs, 4, 54, 79–80, 84–5, 122–4
  organisations, 118–19, 120, 134n
  see also children and young people
'Youth Advisory Service Scheme', 128

EU representative:
Easy Access System Europe
Mustamäe tee 50, 10621 Tallinn, Estonia
Gpsr.requests@easproject.com

www.ingramcontent.com/pod-product-compliance
Lightning Source LLC
Chambersburg PA
CBHW070325240426
43671CB00013BA/2369